# GO! GO! GO!

Rusty Firmin was born in Carlisle in 1950. Adopted at a very young age, he has never known his real mother and father. Caught taking ducks' eggs aged fifteen, he was forced to join up as a boy soldier in the Royal Artillery's Junior Leaders Regiment. Unhappy but unable to afford the £50 to buy himself out, two years later Rusty was posted to 49 Field Regiment Royal Artillery and subsequently to the 29 Commando RA. Getting a taste for commando ops, Rusty passed the gruelling SAS selection and joined B-Squadron 22 (SAS) Regiment in 1977. Following covert tours in Northern Ireland with the SAS, Rusty then led part of the iconic assault to rescue the hostages from the Iranian Embassy in 1980. In 1982 Rusty served with B-Squadron 22 (SAS) in the recapture of the Falkland Islands. A fitness fanatic who represented the British Army at football, he lives in Surrey with Torky, his fiancée, and has two grown-up sons, Matthew and Mark.

*

Will Pearson ran away from home aged fifteen and joined the Royal Navy. Seven years and two world tours later, he won a scholarship to Ruskin workers' education college and then read modern languages at Oriel College, Oxford. After various careers, Will turned his hand to writing. His military experience and contacts lead to a breakthrough book, the bestselling *Tornado Down*, written with the RAF's John Peters and John Nicol. He has also produced and scripted documentaries for Channel 4 and Discovery Channel, and written for the *Financial Times*, the *Daily Mirror*, *Africa Today* and many other publications. Will lives in London with his wife and two children.

*

After fifteen years as a commissioning editor in criminology, Gillian Stern discovered a novel that went on to win a host of literary prizes. With this came a move from academic to commercial publishing. She is now a much sought-after freelance editor of fiction and non-fiction and has worked with a number of contemporary writers. Gillian lives in London with her husband and their three children.

# GO! GO! GO!

**WILL PEARSON and RUSTY FIRMIN**

**with
Gillian Stern**

WEIDENFELD & NICOLSON

A W&N paperback

First published in Great Britain in 2010
by Weidenfeld & Nicolson
First paperback edition published in 2011
by Phoenix
This paperback edition published in 2017
by Weidenfeld & Nicolson,
an imprint of The Orion Publishing Group Ltd
Carmelite House, 50 Victoria Embankment
London EC4Y 0DZ

An Hachette UK Company

3 5 7 9 10 8 6 4 2

A CIP catalogue record for this book
is available from the British Library.

ISBN 978-1-4746-0805-3

Typeset by Input Data Services Ltd, Somerset

Printed and bound in Great Britain by Clays Ltd, Elcograf S.p.A.

www.orionbooks.co.uk

This book is dedicated to the memory of 25061538 Serjeant Paul McAleese, 2nd Battalion The Rifles, killed Thursday 20 August 2009 on active service in Afghanistan. And to all British service personnel who have given their lives in action.

# The Hostages

Dr Gholam-Ali Afrouz – Chargé d'Affaires. Wounded by gunmen.

Shirazed Bouroumand – Embassy Secretary.

Chris Cramer – BBC TV News Producer.

Ahmed Dadgar – Medical Clerk. Wounded by gunmen.

Dr Abdul Fazi Ezzati – Iranian Cultural Attaché.

Abbas Fallahi – Embassy Doorman.

Muhammed Hashir Faruqi – British Pakistani, Editor of Muslim political magazine *Impact International.*

Ali Guil Ghanzafar – Pakistani tourist. Released on fourth day of the siege.

Sim Harris – BBC sound recordist.

Nooshin Hashemenian – Embassy Secretary.

Roya Kaghachi – Embassy Secretary.

Mrs Hiyech Sanei Kanji – Embassy Secretary.

Mustapha Karkouti – Syrian Journalist for Lebanese paper *Assafir.*

Vahid Khabaz – Student, part-time London correspondent for Tehran-based newspaper *Keyhan.*

Abbas Lavasani – Embassy Chief Press Officer.

Police Constable Trevor Lock – Diplomatic Protection Group, Metropolitan Police.

Moutaba Mehrnavard – carpet dealer.

Aboutaleb Jishverdi-Moghaddam – Iranian Attaché

Muhammed Moheb – Embassy accountant.

Ron Morris – Embassy Manager and chauffeur

Frieda Mozafarian – Press Officer.

Issa Naghizadeh – First Secretary.

Ali Akbar Samadzadeh – temporary worker at the Embassy, studying for a computer doctorate.

Ali Aghar Tabatabai – Banker from Central Bank of Iran.

Kaujouri Muhammad Taghi – Accountant

Zahra Zomorrodian – Embassy Clerk

# The Gunmen

Salim Towfigh – alias Oan Ali Mohammed – known during the siege as Salim or Oan.

Faisal Jassem – alias Shakir Abdullah Radhil – known during the siege as Faisal.

Hassan – alias Shakir Sultan Said – known during the siege as Hassan.

Makki – alias Makki Hanoun Ali – known during the siege as Makki.

Abbas – alias Themir Mohammed Hussein – known as Abbas or 'Ugly' by hostages.

Fowzi Badavi Nejad – alias Ali Ahmed Jassim – known during the siege as Ali.

Khuzestan in Western Iran

FOCAB008/30

OO CABINET OFFICE

GRS 212

CONFIDENTIAL
DEFKBY TEHRAN 010330Z
DESKBY ABU DHABI 010400Z
FM FCO 301920Z APR 80
TO IMMEDIATE TEHRAN
TELEGRAM NUMBER 270 OF 30 APRIL 1980
AND TO IMMEDIATE ABU DHABI

ATTACK ON IRANIAN EMBASSY LONDON: MY TELNO 267

1. ASSUMING YOU SEE NO OBJECTION, PLEASE DELIVER AS SOON AS
POSSIBLE THE FOLLOWING MESSAGE FROM THE PRIME MINISTER TO
PRESIDENT BANI SADR.
BEGINS
QUOTE I SHOULD LIKE YOU TO KNOW OF MY DEEP PERSONAL CONCERN ABOUT
THE SITUATION AT THE IRANIAN MEBASSY IN LONDON. THIS INTRUSION
CONSTITUTES AN ACT OF TERRORISM AND AN INFRINGEMENT OF THE
IMMUNITY OF DIPLOMATIC STAFF WHICH THE BRITISH GOVERNMENT FINDS
TOTALLY REPUGNANT AND IS ACTING FIRMLY TO COUNTER. I HOPE THAT
THIS INCIDENT WILL BE RESOLVED SPEEDILY AND I CAN ASSURE YOU THAT
THE SAFETY OF THE LIVES AT STAKE WILL BE A PARAMOUNT CONSIDERATION.
THE HOME SECRETARY IS PERSONALLY IN CHARGE OF THE SITUATION AND I
AM TAKING A VERY CLOSE PERSONAL INTEREST. I WISH TO ASSURE YOU THAT
WE SHALL BE KEEPING IN CONSTANT TOUCH WITH YOU AND YOUR GOVERNMENT.
UNQUOTE ENDS
2.

3. ABU DHABI PLEASE PASS TO IRANIAN FOREIGN MINISTER.

CARRINGTON

NNNN

SENT AT 01/0002Z   PJ
RECD AT 01/0002Z   KS

Confidential telex from British Foreign Secretary Carrington

**EMBASSY OF THE**
**ISLAMIC REPUBLIC OF IRAN**
London

No. 2256/D.                                    Date: 30.4.1980

### Note Verbale
### MOST URGENT

The Embassy of the Islamic Republic of Iran presents its compliments to His Excellency the Foreign Secretary and has the honor to draw His Excellency's attention to the incidence at this Embassy today in which lives of twenty odd Diplomats and staff including Charge d'Affairs and several women is under constant threat of death.

It is requested that His Excellency the Foreign Secretary will appreciate the severity of the threat and will order the security forces to take all possible measures to safeguard their lives.

The Embassy of the Islamic Republic of Iran avails itself of this opportunity to renew to His Excellency the Foreign Secretary the assurance of its highest consideration.

The Foreign and Commonwealth Office,
London.

Urgent telex from Iran Embassy to FCO, London

# DAY ONE: Wednesday, 30 April 1980

It started with a stroll in the park. Six young men from a foreign country, seeing the sights and soaking up London life. But these six were not typical. Nor were they tourists. They were walking through one of the world's most exciting and vibrant capital cities. But their interest began and ended in a single building.

As they sauntered across the vast green expanse of Hyde Park, filling now with innocent people going about their everyday business, each man made what peace he could with his teeming thoughts. Each felt the weight of a handgun pulling down on his pockets.

The six had met at the Albert Memorial many times before on reconnaissance trips. Abbas, who'd gone ahead as the scout, came up: 'It's good news. About twenty-five people have already gone inside.'

'It's enough,' Salim said, checking his watch. 'It is time. We attack now.'

Knife-slim and with a long, intellectual face, the group's twenty-seven-year-old leader was blade quick. Touching the drooping moustache that framed his upper lip, he cast an appraising eye over the men in his charge. He felt a surge of pride. His tall, powerfully-built second-in-command Faisal looked ready for anything, the strong, regular features calm and determined under the Afro bush of hair.

Abbas, their lookout, was squat and barrel-chested, with a face that was never going to win him any beauty competitions – not least because of the scars that marred both cheeks. But he was as strong as a lion, and just as courageous.

Thin and with a hooked nose, Hassan, the shortest member of the team at five foot three, was an accomplished karate expert. With a quick, nervous manner he was never still. Aged twenty-four, he'd met

1

the fifth member of the group, Ali, at school. A year younger than Hassan, Ali least looked the part of a gunman: slightly built and handsome, with thick, glossy hair and large, dark eyes, the role of ladykiller might have suited him better.

The final man was Makki. Of medium height and build, there was little to distinguish him bar his long, bushy sideburns and a plump face.

The group had reached the southern border of the park. Here, they split up as planned. Salim, Faisal and Abbas looped left to approach their objective from the eastern end of Princes Gate; Makki, Ali and Hassan hooked round at the target from the west.

The bright fire of revolutionary idealism burned in their eyes, and they were brimming with confidence. They were young, they were strong, and nothing could stop them. Here, at last was their chance to hit back at the oppressor Iran: to strike a blow for their homeland. It was 1120 hrs.

As they neared their target, the gunmen found it hard to believe their eyes. On each of their surveillance missions, there had been a police officer on duty right outside the building. But this morning, the duty constable was not at his post. The entrance stood unguarded. Surely, this was an omen: a sign that their enterprise was blessed.

Salim exchanged glances with Faisal. Agents of the new Revolutionary Islamic regime in Tehran had tortured both of them horribly. It was payback time.

'*Yalla!*' Salim said. 'The coast's clear! Let's go!' Pulling hoods and chequered kaffiyehs around their heads, they took out the weapons and made them ready. 'Long live Arabistan!' shouted Faisal. With that, the six men charged at the front door of the Iranian Embassy.

They were the Group of the Martyr. And their time had come.

■ ■ ■

If the gunmen were in luck that day, Police Constable Trevor Lock's fortune had pretty much deserted him. The evening before, he had agreed to cover for a colleague who wanted the day off. A constable with fifteen years' service behind him, PC Lock had a large family.

As a surprise treat for his wife, Doreen, he'd bought two tickets for that evening's performance of the hit African musical *Ipi Tombi* at a theatre in London's West End. To help him make the quick change back into civilian clothes after a day guarding the Iranian Embassy, that morning he'd put on green rather than his regulation black uniform socks.

Lock had only been with the Diplomatic Protection Group (DPG) for three months. His firearms training before starting active duty in the branch had lasted only a few days. But, like all DPG officers on duty, Lock was armed: in his case with a .38 Smith & Wesson revolver in a holster on his right hip. He normally stood sentry under the embassy's porch or on the pavement fronting it. Had he been at either of these spots, he'd probably have seen the gunmen approaching – one group from the left, one group from the right. He might also have been able to lock the doors: stop the attackers before they could get in. As it was, the embassy doorman Abbas Fallahi had just invited Lock to step inside for a nice, warming cup of the delicious Iranian coffee he made in his lair, to the left of the small lobby that lay between the front door and the inner steel-and-glass security door. It was a cold day and Lock had gratefully accepted the offer.

There had been a lot of visitors in and out of the building that morning. So at the time of the attack, not only was there no police presence outside the embassy, but the inner security door was standing wide open.

With a jolt of alarm, Lock suddenly heard voices shouting in a foreign language. He came out of Fallahi's ante-room to see three armed men waving guns in the air. Yelling slogans and wielding a sub-machine gun, the tallest of them ran through the door. He caught sight of Lock and charged at him, shouting 'Don't move! Don't move!' in Farsi.

Lock flung himself at the man's waist, managing to kick the outer door shut. As the two of them grappled in the lobby, one of the other gunmen raised his Browning pistol and fired a shot through the plate-glass panel above the front door. The glass shattered. Dozens of razor-sharp fragments flew into Lock's face; one splinter sliced a long gash in his cheek; smaller fragments cut him across the forehead. Temporarily blinded by the runnels of blood pouring down his face, Lock felt as if someone had thrown acid into his eyes. He thought he'd been shot. Overwhelmed as the rest of the gunmen stormed in and grabbed him, the policeman staggered back.

'Go in, go in!' Salim yelled to his men, ripping the police radio from Lock's lapel. He was too late: Lock had already sent out an emergency alarm call. The rest of the attack team rushed past them into the embassy's main hall. Makki slammed the doors behind him and locked them shut. The Group of the Martyr had taken the Iranian Embassy. One of the most famous sieges in modern history had begun.

■ ■ ■

PC Dusty Gray was on duty nearby. The fact that Gray, a Metropolitan Police dog handler, happened to be in the area was a complete coincidence – he normally worked with the Hard Dogs Section at Heathrow Airport. But not quite as great a coincidence as the fact that Gray was a recently retired member of D Squadron, 22 (SAS) Regiment.

As far as Gray was concerned, it was a quiet day. Too quiet: he was fiddling with his police radio, listening to the messages and trying to pick up a job. He was just starting to despair of anything interesting happening that day when his alarm sounded. It was New Scotland Yard relaying an emergency call from a PC Trevor Lock of the DPG. Lock seemed to be in trouble nearby, at No. 16 Princes Gate.

Gray waited for more details. A veteran ex-Para, he wasn't exactly new to trouble. But he wasn't prepared for what followed a few seconds later. The main Met police frequency blipped back on and a gravel-toned voice announced tersely: 'Armed terrorists have attacked and taken the Iranian Embassy.' A short second statement followed hard on the heels of the first: 'The Iranian Embassy's direct emergency link with Scotland Yard has been triggered. All available units attend immediately.'

'Right,' Gray thought, reaching for his radio phone. 'Better give the boss a call.'

Tall, distinguished-looking and known for his dry sense of humour, during his nineteen years with the Regiment, Gray had seen action in Aden, Oman and Northern Ireland. He'd spent the last two years of his SAS career attached to the anti-terrorist team. At 1144 hrs, a few minutes after he'd overheard the first emergency calls, Gray called the SAS headquarters command group at Bradbury Lines, the Regiment's main base on the outskirts of Hereford. As far as Gray was concerned, the sooner 22 (SAS) Regiment's commanding officer Lieutenant-Colonel Mike Rose knew there was a gang of gunmen holding people hostage in a London embassy, the better.

At Bradbury Lines, the ops desk put Gray straight through to Lt-Col Rose. Knowing the former trooper had a reputation for playing practical jokes, Rose said: 'Are you taking the piss, Gray?' Gray protested he was serious. He was on duty and he'd picked up the emergency calls. Rose wasn't about to brush off the news that armed men had seized a London embassy in broad daylight, fired sub-machine guns and taken hostages. He went into immediate action.

First he put in a call to Brigadier Peter de la Billière, DSG (Director, SAS Group), via the Ministry of Defence. He wanted confirmation of the alarm call. Then, without waiting for de la Billière to give the nod, Rose called the ops officer, Major Ian Crooke: 'Send the SP team the live operation code – and where possible, make sure that they double up with a telephone call. You know how patchy those bleepers can be outside of Hereford. Tell them to get their gear ready and report to the hangar for immediate briefing update. Give Major Gullan the heads-up, and if he doesn't already know, tell him to find out what's going on and make the initial brief. And tell them all to step on it, in case we have to move fast.'

The unexpected command left Major Crooke facing a dilemma. At that particular moment, B Squadron had just taken over as Special Projects (SP) team from D Squadron as the Regiment's standing counter-terrorism unit. For operational purposes, the SP team was split into two teams, codenamed Red Team and Blue Team. Through the half-open window of his office, the ops officer could hear the faint sound of gunfire and explosions from inside the 'Killing House' – the Close Quarters Battle facility used to practise hostage rescue assaults – and from the twenty-five-metre outdoor range where members of Red Team were training. But most of the Blue Team soldiers were off-camp, at home spending precious last minutes with their families, or in the case of the single men, their girlfriends. To get them ready for immediate transfer to London meant scrambling the whole team as quickly as possible. It was true nobody had said they were definitely going to London at that stage, but with a live operational callout, ready sooner was better than ready later.

At 1148 hrs, Crooke sent out the 'live op' alert code: 9999. All over Hereford and surrounding districts, sixty-plus electronic pagers sounded simultaneously. SAS men, signallers, drivers and other attached arms who would be involved in the operation stopped dead in their tracks. Checked the tiny screens at their waists. And tried to believe what they read there was true. For many, the prospect of being involved in a live operation was a first.

■ ■ ■

The Iranian Embassy staff had no idea that Wednesday, 30 April 1980 would turn out to be anything other than a typical working day. Neither did the embassy's many visitors. At around 1100 hrs, two BBC men, TV news producer Chris Cramer and sound man Sim Harris, had arrived to continue the slow and frustrating business of obtaining visas for a news-gathering trip to Iran.

Both had experience of working in the world's trouble spots, including a previous trip to Iran. The BBC wanted a nice, snappy update on the revolutionary Islamic regime, as led by the eighty-year-old Ayatollah Khomeini. It was the third time in two weeks they'd come to the embassy; on all their previous visits there had been a police officer outside, but on this occasion the policeman had checked their BBC identity cards in the small lobby between the front door and the inner glass-and-steel security door.

Ambling through into the reception area, Harris and Cramer didn't even bother to show their ID to the uniformed man at the desk. He waved them straight through to the waiting room. 'Not like the US Embassy, is it?' Cramer said. 'Look around: they haven't even got CCTV here.'

The waiting room was quiet and drab. There were a few empty vases in a glass-fronted cabinet, some chairs, a smeared coffee table. The only colour came from a couple of posters, glamorous images of handsome young 'martyrs' of the recent Islamic Revolution. There were three other visitors waiting: Ali Guil Ghanzafar, a large, bearded Pakistani man wearing a black fur hat sat priest-like in the only comfortable armchair. The other two introduced themselves as Iranians: Moutaba Mehrnavard, an elderly carpet salesman; and Ali Tabatabai, who was in the UK on a fourteen-week course organised by the British Midland Bank. Mehrnavard said he'd come to consult Ahmed Dadgar, an Embassy medical officer. Tabatabai was hoping to collect some visual aids to liven up a talk he was due to give at the bank about his home country. Moments later, a slim man in his late forties was shown in. As he sat down he introduced himself in Farsi to his fellow Iranians, nodding his head in quick, anxious bobs.

No sooner had the men sat down than the doorman appeared. Motioning to Cramer and Harris, he said, 'Excuse me, gentlemen. Would you please come to the telephone? You must speak with Dr Ezzati's secretary.'

'Here we go,' muttered Cramer. 'I am not taking no for an answer today.'

The two men stepped out into the lobby. Harris took the phone. 'I apologise to you,' the crisp female voice on the other end said. 'We cannot find your visa application up here. You must please submit the forms again.'

Not for the first time in his dealings with the Iranian Embassy, Harris could feel his blood pressure rising. 'But we know our forms are here. We came to the embassy and gave them in ourselves, in person, just a few days ago. We were assured that they had been telexed to Iran. We came yesterday to get them, too.' He put his hand over the receiver. 'Bloody hell, they've lost our paperwork. You speak to her, Chris.'

Grumpily, Cramer took the phone and asked to be put through to Ezzati in person. 'That will not be possible,' the secretary said officiously. 'He has someone with him. Please call back in fifteen minutes.'

Fifteen minutes seemed like a very short time. But time was about to take on a new meaning.

As Cramer slammed down the receiver, he heard a gunshot. Spinning round, he saw the policeman who'd examined his pass struggling with an Arabic-looking man in a green anorak. Behind him was a wild-eyed group of men wielding guns. As the gunmen burst through and into the reception area, one of them fired a second shot into the ceiling. Harris put his hands in the air, heart pounding. There was no arguing with bullets.

Screaming 'Put your hands up! Stand against the wall!' Salim pushed Lock backwards into the hall. Blood was streaming down the policeman's face. He slowly raised his hands and stood next to Harris and Fallahi.

While Makki and Hassan stood guard, the rest of the gunmen fanned out through the building, shouting and shooting into the air. The sounds of people running down the corridors and screaming echoed around the embassy.

'Please – do not worry. Do not be afraid,' Salim told the frightened men who were now lined up against the wall. 'We get everyone in the building together, make a few speeches and then we go.' Then – as if to totally contradict himself – he wound his kaffiyeh more tightly round his face, took a bright green hand grenade from his pocket and stuck his little finger through the ring of the safety pin. The men backed further up against the wall. Salim smiled. 'Don't worry, don't worry. Nothing is going to happen to you. You are all our friends.'

'Bloody funny way of showing friendship,' Harris thought.

Cramer had run back into the waiting room. The other visitors were on their feet, panicking. It didn't help when they saw the bearded, long-haired Englishman run through the doorway. They stepped back in fright. 'It's not me!' Cramer yelled at them. 'There are Arab gunmen out there. You'd better put your hands up and face the wall.' The Iranians and the Pakistani man did as he suggested. But Cramer was not about to heed his own advice.

Catching sight of a possible escape route, he leapt across the room to the window. He managed to undo the catch – but the frame was stuck fast with paint and refused to budge. Cramer gave it one last almighty heave with his right arm, then stepped back. The gunmen were closing in. He could hear them shouting just outside the door. Raising his hands, he walked out reluctantly and joined the others, now in a long line with their hands up, faces to the wall.

'You walk now! One in front of other!' barked Salim.

Shoving the muzzles of their guns into the captives' backs, the attackers herded the first group of hostages up the ornate marble staircase to the second floor, and then into a small room. Leaving Makki on guard there, the rest of the gunmen spread through the building looking for anyone still trying to hide or escape. Kicking open doors and yelling, they rounded up the staff.

On the first floor, two gunmen were hunting their big prize, Dr Gholam-Ali Afrouz, the embassy's new, revolutionary Chargé d'Affaires. Oblivious to the mayhem, Afrouz was in his elegant first-floor office, enjoying the eminently desirable view through the big bay windows overlooking Princes Gate and Hyde Park. He was in an expansive mood. Muhammad Faruqi, editor of the London-based Muslim magazine *Impact International*, was sitting in front of his expensive polished desk, interviewing him about the repercussions of the recent revolution in Iran. Afrouz was an Ayatollah man through and through. As far as he was concerned, the new Iranian regime was going great guns and he was one of its most important representatives, the kingpin of its London outpost.

All that was about to change. Until now, the office's opulent carpets and fine fittings had deadened all but very distant sounds of the assault. Then he heard voices yelling. 'Ali Afrouz! Ali Afrouz!' They were right outside. The Chargé d'Affaires jumped up and locked the door. There was a huge crash as the gunmen tried to smash through it, kicking and then clubbing it with their weapons; but the solid oak frame and the heavy metal deadlock held firm. Giving up for the moment, the attackers moved on.

A couple of seconds later, without so much as a word to his shocked companion, Afrouz unlocked the door. Rushing to the back of the building, the diplomat unlocked a window, climbed over the sill, sat for a moment looking down, and then hurled himself out. He smashed down on to the paved terrace in the garden below. The impact knocked him out. It also broke his jaw, badly bruised one side of his face and injured his right arm and ribs. The Chargé d'Affaires lay there unconscious, and for the moment, unnoticed.

Faruqi had remained, frozen, in Afrouz's imposing office. As he sat watching in utter disbelief, a gunman with his face partially concealed by a kaffiyeh shot the lock out of the door frame. The sharp smell of cordite reached his nostrils as the attacker burst in. 'Get up!' the man shouted. 'Hands up! Come here!' Then Faruqi too felt the muzzle of a gun in his back. Seconds later, he found himself upstairs, being bundled in through the door to join the other captives in the embassy cipher room.

On the third floor, Mustapha Karkouti, a Syrian journalist writing for the Lebanese paper *Assafir* (*The Ambassador*), had been interviewing the embassy's Cultural Attaché, Dr Abdul Ezzati, and its young, fervently religious press officer, Abbas Lavasani.

Hearing all the noise, the two diplomatic staff excused themselves and stepped out on to the landing. Like Faruqi, Karkouti stayed where he was. But after a further burst of gunfire, he, too, went to investigate. He was astonished to see eight or nine embassy staff members racing past him, making for the building's top floors. One of the women in the group shrieked at him: 'Come on, come with us!' Karkouti ran after them. 'Where are you going?'

'We go to find fire escape!' With armed men roaming the building, that struck Karkouti as a good idea. He joined them in the frantic search for a way out. But there was no time. With the gunmen closing in behind them, firing shots into the ceiling, they piled into an office. Showing great presence of mind, one of the female members of staff locked the door from the inside.

They cowered against the wall, hardly daring to breathe. But then a young secretary, Frieda Mozafarian, began to scream hysterically. Her shrieks echoed right across the fourth floor. In an effort to shut her up, one of her female colleagues leaned forward and slapped her across the face. Mozafarian stopped screaming and sat for a moment, stunned. Her silence came too late.

Seconds later, Salim burst in. Raising the barrel of his machine-pistol, he fired another burst into the ceiling. In the confined space, the noise was deafening. Shouting in Farsi, '*Dastha baalaa!*' (hands on head) and '*Roo be divar!*' (face the wall), he ordered the cowering hostages back. He brandished the Skorpion machine-pistol in their faces. No one dared resist. Still in deep shock, Frieda Mozafarian was too weak to stand. Two of the other captives had to lift her to her feet and hold her upright. With Salim ushering them along before him, the new batch of prisoners trooped downstairs to join the others in the cipher office.

Up in his fourth floor office, Ron Morris, the embassy's long-serving British manager, heard the distant pop of the initial gunshots. He put the noise down to a motorbike misfiring on the street outside. Morris had started working at the embassy as a boy in 1947. He had seen dramatic changes in that time. Before the Iranian revolution of 1979, the London embassy had been a byword for excess and conspicuous consumption: an invitation to the banquets held in its opulent dining room was a guaranteed ticket to the finest food and wines, in the company of the richest, most powerful and most influential people in London. In general, the guests sang for their supper by duly portraying the Shah and his regime in a favourable light. Morris's duties had included chauffeuring Parvis Radji, whom the British press almost invariably described as 'Iran's young and eligible ambassador', around in the embassy's Roll's-Royce Silver Ghost.

Now, with the austere twenty-nine-year-old psychology graduate Ali Afrouz in charge, the days of lavish entertainment were over. Afrouz hadn't got rid of all the old embassy employees yet, but he had fired the SAVAK secret service agents who had infested the place. The deposed Shah had used these thugs – who both behaved and dressed like pimps – to infiltrate Iranian opposition groups in London, report on their activities, and intimidate dissidents with both verbal and physical threats. Dr Afrouz told them all to report immediately to the revolutionary regime in Iran. Needless to say, the SAVAK agents had disappeared without trace. Had they turned up in Tehran as instructed, they would most certainly have enjoyed a warm welcome.

After cleansing the embassy of seedy secret agents, Afrouz, who'd studied at Michigan State University, set about the embassy's wine cellar. He poured all the expensive wines, the champagnes and fine cognac down the drain. But he had not yet had time to change the embassy's interior. Much of it was still decorated in the ostentatious style of the shahs: fine, patterned-marble floors; tapestries and wall hangings depicting ancient Persian scenes; rich brocade curtains; ponderous, old-fashioned furniture and antique Iranian pottery.

'There's a lot of noise out there today,' thought the forty-seven-year-old Morris. Assuming it was just another student demonstration, he didn't really think there was anything to worry about. Even so, still passionate about the embassy he'd served for thirty-three years, he didn't like to think of its hallowed calm being disturbed – or its staff threatened – in any way. As he got up to investigate it occurred to him that he should take one of the ten replica firearms he kept in his desk drawer just in case. Selecting a Diana air pistol, which looked much like a Browning 9mm, he made his way cautiously down the stairs, checking for trouble as he went. If something serious really was happening, then he wanted to do something about it.

Rounding the landing to the first floor, Morris saw two armed men forcing a uniformed police officer and his old pal, doorman Abbas Fallahi, up the stairs towards him at gunpoint. With alarm flooding through him, he thought the intruders in their chequered headdresses looked like Arabs. One had a machine gun, the other a pistol of some kind. Seriously outgunned, Morris quickly tucked his replica away in a pocket. His brain racing, he turned on his heel, ran back up to his office and grabbed the phone. Stabbing at the buttons with his index finger, he dialled 999. But just as he finished dialling the last digit,

Faisal burst into the room. Aiming his Skorpion directly at Morris's head, he shouted: 'English, English! You my friend, come!'

Morris knew better than to argue. Slowly, he got up from behind his desk and moved to the landing. Something very, very bad was going on here. In his heart, he feared the worst.

Morris was the last hostage to be rounded up. As Salim prodded him into Room 9A, he saw a mass of trembling prisoners lined up against the wall with their hands on their heads. The embassy's legitimate visitors were strangers to him, but the other hostages were all people he knew personally – and liked. He stopped in the doorway, and got a nudge in the back with the muzzle of a gun. When he didn't move, Faisal prodded Morris again, this time harder. 'Put your hands up! Stand against the wall!' Morris shook his head. He was furious. How dare these people – this rabble – break into his embassy and order him and its staff around?

As these thoughts were going through his mind the gunmen ordered all the hostages to move through into the much larger Room 9 next door. It was no more comfortable than the waiting room downstairs. There was steel furniture everywhere: filing cabinets, desks, cupboards. The paint was peeling from the high ceiling and the green carpet shone murkily in the fluorescent light. There were piles of blue box files and some out-of-date magazines on a shelving unit. The large windows let in some welcome daylight, but Harris and Cramer were ordered to close the large curtains, plunging the room into darkness until one of the gunmen switched on the lights.

Hassan, who was small and bouncy, jumped on to a desk and tore at a phone, ripping the cables clean out of the wall. The hostages gasped as he hurled the handset across the room. Some of them ducked, thinking it was going to hit them.

Cramer needed to stub out his cigarette in the pedestal ashtray by the door. He crossed the room and offered Salim a smoke. 'What do you want with us?' asked Cramer. 'How can we help you?'

Salim gripped his machine gun so tightly the knuckles stood out white on his hands, but he spoke gently. 'Get back across the room.

Please do not talk. It is best you keep quiet. OK?' He motioned to Makki and Ali. 'Search them now.'

Morris began to protest. Salim barked: 'Put your hands up, or I shoot!' Slowly, Morris raised his arms. When they were high above his head, Faisal stepped close and rummaged through the manager's pockets. All he found was the case where Morris kept his reading glasses. Faisal chucked it on the floor. The case burst open and the spectacles flew across the room. 'Hey, go easy!' Morris shouted. 'That's my glasses!'

The gunmen moved on to search PC Lock next. 'What's this?' Faisal demanded, slapping the bulging right-hand pocket of Lock's uniform raincoat. Thinking on his feet, Lock told him: 'Notebooks, maps and the like.' He drew some of the stuff part-way out of his pocket so Faisal could see. The pantomime seemed to satisfy the gunman – he moved on to the next hostage.

As he went to retrieve his specs, Morris paused next to the captured policeman. 'Did they get your gun?' he hissed in the officer's ear.

'Not yet,' Lock breathed in reply. Lock held an ace. But having the firearm was one thing. Using it was another.

The hostages stared at one other in amazement and terror. In five short minutes, their lives had changed beyond all imagination. Then one of the Iranian men shouted: 'Afrouz has jumped! I saw him on the ground outside. He is just lying there dead!' He began to weep. A group of female embassy workers in the far corner of the room started to weep with him. The sound of crying overwhelmed the room. Lock spoke calmly: 'Look, let's all calm down and keep quiet. I think they are only firing blanks. They aren't going to hurt us, so let's just be as quiet as we can.'

In fact, three members of the embassy staff had managed to escape: Zari Afkhami, head of the medical section, had grabbed an elderly Iranian clerk and together they had scrambled to freedom through the window of Afkhami's ground-floor office. They had then run across the street and asked two builders working nearby to call the police. Another embassy official had bravely made his escape by climbing on to the first-floor front balcony, across the intervening parapet and into the Ethiopian Embassy, next door at No. 17 Princes Gate.

Dr Afrouz was not so fortunate. Still lying on the embassy's rear flagstone patio, he'd just begun to recover consciousness when two of the terrorists came down to get him. Making their way out through the ground-floor library, they grabbed the injured Chargé d'Affaires and dragged him up to a first-floor secretarial office. Afrouz was bleeding from a cut beneath his eye. Groggy with concussion and the pain of his broken jaw and bruised ribs, he had little or no idea what was happening. But as the embassy's chief representative of the Islamic revolutionary regime they hated, to the gunmen Afrouz was the enemy incarnate.

Yelling at him not to try any more tricks, Ali raised his Smith & Wesson revolver and fired a shot into the ceiling directly above the diplomat's head. He was looking to taunt Afrouz, leave him in no doubt as to who was in charge of the embassy now.

Their first thought had been to keep Afrouz away from the other captives, but a few minutes later the gunmen changed their minds, hauling Afrouz along the corridor and across the landing into Room 9. Barely able to stand, he promptly collapsed to the floor. Seeing the blood and his badly torn clothes, the hostages assumed the gunmen had beaten him up. Morris ran and knelt by his boss's side. 'Call a doctor at once!' he shouted at the startled gunmen. 'He is seriously ill. Come on!'

Following a short discussion with the other men in Arabic, Salim said: 'It is not possible. Please be quiet.'

'Well, at least let me get some water for his face,' Morris retorted, refusing to back down. To everyone's surprise, one of the gunmen went and fetched some water in an unused plant pot.

While Morris did his best to clean up Afrouz's injuries, Cramer used some of the water to wash the blood from the cuts on PC Lock's swollen face. The two men had nodded hello to each other on one of Cramer's previous visits to the embassy. Now they had a chance to talk. Lock told Cramer he still had his gun. 'They searched me but they didn't find it. They missed it. I'm not going to use it though. Look how many of them there are. I could only take out two of them at the most. It would put everyone in danger if I used it. But if the bastards shoot me, then take it. It's under my jumper on my hip. You BBC types ever used a gun? There's no safety catch – just pull the trigger.'

There was no way Lock could have known it, but in the BBC Cramer was known as 'Crusher Cramer' after he'd rescued newsreader Angela Rippon from the unwelcome attentions of a male fan who'd sneaked his way past security. The name was ironic: Cramer had simply taken the man by the arm, asked him to leave and then escorted him, unresisting, out of the building – but it had stuck.

They were interrupted by the jangling sound of a telephone. Karkouti, who was nearest, picked it up: 'Hello, who is there please?' Makki cocked his pistol and aimed it at Karkouti's head. The Syrian journalist quickly put the phone down, saying, 'It was a wrong number I think.'

'At least someone knows we're here,' Cramer muttered to Harris. 'And they'll be wondering where we are at the office. Christ knows, we've spent enough time here in the past week trying to get those bloody visas.'

As if on cue, a loud bleeping noise sounded from inside the cipher room. 'That's my Post Office pager,' said Harris hurriedly. 'It's just my office trying to get hold of me. But if I don't answer, they won't know I'm here.'

One of the gunmen went up to the beeping pager and poked it with his toe. Then he pointed his gun at it. For a moment, Harris and Cramer thought the man was going to shoot the device. Instead, he kicked it away.

Salim, seeming calmer now, said: 'How do I phone for doctor?'

'Dial 999 – three 9s,' Lock said. 'Or we can call on my two-way radio, if you let me get it.'

The suggestion alarmed Salim. 'No. You stay here. You all stay here.' With that he left the room.

He came back a few minutes later carrying a large bundle of printed leaflets. Handing one to Cramer, he turned to address the room. 'I want to tell you why we here and what we want. First I read this in

Farsi and then, Mr Chris, please you will read in English.' Quaintly, Salim addressed the British hostages as 'Mr Chris', 'Mr Sim', 'Mr Trevor' and 'Mr Ron'.

The room settled down – it was their first chance to find out what the gunmen wanted, why they were holding them all up – and everyone was listening intently. While Salim read the Farsi script to the Iranians, Cramer glanced through the badly written English version. It was as he feared. If the gunmen's demands were not met by noon the following day, they meant to blow up the embassy and everyone inside. Judging from the squeals of terror from the Farsi-speakers in the room, it was obvious Salim had just reached the same point in his recitation.

Cramer steadied his nerves and began reading in English.

We belong to the Group of the Martyr. We belong to the Democratic Revolutionary Movement for the Liberation of Arabistan.

We, the Group of the Martyr apologise to the British people and government for any inconvenience we are causing. We are seeking to bring to your attention, the plight of the Arab people in Arabistan who are suffering under the Iranian regime. We demand the release of ninety-one Arabs being held prisoner in Arabistan, a plane to fly them all from Tehran to London and the recognition of Arabistan as an autonomous region. The British authorities have twenty-four hours to react otherwise we will blow up the embassy.

To the hostages looking down a selection of gun barrels, the word 'martyr' was especially frightening. Martyrs by definition were prepared to die for their cause. But nobody cared to join them.

Cramer broke the deathly silence: 'It's all well and good telling *us* this, but how are you going to tell the outside world?'

'We have already thrown paper out of window at police,' Salim said. 'We wait now for their response. We shall wait twenty-four hours. If nothing, we will kill you. Now silence!'

Salim made a short tour of his new kingdom. What fell to his gaze pleased him. With minimal violence and bloodshed, he and his band of Arabistani brothers had captured twenty-six hostages. True, some of the women were crying, and several of the Iranians were rocking backwards and forwards praying urgently to themselves. But the British and other foreign nationals were keeping nice and quiet. And the injured Ali Afrouz was dozing in the corner like a little lamb.

. . .

In the Killing House at Bradbury Lines, Pete Winner – Snapper – was patching up the target he'd just shot full of holes when the pagers started bleeping. He looked down. Ops messages featured a sequence of four digits. To his surprise, Snapper saw the number 9999 on his pager. Slapping some more glue on the ferocious cardboard 'Carlos the Jackal' target, he shouted over to the other three men in his team: 'It's the "live op" code. And I bet it's another lemon.'

Only the year before, the entire duty SP team had scrambled to Stansted Airport when an over-excited Irish air traffic controller triggered a full-scale alert in the belief that Ugandan dictator Idi Amin was about to land his personal jet in the UK – without permission and without warning. And without anyone having the slightest idea what the brutal dictator might be planning to do. The alarm had turned out to be entirely false. Snapper had no expectation that this latest call to arms would prove any less 'Mickey Mouse'. Still, a call-out was better than schlepping off on another routine exercise where the good guys win in the end.

Lance Corporal Rusty Firmin was at home drinking coffee and leafing through the morning newspaper. Unmarried, Firmin lived within five hundred metres of the camp's main gate. When his pager went off, he looked down, swallowed the last of the coffee and set out at a quick walk. Whatever was going on, he'd be one of the first to find out. During his three years with the SAS, Firmin had already seen his share of action. It might be that he was about to see some more.

Lance Corporal John McAleese had just enjoyed a leisurely full English breakfast of best Herefordshire bacon – and as far as he was concerned, it was the best in the world – easy-over fried eggs and grilled tomato. Then he'd played silly games with his sixth-month-old son, Paul, his firstborn child and the apple of his fatherly eye. McAleese smiled to himself. The little plastic frog he'd bought earlier in town was a big hit: when he pulled the string that moved its arms and legs, his baby son gurgled and shrieked with delight. As he strolled in towards camp, he thought it was a bit of a shame the exercise was probably going to stretch right through the May Bank Holiday weekend. He might be in the SAS, but when he was away from home he missed the boy. And just as he was thinking that, his bleeper went off.

McAleese stopped and glanced down. Seeing the '9999' code for a live operation, he shook the device to see if it had displayed the message in error. It hadn't: less than one minute later, the same operational callout code flashed into view again.

His next reaction was a moment of elation. You trained and trained, and nothing happened. Some blokes trained their whole careers and never fired a shot in anger. McAleese had fired plenty in his time: several covert tours of Northern Ireland had seen to that. But there was nothing like the chance to hone your fighting skills in a real battle. Bloody lucky, he thought, that B Squadron had just taken over SP team duty from D Squadron.

In those rare cases where 22 (SAS) Regiment's extra firepower and expertise were needed as a 'military aid to the civil power', it usually came in the shape of the SP team – the cutting-edge, immediate response anti-terrorist unit responsible for combating armed terrorist attacks on the British mainland. Each of the Regiment's four fighting Sabre squadrons – A, B, D and G – rotated six-month stints of SP duty, with one team on thirty-minute standby to move, the other at three-hours' notice. But when all the bleepers sounded at the same time it was a case of: 'get as many team members in as quickly as you can'. At the time of the callout, B Squadron had some men away on training courses in the UK. Other SP team members were abroad training foreign nationals. So when the call came, B Squadron was slightly below the complement it needed for a full SP team. With several senior corporals and sergeants deployed in the Middle East,

Blue Team was most affected. Unlike Dr Who, the Regiment did not have a Tardis at its disposal. To bring B Squadron up to strength, extra snipers from A and D Squadrons would be attached for the duration of the operation.

With a new spring in his step, McAleese picked up the pace and headed for the camp's main gates. By the time he reached them, he was moving at a dog-trot. The second he got into camp, McAleese knew the call-out was for real. The whole place was buzzing, on fire with a new purpose. It was in the body language of everyone he saw; he could see it gleaming in their eyes.

As he drew near the Paludrine Club – as some wag had named the NAAFI canteen after the bitter anti-malarial medicine the coffee resembled – he bumped into Snapper. 'All right, mate?' McAleese nodded down at his pager. 'There's a live op?'

'Looks like it,' Snapper said. 'They want us in the hangar now for briefing.' They set off at a brisk pace.

When they reached the big hangar in the centre of the camp, the men of both Red and Blue Teams were pouring in through the doors. Confident the information would be passed on to any latecomers, B Squadron's OC, Major Hector Gullan started the briefing:

'Morning, gentlemen. The intelligence we have so far is very sketchy. But I can confirm we're looking at a live op. It appears that an unknown number of men, most likely of Iraqi origin, have stormed the Iranian Embassy in central London at approximately 1130 hours. They're armed – shots were fired as they made entry. Early estimates suggest they have taken everyone inside the building hostage, but the exact number of hostages is as yet unknown. We do know that one of the hostages is a Diplomatic Protection Group officer, Police Constable Trevor Lock. We also know that Lock is – or was – armed with a .38 Smith & Wesson revolver. *Do not repeat this information for the present.* There are no reports so far of any casualties. We have no idea who is behind this attack or what they want. Our orders are to move up to Regent's Park Barracks and prepare for an immediate action. In the meantime, get on with checking and packing your kit. I will keep everyone up to speed as more information comes in. Any questions?'

There were none. You could tell by the pin-drop silence that every-one was raring to go. Like John McAleese, they felt they trained and they trained – but you could only sharpen a knife so much. What they wanted was to use the edge. And for that you had to be lucky. Today, it looked as if they might be lucky.

The SP team's seven white-painted Range Rovers and its motley collection of Ford Transit vans were parked in a neat row along the far side of the two hangars. A pallet loaded with equipment for immediate use sat directly behind each Range Rover. It included boxes of operational ammunition; operational weapons such as Remington 870 pump-action shotguns, MP5 machine guns, Polecat gas-canister launchers and British Army-issue hand grenades; food supplies; water; tool-rolls; radios and spare batteries; model S6 gas respirators; night-vision goggles; boxes of CS and stun grenades; medical equipment; method-of-entry kit and explosives; and – although there weren't enough of them to go around every member of the team – Maglite MP5 gun-torches on permanent charge ready to be picked up prior to departure.

All team members had a green army-issue holdall bag that travelled with them in the operational vehicles. It held their gloves, NBC hood, balaclava, S6 respirator, coveralls, boots, belt kit, ops waistcoat, weapon-cleaning kit, 4 by 2 body armour and ceramic plates for body armour, and abseiling essentials. The bag also held personal weapons like the MP5 and 9mm Browning semi-automatic pistol and a couple of shell dressings; not to mention four MP5 thirty-round magazines and one twenty-round mag, two twelve-round mags for the Browning, and individual operational ammunition. This meant as soon as they got to an incident they could be operational in a matter of minutes.

Everyone on the SP team also had a personal 'go' or 'ready long-stay' bag with him. It held things like spare clothing; shaving gear; toothbrush; extra black assault kit; sleeping bag or green maggot; tracksuit; training shoes; underwear, etc.

A big pantechnicon loaded with the heavy gear was on standby in a nearby hangar. The van contained a vast assortment of ladders including caving ladders; drums of climbing ropes and abseiling gear;

high-powered lighting rigs; large tools; specialist battering rams; extra water and food and other, more secret specialist equipment. The van also transported the personal long-stay bags.

Each member of the SP team had his own dedicated personal weapons stored on his pallet. Any extra weapon requirements could be signed for from the small SP team stores and the armoury right there in one of the hangars. Like all legally held firearms, each gun came stamped with a unique serial number.

Following Selection – the notoriously difficult process in which nine out of ten SAS recruits fail to make the grade – all new troopers trained on a vast range of foreign weaponry collected from all quarters of the globe. In a tight situation, they had to be able to identify and use what came to hand if required. Their primary, preferred weapon for close-quarters anti-terrorist work was the Heckler & Koch MP5 in all its variants. The Regiment had adopted the MP5 about three years before. This had changed the whole game in favour of the good guys. For Special Forces everywhere, the MP5 was a Rolls-Royce weapon.

Most men had the basic model. A few had the MP5-K, or Kurz ('short' in German); two of the Blue reserve team had the MP5-SD, or silenced version: but only because there weren't enough of the basic model to go round.

Far more accurate out to 300 metres than the Sterling SMG it replaced, the MP5 had a rolling-locked bolt system, making it quicker, easier and safer to fire. Its magazine, which came in fifteen- or thirty-round variants, projected downwards, not sideways, which helped to prevent misfires, and the spent shell cases ejected sideways and not down.

The sighting system on the MP5 was also a huge improvement on the Sterling's. Based on the principle of concentric rings, which channel human eyesight naturally, the MP5 had a rotary drum rear sight and a hooded post fore sight. Along with its many other merits, the weapon was superbly engineered; it tolerated not being cleaned as much as it should be, and it was very reliable.

When it came to ammo, the SP team – like the rest of the

Heckler & Koch MP5 (1980 model)

MP5-SD

MP5-K

Regiment – chambered full metal jacketed Mk.2z 9x19mm NATO standard Parabellum rounds in both the MP5 and the Browning High-Power semi-automatic pistol standard close assault weapons. The name 'Parabellum' comes from the old Roman motto: *Si vis pacem, para bellum* – 'If you seek peace, prepare for war'.

Like the Sterling, the MP5 had a low muzzle velocity (400 m/second) compared with an assault rifle like the AK-47 (715 m/s). It might sound counter-intuitive, but a low-velocity round generally inflicts more damage at short range than its high-velocity cousin: the whole of the slower bullet's destructive energy tends to explode inside the target's body mass instead of making a neat, and often more survivable, 'through and through' wound.

Some of Blue Team were fresh from live-firing training in the Killing House. They got busy now, checking and cleaning their weapons. Others set about the gargantuan task of making a Sabre squadron ready for a live op. With most of the men prepared for the upcoming exercise anyway, that didn't take long.

At 1458 hrs, the SP team command group or 'head shed' set off for London. At this time most people weren't any the wiser as to what was happening. There had been a few rumours as the day progressed, but no solid info. At 1700 hrs, the command group arrived at the Defence Situation Centre (DSC) in London, where they were briefed. At 1830 hrs, the head shed moved on to Regent's Park Barracks, which became the main base station or MBS for the duration of 'Operation Nimrod' as it was now codenamed.

This did take some time. It wasn't until 1930 hrs that evening that the SP team Range Rovers slipped out of the camp in pairs, the intervals deliberately irregular to prevent any watchers realising there was something serious afoot. The pantechnicon would follow in its own time and would eventually rendezvous at the MBS.

Still travelling at widely spaced intervals, the seven white-painted Range Rovers rolled steadily towards London. There was a police radio fitted to each of the vehicles, but there was no speeding or blue flashing lights and no police escort. As they made ground, the SP team's dedicated specialist signaller, Stuart 'Squash Ball' McVicar, checked in with each of the police area controllers in turn to let them know the SAS convoy was passing through. A safety and security measure if something went wrong, it also meant the police knew the type of cargo the SAS vehicles were carrying: frightening. McVicar's shape had earned him the nickname: he might be a bit on the short side, but he was almost as broad as he was tall.

After about two hours on the road, the first vehicles pulled into the Army School of Languages in Beaconsfield. The other SP vehicles came in over the next hour or so. In all the excitement, most of the SP team hadn't eaten lunch. Hungry, and looking forward to a good meal, they made straight for the camp canteen. The sorry fare that awaited them fell well short of expectations.

'What's this, Chef? Breakfast?' said the man at the head of the queue.

The chef was a sergeant; a big man, but running to fat. By the time the SP team turned up wanting food he seemed the worse for wear. 'Take it or leave it,' he said. 'That's all you're getting.' Clearly the chef had no idea who his long-haired visitors were or what they were doing in a short-haired Green Army base.

'You what?' 'Tak' Takavesi was a big man, too – but in his case, the size was made up of solid muscle. Renowned for his spicy but flavoursome curries, Tak enjoyed cooking – and eating. He tried again, politely asking the chef if he wouldn't mind rustling the men up some fresh grub.

The chef said, 'You heard me,' and stalked back to his kitchen.

Which was rude of him. And unwise. The Regiment takes the old adage, 'an army marches on its stomach' seriously; the sixty men lined up in front of the counter had no time for bad food.

The queue started to move forward. Being big hungry SAS men, the first ten blokes in line saw off everything on offer. Lance Corporal Tommy Palmer, who was next in line, looked down at the empty trays. 'Chef!' he called, doing his best Oliver impression. 'Got any more grub?'

The chef came back up to the counter. 'I already told you – that's it.'

Palmer's eyes narrowed. He looked ominous that way, like Clint

Eastwood when the bad guys have just insulted him. The chef started cleaning up, banging noisily about as a sign for his unwelcome visitors to leave. Now Takavesi's gaze flattened, too. Tak was an easy-going sort – except when you got between him and his food. He said mildly: 'Look, mate, there are a lot of us, and we're bloody starving. Someone rang ahead to say we were coming. Now, are you going to rustle up some fresh scoff, or what? We don't need anything fancy. How about some egg and chips?'

The chef leaned forward. 'How many times do I have to tell you? You've had your chips – I'm off duty.'

A collective sigh ran down the line of waiting men. Nobody said a word. Two men stepped out of line, lifted the access hatch and walked through. Grabbing the chef, they frogmarched him to the nearest stove. One man caught the chef's left hand, applying a lock that bent him double and made him more amenable. The other switched on a hotplate, then turned and grabbed the goggling chef by the wrist. As if it was the kind of thing he did every day, he placed the chef's hand palm down on the slowly warming ring. The chef's face had turned pale. His mouth opened and strange sounds that might have been words spluttered from his lips.

As the heat from the hotplate began to seep into the skin of his palm, the chef found his voice: 'All right!' he yodelled. 'I'll cook for you! Let me go!'

The men who'd been holding the chef let him go. One brushed him down. 'Didn't hurt you, did we, Chef?' he asked politely.

'No,' stuttered the chef. 'I'm fine. But I'd like to get some help – there are a lot of you.'

'Fair enough, Chef: you go right ahead and do what you have to do.'

Half an hour later, the SP team sat down to a freshly cooked meal.

■ ■ ■

PC Lock's emergency signal had triggered something akin to warfare at New Scotland Yard. When one of their own was in danger, the police pulled out all the stops. Their task now was to get officers to the location as fast as possible; identify the threat to their man; and neutralise it.

At 1126 hrs, the local police station at Gerald Road put through a second emergency call to the Yard. This one had a measure of detail: there was trouble at the Iranian Embassy in Princes Gate: armed men had forced their way inside, and a police officer had been injured.

Sirens wailing, four armed DPG motorcycle officers roared to the scene, clearing the startled London traffic from their path. They were outside No. 16 Princes Gate by 1131 hrs. DPG commander Chief Superintendent Roger Bromley, who happened to be nearby, arrived a minute later. Another three DPG officers arrived shortly after him. Jumping off their motorbikes, the seven officers moved to surround the embassy, then began probing forward in an effort to discover what was happening.

Residents of nearby apartments were astonished to see armed policemen rushing through the garden behind the embassy. Disturbed by the commotion, the novelist Dame Rebecca West started up from her desk: fiction was all very well, but here, unfolding before her very eyes, was what seemed to be an extraordinary real-life drama.

One police officer approached the embassy's rear. Looking up, he saw a gunman standing at one of the first-floor windows. 'Who are you and what do you want?' the officer called.

'If you take one more step you'll be shot,' the gunman called back. The officer wisely retreated.

The Met's Deputy Assistant Commissioner (DAC) John Dellow arrived outside the embassy a few minutes after midday. Head of Scotland Yard's day-to-day operations, Dellow, who'd joined the police force at the age of eighteen, had been in the Met for twenty-nine years. Tall, slim, aquiline and crisply turned out, with a military bearing and an air of confident, relaxed authority, he was the very model of a modern police commander.

Setting up temporary command in his car, Dellow's first action was to initiate the emergency protocol the Metropolitan Police employed in the event of sieges, hostage-taking and hijackings. Known by the acronym 'ICC' the emergency protocol's immediate provisions were to: Isolate the incident; Cordon off the perimeter; and Contain and negotiate the crisis to a peaceful conclusion.

Dellow's priority was to create a sterile area around the embassy: isolate the gunmen inside, and make the isolation tell on them as much as possible. To this end, Dellow ordered his men to set up inner and outer cordons around Princes Gate; to evacuate neighbouring or tactically useful buildings; and deploy the police dog section from Heathrow to help cut off any gunmen who might try to make an early run for it.

Ch. Supt Bromley and Ch. Supt Fred Luff, former head of the Met's Drug Squad and now based at Gerald Road police station, approached the front of the embassy. The last element of the ICC protocol, 'Contain and negotiate to a peaceful conclusion', was in many ways the most important. Both policemen knew it was essential to make contact and start negotiations with the hostage-takers as soon as possible. They began shouting up at the embassy's front windows, hoping for some response. A gunman appeared at a first-floor front window. Face shrouded in a kaffiyeh, the man leaned out and threw a sheaf of leaflets down into the street. Bromley picked one up. It was in Farsi. With no translator yet on the scene, the statement made no sense at all.

As he puzzled over the words, a new face appeared at the window. Waving one of the leaflets, Luff shouted up: 'What does this mean?'

Salim called back: 'We are the Group of the Martyr. We demand the release of ninety-one of our brothers held in Iran. We want a plane when the hostages are released.' There was a slight pause while the police absorbed the demands. Then Salim added a chilling coda: 'If these demands are not met within twenty-four hours, the hostages will be killed. The embassy will be blown up if there is any police interference.'

The leaflet might have been inscrutable. But the gunman's last statement left the police in no doubt about the Group's intentions.

■ ■ ■

As the police stopped and rerouted the traffic away from the roads surrounding Princes Gate, Independent Radio News (IRN) reporter

Simon Prebble found himself caught up in the jam. When he saw the ever-increasing number of police officers swarming around the scene, Prebble grabbed his press card, jumped out of his car and tried to find a telephone box. In the days before mobile telephones, contacting the newsroom at a moment's notice was no mean feat. With no red telephone box in sight, Prebble ran into the Thai Embassy. He was astonished to find all the staff lying on the floor under tables and desks, or hiding in cupboards. Terrified by the sound of shooting from the nearby Iranian Embassy, they'd decided that discretion was the better part of valour.

Picking up one of the numerous unused phones, Prebble filed his report. 'At about 1145 this morning, I was coming out of the park when I was suddenly caught in a wedge of police cars, vans and so forth with a lot of plain-clothes police and policemen busily putting on bullet-proof vests. They stormed across the road to Princes Gate.' Prebble went on to say a gunman had stormed into the Iranian Embassy and shots had been heard. But he did not know whether anyone had been hurt, or who the gunman might be. 'I gather he's not English, that's all I know. As you can imagine, the police have clammed up. Since the first few moments, nobody is speaking to anybody. It has all the appearance of a siege.'

With that last assessment, at least, Prebble was spot on.

IRN broadcast the report at 1210 hrs. It was the first public news of the Iranian Embassy siege.

■ ■ ■

New Scotland Yard now issued an 'official warning order'. This was a heads-up to all Metropolitan police agencies likely to be involved in resolving a major terrorist incident. They included C11, or Special Branch, the armed unit that works in close conjunction with the British Intelligence services; and C13, the Met's own criminal intelligence and surveillance branch. With specialist knowledge of the world's political terrorists and terrorist movements, they brought in Arabic and Farsi translators. No one knew for certain yet where the gunmen were from, but there was every chance the police hostage negotiators would need someone who could translate Iran's official language, Farsi, into and out of English accurately.

Other specialist squads raced to the scene. The Met's elite D11 Blue Berets, who trained the force's armed officers, began taking up positions on both sides of the Iranian Embassy: behind the chimney breasts of surrounding flats and houses; on the roof of the Royal Geographical Society opposite; and behind any other available cover that offered a clear field of fire.

Like the SAS, the Blue Berets trained intensively for trouble that rarely came. Now, as they slid the long barrels of their high-powered sniper rifles forward from their points of vantage, they had the same feeling: all the relentless training had been worth it.

In the streets adjoining Princes Gate, Special Patrol Group (SPG) officers from A9 branch pulled up in Transit vans and sat waiting, ready for action. Known for their strong-arm methods, the SPG enjoyed a mixed reputation in the British media. What they weren't known for was keeping a low profile. But on this occasion, as part of the effort to make the gunmen feel alone and friendless in an empty, hostile world, they stayed well back and out of sight.

Scotland Yard's Technical Support Branch, C7, coasted up in plain vans that held some of the world's most advanced electronic surveillance equipment behind their nondescript exteriors. Their state-of-the-art equipment included a long-range listening device that used a laser beam to pick up the tiny vibrations in window panes produced by voices speaking in the room beyond, and bounced it back off the glass to a speech-decoding unit.

As they began assessing how best to bug the embassy, the C7 men were dismayed to see someone going round the building systematically drawing its wooden shutters and heavy brocade curtains. At a stroke, and almost certainly without being aware they'd achieved it, the gunmen had rendered the Met's secret, hi-tech laser listening devices useless.

Within one hour of Lock's initial alarm call, the Met had established secure inner and outer cordons around the embassy. Their taped-off perimeters would be policed around the clock. The cordons were as much to keep people out – especially the press and the expected pro- and anti-Iranian government protesters – as they were to make sure none of the gunmen escaped. The *cordon sanitaire* was also there to assist and protect any hostages who might be released or succeed in escaping. All roads in the vicinity were closed to traffic.

■ ■ ■

After issuing orders for the SP team to deploy to London, Lt-Col Rose whistled up a Special Forces Flight helicopter. Major Gullan went with him. They circled over the Iranian Embassy for a few minutes to get the lay of the land, then flew on and set down at Northolt RAF base, some ten miles to the west of the capital. Rose asked for, and got, the use of the station commander's car.

Using all her fast-driving skills, the driver whisked Rose and Gullan to Kensington at top speed. With the two SAS commanders in plain clothes, Dellow was the only police officer at Princes Gate who knew they were on site. As always when an SAS unit was deployed, the need for secrecy was paramount. Rose and Gullan wasted no time in getting to work. They quickly established that the narrow passage at the eastern end of Princes Gate led into the gardens at the embassy's rear. Once inside, a partially covered culvert led along the back of the terrace and close to No. 16. It wasn't the wholly covert approach the SAS would have wanted, but on the other hand, it wasn't bad.

In the neighbouring streets, ambulances parked up next to the SPG wagons; with them came a team of doctors, at least one of whom would now be on call twenty-four hours a day. The police had learned a lot of useful lessons from the two sieges they'd had to deal with in 1975. In October of that year, three criminals had taken six waiters hostage at a Spaghetti House restaurant. The second siege had flared in December, when an IRA active service unit had held an elderly couple at gunpoint for six days in Balcombe Street, Marylebone. On both occasions, the police had employed psychological profilers to great effect. And in both cases, all the hostages had been released without harm.

The Met asked Professor John Gunn, a psychologist based at the

Maudsley Hospital to begin work on profiling the embassy gunmen. The first thing Gunn would try to establish was the type of person they were dealing with. Were they students? Highly trained and fully committed members of a known terrorist organisation? Amateurs? Or madmen?

Police catering units set up mobile canteens to provide vital refreshments for the small army now assembling to scotch the snake of terrorism.

It wasn't long before the inside of Dellow's car proved much too small a space from which to run such a complex and rapidly evolving operation. The police needed a Forward Control Point – fast.

At the same time as the Met forward control and negotiating teams were looking for somewhere to set up shop, Squash Ball McVicar, the specialist signaller started scouting for the best place to establish a secure local area radio net. With all the houses in the terrace now in the process of evacuation, he had free rein. The layout of the Royal College of General Practitioners at No. 14 was almost identical to that of the Iranian Embassy. McVicar discovered only two serious dead spots in the RCGP, or 'Doctors' House', as he now dubbed it: one in the basement and one on the building's top floor. Thorough to the last, he repeated the procedure at the Ethiopian Embassy on the other side of No. 16, and then went off down the street to try the Royal Needlework School.

The moment he rang the doorbell of the 'Needlework Factory', McVicar realised he was up against a tough enemy: the women who ran the place. Founded in 1872, the school – which is now at Hampton Court Palace – has a large and very precious archive. Its walls were festooned with antique needlework – sewing samplers dating back centuries, rare tapestries and hangings, all unique, all more or less fragile and in need of constant care. The ladies now in McVicar's face looked after more than five thousand priceless artefacts. Unimpressed by the rather scruffily dressed visitor who said he was in 'the SAS' – an organisation they had never heard of and, judging by its current representative was in any case thoroughly dubious – the two women gave McVicar short shrift. The last thing they wanted was a lot of very large men in hobnails thundering around the place, banging into their treasures.

Before retiring, McVicar took readings on his instruments. It turned out that the signal strengths and weaknesses in the Needlework School, the Ethiopian Embassy and the Doctors' House were almost identical. It was therefore reasonable to assume that the Iranian Embassy's signal profile would be the same.

Sticking to McVicar like glue, the needlework ladies told him in no uncertain terms not to move or touch anything, not to tread on anything, and to be careful where and how hard he breathed. Talking of breathing, he wasn't allowed to smoke anywhere on the premises either. He went outside to snatch a crafty cigarette.

Here he bumped into DAC Dellow, who was on his way in to ask if he could use the building as a forward control point. 'Good luck,' was all McVicar said when Dellow told him what he was doing. But the arrival of a senior Metropolitan police officer in full uniform and with a small retinue in tow had a positive effect. The custodians agreed to allow the police the run of certain rooms, but only if Dellow adhered to the same strict conditions.

Following delicate and protracted negotiations, the Met Police command group clumped into the building, moved into the agreed areas of access, and started establishing what they now called Zulu Control. The arrangement lasted no more than a few hours. By late afternoon, the police officers in the newly created forward control point were pasty-faced and sweating. Not because they were ill, but because they were all dying for a cigarette. Most of them smoked. A lot. Recognising the effect the lack of regular nicotine intake was having on his team's morale, Dellow decided to shift Zulu Control next door to the Montessori Nursery School at No. 24. There was a second major advantage to moving: he'd no longer have to worry about all that blasted needlework.

The teachers at No. 24 were charming and helpful. All they wanted the police to do was feed the school's pet gerbil, Mr Nibbles, on a regular basis. With Mr Nibbles' future feeding programme duly agreed, the police forward control team moved in. They set up a main incident room on the ground floor, complete with information boards, radio communications, a tea urn and extra telephones.

The initial four-man police hostage negotiation team took up residence in the attic. They were: Detective Chief Inspector David Veness, one of the Met's youngest and most able senior officers; Ch. Supt Fred Luff; Det. Supt Ray Tucker of the Special Branch; and Det. Supt Trevor Lloyd-Hughes from the Stolen Vehicles Section. Such was the stress on these four men that two extra negotiators, including DCI Max Vernon, were later brought in to share the load, reducing the team's twelve-hour shifts to a more reasonable eight hours.

The hostage negotiators were now the most important people at the scene. Their job was to form a relationship with the gunmen inside the embassy – the closer the better – and talk the siege to a peaceful conclusion. The essential tactic in the negotiating process was delay. Previous hostage negotiations had shown that the more time went by, the more the hostage-takers would realise the futility of their position. It was also well established that the longer the negotiators could stall and prevaricate, the more tired the gunmen would get. Tired people make mistakes, and fatigue lowers morale. The police could change personnel at will. The gunmen could not.

The negotiators didn't quite work to a script, but they did employ a number of default tactics: never give a straight answer to a direct question; convince the gunmen that as a negotiator you have no power, but can only act as an intermediary; and to reinforce that, always tell them you have to refer decisions to a higher authority; never give the gunmen anything without getting something back; make it clear from the outset that either they deal, or there's no deal; befriend the gunmen; never engage in an argument or lose your temper; and above all never lose sight of the goal: to end the siege without violence.

One very important thing the negotiators had to do was to try and create conditions in which the gunmen's dependence on the authorities was absolute. The idea was to reduce the hostage-takers to the status of needy – and, if possible, rather frightened – children. If they wanted food, they had to ask the negotiators to supply it. If they needed a doctor, or medicine, or a plane to fly them to some exotic terrorist haven, whatever it might be, the gunmen would have to ask the police if they could have it. And the moment they asked, they were in the negotiators' deceptively friendly, invitingly emollient grasp. A clutch that was in reality utterly cold-hearted.

The key factor in all this was communication. There must be one way, and one way only in which the gunmen could contact the outside world: through the police. As part of the isolation process, Dellow ordered Post Office engineers to cut all telephone and telex links from the embassy. Assuming the work had been correctly and fully carried out, Dellow then had a green, military-style field telephone passed into the embassy by means of a shoe-box on the end of a long wooden pole. Unless they resorted to shouting out of the windows, the gunmen now had to rely wholly on the police for all and any communication. From here on it would be the police and not the gunmen who determined the pace – and even the fact – of any negotiations.

Dellow got the gunmen to accept the field telephone by convincing them that it was the only way in which their negotiations would remain private and secure.

On the face of it, the field telephone was very simple. It consisted of two handsets joined by a long length of wire, which the police could pay out as necessary. Thus Salim – who acted as the gunmen's sole negotiator – could move up and down the embassy with it at will yet always remain in touch. Each handset had two buttons: a red one to call the other end, and a black one to speak.

What the terrorists didn't know was that the handset on their end of the landline never, ever switched off. It was a listening device: a bug that was always on. Not only that, the police had discreetly marked the phone line between the two handsets at metre intervals. The length of phone line they had to pay out as he moved up and down the embassy told the police which floor Salim was on at any given time. They could even take an educated guess as to whether he was at the front or the rear of the building.

By the end of the afternoon on Day One, Zulu Control was fully operational. The only problem was the furniture: designed for nursery-age children, it was tiny: there was no way Met officers were going to fit their large, serge-covered bottoms into those miniature seats. Dellow ordered up some replacement furniture, and told his men to stack the nursery stuff to one side. There was nothing he could do about the ankle-level toilets. They'd just have to manage as best they could.

McVicar had been hard at work setting up the SP team's forward comms hub and temporary forward operational HQ on the second-floor landing of the Royal College of General Practitioners. Its call sign was 'Sunray'. Off-radio, the members of the SP team called it 'The Desk'. The call sign for Major Gullan personally, or for whoever had operational control in the event of his being replaced, was 'Lysander'. For the next five days and nights, McVicar would sleep, eat and live on the landing. To him this was no hardship: wherever he pitched it, mountaintop or moor, once he crawled inside his 'green maggot' sleeping bag he slept like the proverbial.

The Doctors' House would also act as the SP team's Forward Holding Area and sleeping quarters. Alternating twelve-hour shifts, when they were on standby Blue Team or Red Team would make themselves as comfortable as they could in the large and beautifully furnished first-floor reception room.

■ ■ ■

Within minutes of Prebble's initial radio broadcast, the newly installed police CCTV cameras were relaying real-time images of the embassy and surrounding area. At once, the police saw that the area around the embassy was crawling with journalists, probing the edges of the police cordons in an effort to penetrate and cover the story. But it was essential to prevent the press from broadcasting live footage that might prove useful to the gunmen. Even the newly austere Iranian Embassy might still have a television on the premises. The last thing the police wanted was the gunmen seeing what they – or any other official forces on the scene – were doing.

Determined to keep the media under control, Met Police press relations officer DAC Peter Nievens set up 'Pressville', a small, fenced area on the corner of Kensington Gore and Exhibition Road. Within a few hours, Pressville had taken on the look of a teeming, ramshackle adventure playground, as national and international TV news crews vied to erect the tallest scaffolding towers or bring up the tallest mobile 'cherry-picker' camera cranes from which to get the best view of the siege. Outside broadcast vans arrived, and with them mobile food canteens: the international press pack was on the scent of a momentous story, and they would not leave until they got it.

■ ■ ■

In an ironic twist, at the very moment the gunmen blasted their way into the Iranian Embassy, several key Home Office officials with responsibility for counter-terrorism were in central London attending a conference on Terrorism and the Media. The proceedings were interrupted so that they could be told of the siege, and go to their places of duty as required.

As it became clear that the siege was developing into a major incident, the forces of the British state shifted into high gear. Chief among these was the recently established national crisis office: the Cabinet Office Briefing Room (COBR, or more easily, COBRA). Housed in the basement of a magnificent Renaissance-style building just around the corner from Downing Street on Whitehall, COBRA had been established precisely to deal with national emergencies of the kind that was now unfolding in Princes Gate. It had a long central table and chairs, and a wall of television monitors tuned to both domestic and foreign stations. It also had various 'hot-line' telephone links, including one to Number 10 Downing Street, the Prime Minister's residence, and another to the office of the Home Secretary.

Chaired by the Home Secretary, William 'Willie' Whitelaw, COBRA both managed a given national crisis and acted as the direct conduit between the ultimate power in the land, the Prime Minister, and all the other arms of state.

In the absence of Foreign Secretary Lord Carrington, who was absent on official business, Foreign Office Minister of State Douglas Hurd acted for COBRA in the matter of foreign relations. Barney

Hayhoe arrived to represent the Ministry of Defence. He was joined by senior staff from the British Security Services, MI5 and MI6; Brigadier Peter de la Billière, Director, SAS Group (DSAS); the senior managers of the British Airways Authority, the public utility companies and other key institutions of state.

It was some time before all the key members of COBRA could get together in person – it was 1500 hrs before it convened for the first time – but once in session, the committee was quick on its feet. Later that same afternoon, following extensive telephone consultation between Whitelaw and Prime Minister Margaret Thatcher, COBRA agreed an initial response to the gunmen's demands. It stated:

1. That no terrorist will leave the UK under any circumstances.
2. That all terrorists will be answerable to the law of the UK for their actions.
3. That no hostage will leave the UK under pressure.
4. That the police will negotiate for as long as necessary to reach a peaceful conclusion to the siege.

Living up to her nickname, the Iron Lady made sure the COBRA statement now became official UK government policy. They might not know it yet, but the gunmen were in a prison whose walls were gradually crowding in on them.

After the meeting broke up, Whitelaw made a statement to the House of Commons summarising the agreed strategy. In essence, COBRA's statement was a direct refutation of the gunmen's demands.

Everything was in place for a head-on and bloody collision between the two sides.

■ ■ ■

By early afternoon, things were hotting up in the section of Hyde Park between the Albert Memorial and the Iranian Embassy that the police had set aside for the anticipated demonstrations. Large numbers of pro-Khomeini demonstrators were gathering behind the crush barriers, shouting slogans such as: 'Death to Carter! Death to the

CIA! Death to America!' their cries echoing across the park and into Princes Gate.

A smaller, but no less vociferous band of anti-Khomeini protesters faced them, singing 'Ten ayatollahs standing on the wall, ten ayatollahs standing on the wall. And if one ayatollah should accidentally fall, there'll be nine ayatollahs, standing on the wall . . .' to the tune of 'Ten Green Bottles', and chanting, 'Go home you bums, Go home you bums' to the tune of 'Auld Lang Syne'.

It wasn't long before the pros and antis got to pushing and shoving. Extra police were deployed to keep the two groups apart lest they came to blows, or, in the case of the pro-Iranian demonstrators, broke through the police lines and carried out their threat to storm the embassy and rescue their beleaguered fellow nationals. As the police tried to drive a wedge through the opposing forces, fighting broke out.

These skirmishes were of little concern to DAC Dellow and his fellow Met commanders. They assumed Post Office telephone engineers had cut all the embassy's communications, but they'd missed the main telex line and the telephone in Room 9 was still operational.

The hostages in Room 9 were still adjusting to the group's newly declared timetable. Twenty-four hours didn't seem like such a long time. But supposing the police hadn't picked up the leaflets Salim had thrown out of the window? Suppose he had only thrown out the ones written in Farsi? Knowing how slowly the machinery of the British state could operate, Lock and the other British hostages feared it might take a day just to get the demands translated.

In a sense, the gunmen were in luck: although they hadn't realised it yet, of the twenty-six people they now held captive, no fewer than five were journalists, and two of the embassy staff were press officers. Surprised by the gunmen's naivety – did they really believe that chucking a bunch of leaflets out of the window was an effective way of publicising their cause? – the much more media-savvy Mustapha Karkouti asked if he could make a suggestion. 'I am a journalist,' he said. 'Why don't we telex my newspaper in Beirut and get them to print your demands?'

'They will definitely take the story,' Cramer agreed. 'The BBC will be interested, too. I can get you a direct line to the news desk.'

Salim appeared interested. After hissing some instructions to Abbas and Ali to 'barricade the corridors', he beckoned to Karkouti: 'Come with me.' Pushing the journalist at gunpoint along the corridor to the telex room, Room 10, he told him: 'You speak only to your paper. No funny business.' Karkouti began dialling out on the embassy telex machine. But at the precise moment he attempted to get through to Beirut, John Hooper, a reporter with the *Guardian* newspaper, succeeded in dialling in.

Hooper had been trying repeatedly to get through, but on each attempt he'd received either the OCC – Customer Engaged – or the ABS – Office Closed signal. He was just about to give up and try something else when an 'answerback' code chattered out of the *Guardian*'s telex. It was the Iranian Embassy. Hardly daring to believe his luck, Hooper typed: 'What is happening in there?'

For several minutes there was no response. 'What is it, this *Guardian*?' Salim asked Karkouti suspiciously. Karkouti told him the *Guardian* was a truthful and responsible newspaper, one that didn't simply parrot the official British line, and of all newspapers would be most likely to publish the group's demands verbatim.

Salim told Karkouti to send Hooper the list of demands he had formulated earlier. In the *Guardian* newsroom on Faringdon Road, Hooper was astonished to see the gunmen's demands tumbling out. What a scoop! He typed back a series of questions: 'How many people are occupying the embassy?'

Salim shook his head at Karkouti. 'Do not reply.'

Hooper tried again: 'Are you a spokesman for the group occupying the embassy?'

'Yes.'

'Why did you occupy the embassy?'

'For our human and legitimate rights.'

'What are your rights?'

'Freedom, autonomy and recognition of the Arabistani people.'

'How do you intend to secure your rights with this occupation?'

'This is only one mean[s] to make public opinion know and hear us.' Rattled by how much Hooper had managed to draw out of him, Salim suddenly became agitated: 'No!' he said, stooping and ripping the electrical plug from the socket.

■  ■  ■

Returning to Room 9, Salim felt the need to assert his authority. Angered by the increasingly loud and fervent communal prayers they were committing to Allah, he ordered the Iranian nationals to form a circle on the floor. He told the non-Iranians that they could sit on chairs. Ron Morris said: 'I want to sit in the circle with my friends. This is Iranian soil.'

Salim stared at the embassy manager in amazement. 'No. You British. You must not sit with those people.'

'They are my friends,' insisted Morris, 'I want to be with them.'

Salim's mouth stretched in a tight smile. 'You do not want to sit with them. I tell you why?'

'Why?' demanded the angry Morris.

'Because later, maybe I have to shoot them.'

Morris moved across to sit with the non-Iranians. Altogether there were seven non-Iranian hostages – four British, two Pakistani and one Syrian. On the other side of the room on the floor sat the Iranians: six women and thirteen men.

Lock pulled up a large Queen Anne armchair from its position at the side of the room. From that moment on, occupying the chair almost as a kind of throne whenever they were held in Room 9, he would act as a kind of touchstone and support for the other hostages.

Leaving Faisal and Makki on guard, Salim and the other gunmen disappeared. The Iranian hostages sat uncomfortably in a ring, praying, smoking and talking quietly together. Karkouti told Lock: 'I don't think they anticipated there would be so many of us in here. You know they keep apologising to me about your injuries. They do not wish to harm us.'

'It's a bit late for that,' Lock said, touching the gash on his cheek.

'They're a bit strange aren't they? First they take us at gunpoint, round us all up, force us in here against our will and then they apologise. What's going on? They're a total contradiction.'

Harris was amusing himself with a Saccone & Speed wine list that he had found lying on the floor. 'Hey, aren't they supposed to be teetotal in here?' The BBC sound man had already been to Iran on a news job. He knew how volatile young revolutionary hotheads could be. On top of that, he'd been among the news crews at both the Balcombe Street and Spaghetti House sieges in 1975, and he'd done a lot of work covering the Troubles in Northern Ireland. The sight of weapons didn't faze him quite so much as it did those hostages who had never seen a gun.

Cramer, however, was in no mood for banter. He was chain smoking and thinking. What if he didn't survive this, didn't get out alive? He had been in dangerous situations before but this one felt particularly menacing. Beneath the outward politeness, the group's leader struck him as volatile. He decided to write a letter to his parents:

*Dear Mum and Dad,*

*This seems strange sitting on the floor here in this strange office in the embassy writing to you all. Just think – I had no particular reasons to come here this morning. Another few minutes and I would have been out of the place.*

*My feelings now are difficult to describe. You have the need to keep talking the whole time and don't really care about anyone else except yourself (predictable really!!). I'm obviously frightened but I figure the gunmen are as well. None of us is saying much really.*

*God knows how this will end – all I can think about is what I can tell the lads in the bar when this is all over. The trouble is I can't see an end to it. They have their demands and we know they will never be met.*

*I think the reason I'm writing this is to say that I love you all deeply although I've probably never showed it too much. I know now how really good you have been to me always. Please tell Sue and Bev that I love them both very much. Sue I will always love and Bev*

*could have made me very happy I think. Please take care of yourselves.*
*I am thinking of you the whole time. God bless,*
  *Chris*


As Cramer folded the note up and placed it in the depths of his wallet, Salim reappeared carrying a portable radio. He was jumpy, asking someone to help him tune into a news station. As he listened, he became incensed at a BBC report stating that 'Iraqis' had taken the building by force. He and his brothers were from Arabistan – or Khuzestan if they had to describe it in the enemy's terms.

The reports and Salim's reaction to them did nothing to ease the hostages' state of mind. Fearing the worst, like Cramer, those with families were desperate to let them know what was happening. Frieda Mozafarian started wailing again. It was getting quite difficult to ignore her, especially when she bent and began vomiting into a waste-paper bin. In between times, she was shouting, weeping, fainting and screaming. Bracing Salim up, Morris yelled: 'Can't you see this woman is seriously ill? Let her go at once. Let all the women go!'

'No,' Salim said. 'You must all stay here. No one leaves. We make demands, not you. When police say yes, we let you all go.'

'You coward,' Morris hissed back. 'At least call for a doctor. You aren't very brave, are you?'

Faisal moved forward. He raised his arm as if to strike Morris, but Salim held him back. Morris's words had done the trick. 'Guard them!' Salim snapped at the other gunmen and went downstairs to the field telephone. 'Get me a doctor: woman doctor,' he told the police.

In the same calm, unruffled voice he and his colleagues invariably employed, the negotiator said: 'OK, we'll see what we can do.' An hour later, he called back. 'Sorry – there are no doctors available. But may I make a suggestion? If Mrs Mozafarian needs urgent treatment, then what about showing your humanity, and releasing her so that she can receive it?'

While Salim, the only gunman who understood fluent English, was busy on the phone, the hostages got busy forming a new plan. Salim had been told that one of the female hostages was pregnant, but he didn't know which one. In reality, it was the beautiful embassy secretary, Hiyech Kanji. What if they told the gunmen's leader it was Frieda Mozafarian, instead? Kanji, who was a much calmer and steadier character than her colleague, had courageously volunteered to swap places.

When Salim returned, Lock asked to have a quiet word with him. 'Look, Salim,' Lock said gently, 'you won't do your cause any favours by holding on to a sick, pregnant woman, will you?'

Coming on the heels of the negotiator's suggestion, the comment worked. At 1630 hrs, Hassan and Makki half-led, half-carried Frieda Mozafarian downstairs, opened the front door a fraction and pushed her out on to the embassy porch. Screaming hysterically, she collapsed. Two policemen carried her to a waiting ambulance, then went with her to St Stephen's Hospital, Fulham. It was their crucial first opportunity to talk to someone who had been inside the embassy. The police hoped that, once she calmed down, gentle questioning would draw from Mozafarian vital intelligence on the gunmen and their setup within the embassy.

They were wrong. Even under sedation, all Mozafarian would say was: 'I don't remember anything. I can't remember anything.' It was disappointing, to say the least, for the police.

■ ■ ■

Now some five hours into the siege, the hostages were cheered by Mrs Mozafarian's release. They relaxed a little. In pairs and small groups, they introduced themselves to one another. 'Which one of you is Dr Ezzati?' Cramer wondered. 'The man who refused to give us a visa?'

An elegant man in his late forties identified himself. 'That is me.' He smiled. 'But you don't need to go to my country now to report on the news. You are making news in here yourself.'

Salim took exception to the remark. Aiming his gun at Cramer, he said: 'This is not the news. This is real life. You are in here, captured. Remember that.'

Harris, remembering his car was parked on a meter in Exhibition Road, couldn't resist a further quip: 'Do you think they'll let me nip out and feed the parking meter? Or will the police cough up and pay the fine?'

'Don't worry,' Lock replied. 'We'll overlook the fine just this once.'

The Pakistani agriculturalist Ali Guil Ghanzafar, known as Gul, took an airline ticket out of his pocket and waved it around the room. 'Speaking of tickets, I have a flight to catch on Monday. I must be let out before then to make this flight. This is most important.' Faisal told him to shut up. One of the Iranians couldn't resist joking: 'I have a return underground ticket to Highgate. I need to use it by midnight otherwise it expires. Do you think they'll let me go, too?'

This lightness of mood wasn't to last long. Karkouti heard Salim bark his name: 'Mustapha! Come, my friend, to telex.' The terrorist leader was in a state, angered by the seeming inactivity of the police and the sketchy, inaccurate news reports. He had been told that the British police and press were a pushover, that the whole operation would be over within twenty-four hours. But time was ticking by and still the group's demands had not been transmitted to the outside world. Salim wanted Karkouti to try a different route: call the BBC Arabic Service and ask them to broadcast his message to the Arab world. Karkouti kept trying the main BBC News telephone number Cramer gave him. Nobody answered.

Salim began to grow even more impatient. The BBC was supposed to be a twenty-four-hour news service. Were its staff all asleep at their desks? He paced up and down the telex room shouting at Karkouti. 'I must have BBC! Get me BBC!' Showing Salim the working telephone, Karkouti suggested trying the English language news desk at Bush House. 'Do it!' Salim yelled. 'But don't trick me and don't make any mistakes!'

This time Karkouti managed to get through. With Salim breathing down his neck, he put forward the group's demands. But when the journalist on the other end asked, 'How many people are in the embassy?' Salim got angry and again severed the connection.

With Salim's consent, Cramer had a go at calling BBC TV news direct. One of the journalists on duty answered. But as soon as Cramer started responding to questions about the number of hostages, Salim slammed the phone back on its rest, enraged that none of these news services would do as they were asked and simply broadcast his message without asking impertinent questions.

At 1730 hrs, Salim decided it was time for another stab at getting his message out to the world. 'Mr Chris, Mr Mustapha. You help me. Come now to telex room and call BBC.' This time, Karkouti managed to get through to the BBC World Service at Bush House. Cramer reached BBC TV news at Shepherd's Bush. Both hostages set out the gunmen's demands, which now included a call for Arab ambassadors to mediate in settling the crisis. Pleased that the world's foremost broadcaster at least now had accurate information about the group's cause, Salim told Cramer to say that the gunmen had no intention of harming the non-Iranian hostages. Then, flatly contradicting himself, the terrorist leader repeated his threat to blow up the embassy and everyone inside it if his demands weren't met. He set a deadline of twelve noon on the following day.

Later that evening, everyone inside the embassy realised that, in all the excitement, they'd had nothing to eat. The women – five of them since Mozafarian's release – were taken at gunpoint down to the basement kitchens to search for food. They found a bowl of rice and some tinned figs in syrup. The gunman Makki found some sealed packs of pitta bread.

Morris remembered he had cigarettes in his office. 'I need to get up there,' he told Lock. 'I have £2,300 in cash at the back of my desk. My life savings. My missus would never forgive me if that was lost.' Raising a hand – the agreed signal if one of the hostages wanted to go to the toilet or to move for some other reason, he volunteered to get the cigarettes. Since most of the hostages and all of the gunmen except Makki smoked like chimneys, Salim agreed that Morris should fetch them.

With Ali and his Browning close behind him, Morris stepped out into the corridor. When he reached the third-floor landing, he was disconcerted to find that the gunmen had erected a barricade across the foot of the stairs. It included chairs, tables – and a fridge. Morris studied the obstacle for a few seconds: it really hadn't been all that well done. Reaching round and grabbing the banister, he hauled himself up and over.

A few minutes later, Morris came back down to Room 9. He'd brought a stash of biscuits, 200 Kent cigarettes and a bag of chocolate raspberry truffles, which he distributed among the crowd.

The barricade was clearly meant to discourage a top-down rescue attempt. But like a lot of other things the embassy gunmen were doing, its makeshift and not very effective nature highlighted their lack of professionalism.

■ ■ ■

Listening in to the police negotiator tapes at Zulu Control, Professor Gunn gave the police his assessment of the gunmen: 'They asked me my view as to whether they were serious terrorists or nuts,' he later told the *Observer*. 'They didn't really need to ask, because everybody was convinced we were dealing with terrorists. They were very stable people. That, actually, was one of the most remarkable things about it. In a way, it was a kind of tribute to the leader of the terrorists.

'The six negotiators on our side were under great stress. The twelve-hour shifts they worked proved to be too long. The terrorists, meanwhile, had just one chap. He did the lot from beginning to end, all on his own. He was the only one who spoke English. It was incredible. He never really cracked – although obviously towards the end he was behaving in a dangerous way.'

When everyone had eaten, Salim again called Cramer to the telex room. Faisal helped keep guard. This time, Cramer got hold of the Deputy Home Editor, Richard Ayre. Salim snatched the phone. Ayre, thrilled to have the terrorist on the line – having BBC men inside the embassy had its uses – recorded the exchange:

Ayre: Can I ask what is happening in the embassy?
Salim: Nothing happen.
Ayre: You have a number of hostages?
Salim: Yeah.
Ayre: Why have you taken hostages inside the embassy?

Salim: Because we have some demands and just we took them
   to get what we want.

Ayre: What is it that you want?

Salim: The free of ninety-one prisoners.

Ayre: You want ninety-one prisoners in Iran to be set free?

Salim: Yeah. And the recognising of our region as an autonomy.

Ayre: What makes you believe that taking over the embassy in
   London will force the Iranian government to carry out your
   demands?

Salim: You know it is one of the means that we want to send
   our voice to the world.

Ayre: Tell me a little more about the group that you represent
   in Iran?

Salim: You know that group who are fighting for their legitimate
   rights and they're fighting for the autonomy of Arabistan.

Ayre: Does this mean you are opposed to the new regime?

Salim: We aren't against Ayatollah Khomeini. We are against
   every leader who don't want to give us our legitimate rights.
   Any leaders it makes no difference for us.

Ayre: Are you saying that all the hostages are safe tonight?

Salim: What?

Ayre: Are all the hostages safe tonight?

Salim: Yeah.'

■ ■ ■

Since early afternoon, the female hostages in the embassy had been
taking it in turns to try and make contact with the Foreign Ministry
in Tehran. At 2300 hrs, the call came through. Dr Afrouz's broken
jaw meant that he'd been unable to speak all afternoon. But the
gunmen dragged him along the corridor to take the call.

Iran's Foreign Minister, Sadegh Qotbzadeh, was on a visit to Abu
Dhabi, so one of his deputies took the call. 'Tell him our demands,'
Salim said. Speaking slowly and painfully, Afrouz told the astonished
official that the gunmen holding the London embassy were responsible
people, all Muslim brothers. All they wanted was a measure of

autonomy for Khuzestan/Arabistan, not full independence. If Tehran made an encouraging response to their demands, then the hostage-takers would back off, release all the hostages and end the siege. The official said that Mr Qotbzadeh would return the call as soon as possible.

Salim now ordered that Room 9 be prepared for sleeping. He offered Valium for those who felt they needed it to calm down. No one took up the offer. Afrouz, who'd taken two of the pills as soon as he'd finished the stressful conversation with Tehran, had already conked out. To most of the hostages, sleep seemed a ridiculous idea. Who knew what the gunmen might get up to in the small hours? No one wanted to risk letting their guard down.

The gunmen didn't exactly help create a restful atmosphere. Without warning, they began moving the desks out of Room 9 to make more barricades at weak points around the embassy. Struggling to get the desks through the door, they looked expectantly at the hostages for help. No one moved. Why would turkeys vote for Christmas? As a drawer from one desk slid out of its runners, paperclips and other debris fell to the floor. Cramer, pretending to clear up, managed to find a razor blade and two large hatpins. Nifty little weapons, he thought. And the boxes of paperclips might come in useful for killing time.

Later Salim ran in and began shaking Afrouz awake, shouting that Qotbzadeh was now on the phone in person. Dragged back to the telex room once more, Afrouz said: 'Please, sir, release the ninety-one prisoners in Khuzestan so that we can be freed.' But Iran's Foreign Minister was having none of it. Launching into the kind of intemperate rant that had already come to characterise the Iranian revolutionary regime, Qotbzadeh gave the hostages short shrift. He said that the gunmen were agents of US President Carter and the CIA; that the hostages should and no doubt would view it as an honour and a privilege to die as martyrs for the revolution; and there would be no concessions or negotiations in respect of Khuzestan.

Salim, who'd been listening in, grabbed the receiver. In a few pithy and well-chosen words, he told Qotbzadeh what he thought of him and then slammed the phone down.

Faisal pushed Afrouz back into Room 9 where he collapsed on the floor. Hassan jumped up, assuming the Chargé d'Affaires was faking his physical distress, and made as if to kick him. Faisal held him back.

There was dismay at the Iranian Foreign Minister's response. It was all very well him telling them to die for the Revolution – he wasn't there with them in Room 9. The tension ratcheted. Seeing their boss frightened and in pain, some of the female hostages began to cry. Dadgar picked up a copy of the Koran and began to pray. The other Iranians joined him, facing eastwards and touching their heads to the floor.

Salim insisted the women must not sleep in the same room as the men. He ordered Ali to move them next door to Room 9A. The women gladly obeyed, counting themselves lucky to be leaving: Gul had fallen asleep and was snoring loudly.

Lock, Karkouti, Morris, Cramer and Harris sat together, talking softly. Karkouti said he had already started negotiating with the gunmen: 'I don't think Salim means too much harm. He just wants publicity for his cause.'

Lock stared ahead. He seemed detached, perhaps still in shock from the trauma of the assault and his injuries.

'Are you OK, Trevor?' Harris asked. 'Tell me a bit about yourself. You married?'

'Yes.'

'Been a policeman long?'

'About fifteen years.'

'Do you like it?'

'Yes.'

Lock wanted to be left alone to think. Angry with himself for not stopping the gunmen from taking over the embassy, he worried he might get the sack: it was unlikely his bosses would view his unauthor-ised coffee break favourably. 'My police days are over,' he thought. But gradually, Harris brought the policeman out of himself. He began to entertain the others with a collection of bawdy jokes, picked up from his colleagues while they waited to deploy at demonstrations. 'Not a clean one among them,' Lock laughed.

At about 0100 hrs a single pistol shot rang out from the ground floor. Salim rushed up the stairs. 'Do not worry,' he said. 'This was a mistake. You can all sleep now.'

'Bloody hell, those weapons freak me out,' Lock said. 'Brownings are bad enough, but those machine guns!' Like the others, he'd never seen a Skorpion machine-pistol before. 'If they're anything like the Uzi, they're deadly. They can fire eight hundred rounds a minute. We wouldn't stand a chance.'

'It's the hand grenades that get me,' Harris said. 'Especially when they wind their fingers round the pin. Are they Russian or Chinese, do you think?'

'Russian, I think,' said Lock. 'If they chuck one of those at you, just hit the deck and start praying.'

Leaving Lock on his throne, the other non-Iranians lay down on the floor to sleep. Shivering in cold and fear, for most of them it did not come easily.

As they slept, Qotbzadeh was busy issuing more statements: 'Iran will not give in to blackmail either from the superpowers or a small number of terrorists.' He saw no parallel between the fifty-three American diplomatic prisoners held hostage in the US Embassy in Tehran and the Iranian hostages in London: 'The occupation in Tehran is in reaction to twenty-five years of oppression and killings in Iran. We condemn the occupation of our embassy which is totally a foreign land of foreign people and has nothing to do with the issue [sic].' Qotbzadeh added that he'd given the British government full authorisation to act in whatever way it deemed best to end the siege.

The Iranian authorities had washed their hands of their London hostages. It was up to the Brits to sort things out.

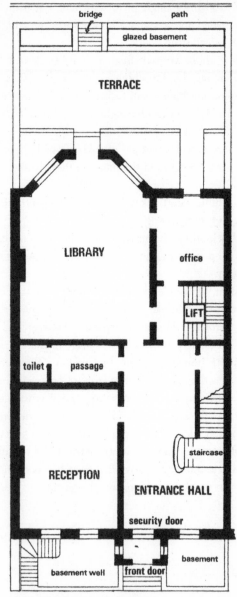

## GROUND FLOOR

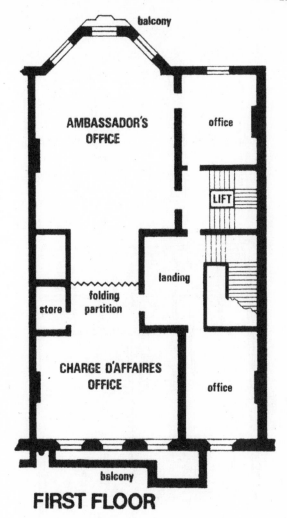

**FIRST FLOOR**

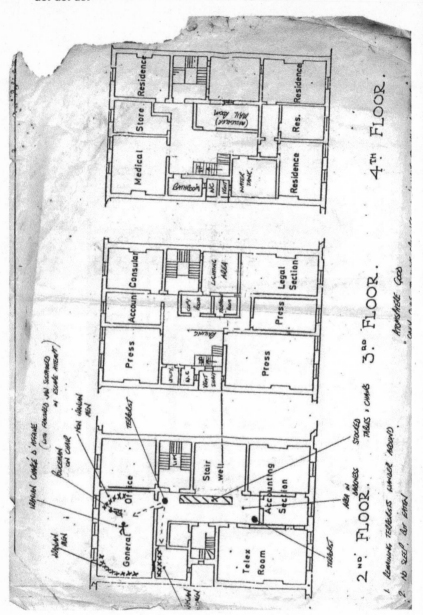

Original SAS intelligence notes of embassy floor plan.

# DAY TWO: Thursday, 1 May 1980

Red and Blue teams arrived at Regent's Park Barracks at approximately 0300 hrs on Thursday morning. It was pitch black and dead quiet, conditions that suited the SP team perfectly. Even better, there were no journalists hanging around the barracks. Rapidly off-loading their weapons and equipment, they dumped their kit in the rooms allocated to them, then gathered in the barracks conference room for an initial 'green-slime' (Military Intelligence) briefing.

Following his personal close target reconnaissance earlier, Lt-Col Rose had decided one team would have to move closer to the embassy. If things went downhill and the IA plan had to be implemented at short notice, Regent's Park Barracks was three and a half miles by road: much too far. Red Team (the Anthill Mob) got lucky: they'd be moving into the holding area first.

Ideally, the SAS wanted to be going in on the embassy's upper, as well as lower floors. Best of all would be attacking from the roof down. The British Army has an old saying: 'never fight upwards'. In a confined space, the adage was especially true.

The initial IA plan was 'bloody'. It came down to semi-sophisticated thuggery. The idea was to get seriously tooled up, jump into the wagons, race up to the front of the embassy, smash as many windows as possible and fire in stun and CS gas grenades; shotgun and batter the front door clean off its hinges; fling double scaling ladders up against the windows and charge in. At the same time, separate teams would attack downwards by whatever means they could.

Though no one present was aware of it, there was a problem with the 'bloody' IA plan. The previous year, at the exiled Shah of Iran's request, a small team of SAS men had made a detailed security survey of the building. One of its recommendations had been to install armoured glass in the embassy's front windows.

It may have lacked subtlety, but the initial IA plan would only be triggered if the gunmen killed a hostage. As they gathered more intelligence, the plan would get much more sophisticated. To this end, Red Team set out to make its own reconnaissance run and carry out a closer examination of the embassy and its surrounds. Several battered and innocuous-looking vans bearing the logo of a well-known hire company stood ready at the side of the large parade ground.

In casual civilian clothes, the team jumped in the vans and set off, leaving at staggered intervals so as not to alert any watching eyes. Coasting through the silent streets of central London with police drivers at the wheel, they made a drive-by reconnaissance of the embassy and surrounding area. Then they got out of the vans at a discrete distance, regrouped and made their way on foot towards the rear of Princes Gate. They looked like a bunch of guys coming home after a late night out. Uniformed police officers already familiar with the area led for some of the way.

Situated in the fashionable – and ferociously expensive – South Kensington district of central London, the Iranian Embassy occupied a large Georgian town house in a row of identical properties with white stucco overlaying their façades, Italianate porticoes supported by statement pillars, first-floor balconies and big, handsome windows overlooking Hyde Park.

Princes Gate formed a short loop or access road running parallel with Kensington Road. Separated from the main road by a four-foot stone and brick wall, it offered street parking for both private and diplomatic vehicles.

Laid out in the shape of a capital 'H,' the embassy was five storeys tall – around eighty feet high. A short, transverse section of flat roof ran north–south and joined the main longitudinal wings. The centre of the flat section had a small skylight. There were fifty-six rooms, including those in the attic space. It also had a basement level. Enough to make life interesting for anyone attempting a hostage rescue.

Nos. 13–25 Princes Gate, typical elevation. H. L. Elmes, architect;
John Elger, builder; 1846–50

Lt-Col Rose had discovered a partially concealed path at the rear leading to No. 14 Princes Gate, which adjoined the embassy's eastern side. Slowly and with due stealth, the recce teams made their way in through the enclosed back garden, then along a sunken communal walkway until they came to the back basement door of the 'Doctors' House'. Once inside, room by room and floor by floor, the recce teams took a long, detailed look at the building, its floor plans and all its works.

The SAS were very interested to discover that, inside the hollow rectangle at its heart, the embassy had a central well or atrium that ran from the ground to the third floors. Even better from an attacker's point of view, the atrium in question culminated in a shallow, four-sided glass pyramid. While any competent abseiler should be able to reach the apex of the pyramid from the narrow parapet on the western side of the flat roof, it would be easier to suspend an explosive charge on a length of rope and blow the atrium skylight in with that, if necessary.

The embassy's front first-floor windows had a stone balcony. There was a similar balcony fronting the first-floor windows at the building's rear. It was immediately clear these would make useful assault platforms.

By 0330 hrs, Red Team had carried out their close target reconnaissance, they hadn't been compromised and they had an updated IA plan in place. Rose was happy: so far, so good.

With a policeman on duty 24/7 to provide security in the holding area, Red Team set about making themselves as comfortable as possible in the Doctors' House. Camp beds and roll mats were soon laid out in the large, ground-floor rear reception room. Everything in the place was gleaming; all the woodwork was highly polished and every surface as clean as a new pin. It wasn't long before the brew kit was out. The food supplied was great. Someone else found the TV room, and switched the set on hoping that BBC Sports was already up and broadcasting. The 1980 Embassy World Snooker Championship was in full swing. Most of the SP team were rooting for the home favourite, Alex 'Hurricane' Higgins. Once they'd arranged the makeshift accommodation, the duty standby team snuggled into their sleeping bags, cuddled up to their weapons and respirators and nodded off.

Back at Regent's Park Barracks MBS, Blue Team grabbed some breakfast and then got straight into training for action. From then on, alternating twelve-hour shifts of duty, the team at the Forward Holding Area would try and sleep, while the other team trained, rehearsed, and planned for a possible hostage rescue mission.

■ ■ ■

The British tabloid newspapers seized on the terrorists' noon deadline with gusto. The *Daily Mail*'s banner headline was: THEY DIE AT NOON. The *Daily Mirror*'s read: DEADLINE HIGH NOON.

The *Daily Telegraph*, *Guardian* and *The Times*, having complied with the police request not to publicise the deadline, were understandably furious. So was DAC Dellow. The last thing he wanted was the weight of public opinion bearing down on his already highly pressurised negotiators.

The newspapers all wanted answers to a number of burning questions. Chief among these were: how – and why – had six young men from the western Iranian province of Khuzestan come to launch an attack on an embassy in London?

To find answers, they would have to look to a small island in the Tigris–Euphrates delta; to the bloody and chequered history of Khuzestan province itself; and delve into the dark and devious mind of the Iraqi dictator Saddam Hussein.

While it might have been under Arab rule in its more distant past, Khuzestan had been Persian territory since the seventeenth century. Treaties between Iraq and Iran in 1937 and 1975 had reaffirmed that status. But whoever ruled its oil-rich sands, one thing never changed: its ethnic Arab – and Arabic speaking – majority always came off worse.

Successive Iranian governments had kicked Khuzestan's Arab population squarely in the teeth. A concerted 'Persianisation' programme instigated by Shah Reza Pahlavi in 1925 aimed to stamp out Arabic language and culture and replace it with the official Iranian language, Farsi. There was a systematic programme of 'resettlement', or ethnic cleansing; Khuzestani Arabs – who, like the embassy gunmen, persisted in calling their homeland 'Arabistan' – suffered relentless economic and political discrimination. Denied jobs in

Iranian government service or in the hugely lucrative oil industry, the province's Arabic-speaking population was largely confined to a traditional, village-based and poverty-stricken existence. Arabs suffered routine abuse at the hands of the Iranian police, and their land was often confiscated without recompense. The wealth gap between the majority Arab-speaking community and the Iranian minority was wide, stark and ever-growing.

But Khuzestan was a prize. A barrel-shaped one, with massive oil reserves. The entire province sat on vast underground lakes of crude oil – more than 70 billion barrels. It held about 90 per cent of Iran's total oil reserves, which amounted to more than 10 per cent of *global* reserves. About 50 per cent of Iran's national income came from the Ahvazi Arab's oilfields. Without Khuzestan's oil fuelling its economy, Iran would have been just another run-of-the-mill Middle Eastern country.

Iranian repression grew worse when Shah Reza's son, Mohammad Reza Shah Pahlavi, took over in 1941. The new Shah's secret police force, the SAVAK, was brutal: Ahvazi Arabs suffered unexplained arrests, imprisonment without trial and summary executions. Torture was almost routine.

When Ayatollah Khomeini's revolutionary Islamic government came to power in February 1979, many Khuzestani Arabs expected life to improve. They were to be bitterly disappointed. Khomeini's Iran was business as usual. The only difference was that the new regime's 'Islamic Revolutionary Guards' and police took over the dirty work instead of SAVAK.

On 29 May 1979, protests broke out in the port of Khorramshar and other Khuzestani cities. In the running street battles that followed, the Iranian Revolutionary Guards and the police shot dead more than 200 – some reports estimate as many as 850 – unarmed Ahvazi Arab civilians, many of them women and children. 'Black Wednesday' saw the rise of a ferocious anti-Iranian opposition movement which persists to this day.

Scores of young Khuzestanis joined the main opposition group, the Democratic Revolutionary Movement for the Liberation of Arabistan

(DRMLA). Picking up where the deposed Shah had left off, Ayatollah Khomeini's regime began arbitrarily arresting large numbers of young Khuzestani Arab men, imprisoning them without trial, torturing them; and in some cases, executing them. As the *Sunday Times'* excellent Insight team and other journalists delved ever-deeper into the reasons behind the embassy seizure, they discovered that this was where the Group of the Martyr had its beginnings.

The leader of the six-man team now holding the Iranian Embassy was Salim Towfigh, a twenty-seven-year-old Tehran University graduate in law and linguistics. With his open, intelligent face, thick, glossy black hair, neat moustache and long sideburns, Salim wasn't what you might first think of when you heard the word 'terrorist'. He was cultured, middle class and, when not riled, had a uniformly pleasant and courteous manner.

Salim spoke four languages fluently: Arabic, Farsi, English and German. As a young student, he had played an active part in the DRMLA. As a result, Salim had come to the attention of the Revolutionary Guards. One night, they came knocking at his door – with their boots. Dragging him outside, they bundled him into a van and drove him to Tehran's notorious Evin prison. Standard treatment for political detainees at the time was beating on the soles of the feet with electrical cable. By way of variation, Evin's torturers tied Salim to a wooden frame and whipped him. The beating inflicted massive scars on his back; Salim was never slow to display them. Embittered by this brutality, he was also marked out by his steely determination, high intelligence, competent English and his obvious capacity to lead. Salim stood ready and willing to die for the cause.

At 6'2", Salim's second-in-command Faisal was the tallest of the gunmen. Well educated and English-speaking (though less fluent than Salim), he entered the UK under the false name of Shakir Abdullah Radhil. The source of Faisal's militancy wasn't hard to find: he, too, had suffered at the hands of Evin's sadistic torturers. In his mid-twenties and seldom seen out of jeans or his highly prized cowboy boots, Faisal had an explosive and violent temper.

At nineteen, Themir Mohammed Hussain – real name Hassan –

might have been the youngest member of the group, but as the burliest and strongest, he most looked the part of the terrorist hard-man. Constantly pumped-up, Hassan was a bit like the 'Cato' character in the *Pink Panther* films: forever breaking into practice karate kicks, shouting out warnings that he was about to strike and generally making a nuisance of himself.

The fourth member of the group travelled under the alias Shakir Sultan Said. An incurable romantic, he talked incessantly about his girlfriend whom he planned to marry. Short and stocky with distinctive fair hair that curled down over his ears, he looked the most European of the group. He was known to his fellow gunmen as Abbas. The hostages, who didn't know that, called him 'Ugly'.

The fifth conspirator was Makki Hanoun Ali, known as Makki. He had long sideburns and a full round face. Good at running the domestic side of things, he'd been helping the female hostages rustle up food and drink in the embassy.

A slim, handsome man with soft, Bambi-like eyes, twenty-two-year-old Fowzi Badavi Nejad – known during the siege as Ali – was the group's final member. Having served in the Iranian army before his most recent job as a labourer in Khorramshar's busy docks, Nejad was an experienced soldier. An eyewitness to the massacre in Khorramshar on Black Wednesday, Nejad, like Salim, had been radicalised by the systematic brutality of the regime.

Another question journalists across the world were starting to ask was: had the six been especially recruited for the embassy hit? And if so, by whom? Iraq was the prime suspect. But the true picture proved to be a little more complex, as Fowzi Nejad's path to the embassy seizure showed.

Realising that the Ayatollah's thugs were busy rounding up hundreds of young Arab men like himself, imprisoning, torturing and killing them, Nejad quit Khuzestan in a hurry and headed for the Iraqi border. Iraq's major cities, in particular Baghdad and Basra, were home to an ever-growing and increasingly vociferous community of Khuzestani political refugees. At the border, Nejad handed himself in to the Iraqi police and asked for asylum.

Finding that he was well-educated and fluent in both Farsi and Arabic, the Iraqis took Nejad to Basra, gave him a house to live in and put him to work translating Iranian radio broadcasts. In the space of a few weeks, Nejad had been transformed from a dock labourer into a low-grade member of Iraqi intelligence.

But he had neither forgotten nor abandoned the Khuzestani cause. One day, there was a knock on his door. Three men stood on the threshold. Two were obviously bodyguards. The third, an austere-looking, imposing older man with a long beard, introduced himself as Said Hadi, Sheikh of Shalamcheh, Chief of the Ahvazi Arab political movement in Iraq. Shalamcheh was a small island in the Tigris–Euphrates delta and Sheikh Hadi's home when he wasn't in his Iraqi-provided offices in Baghdad. Hadi told Nejad that the Iranian Revolutionary Council had sentenced him to death *in absentia* as a traitor and a threat to state security. The news came as no surprise.

The two men got on well. Hadi could see at once that in Nejad he had someone who believed passionately in the cause of Arabistan. Talking quietly into the night, he spun golden dreams of glory in Nejad's mind.

Having heard him out, Nejad asked, 'What can I do to bring justice and peace to the Arabs of Khuzestan?'

'I was wondering if you might like to go on a trip to London?' Hadi said.

Nejad did a double-take. 'London? How can it advance the cause if I go there?'

'Well,' Hadi said, 'I have a plan ...'

■ ■ ■

It had been immediately obvious to Fowzi Nejad that Sheikh Hadi was hand-in-glove with Iraqi intelligence – and that behind him lurked Saddam Hussein. Saddam had not only welcomed Arabistan's political refugees, but, as in the case of Nejad, given them homes, jobs and in some cases serious financial backing. Saddam's reasoning wasn't hard to fathom. Iran and Iraq were natural opponents in the struggle to become regional top dog. With dreams of a pan-Arab, Ba'athist superpower – with himself as leader, naturally – Saddam saw his role as that of a latter-day Gamal Abdel Nasser, the Egyptian leader who had defied the West in seizing – and holding – the Suez Canal. Nasser had tried hard to weld the disparate Arabic-speaking nations into a politically meaningful whole.

As an enemy of the Shah of Iran's Western-friendly regime, Saddam had hastened the handsome 'King of Kings' downfall by having his own intelligence services fund, train and support dissident Iranian activists. In the final months of the Shah's reign, Saddam's agents had fomented strikes in Khuzestan's oil industry. They had also sent dissident teams in to sabotage the oil-rich province's infrastructure: blowing up pipelines, storage tanks, bridges, police stations and the like. In the last year of his reign, the Shah's revenues from oil had plunged by 90 per cent.

When the Islamic Revolutionary regime seized power in Iran, Saddam discovered he had merely traded out of the frying-pan and into the fire. The ayatollahs weren't merely opposed to all things Western, they wanted to export the revolution's new, fundamentalist interpretation of Islam. They wanted to build a Caliphate, or global religious hegemony in which Iran and its ayatollahs, not Saddam Hussein, would wield absolute and final power.

Already, Ayatollah Khomeini's agents were at work among Iraq's disaffected Shi'ite majority, whipping up opposition to the devil Saddam Hussein and all his works. For his part, the Iraqi leader was more determined than ever that Iraq would be the regional super-power – even if it meant going to war.

And Saddam Hussein also had his eyes on the main prize – Khuzestan's oil. While Iraq had its own oil and made many billions a year from exporting it, Khuzestan's crude reserves were in a league of their own. If he could get his mitts on that extra income, it would help Saddam gain the international status he so craved.

Then there was the Shatt al-Arab waterway. This ran 120 miles up the Tigris–Euphrates estuary, from the head of the Persian Gulf to Basra, Iraq's most important port. The Shatt al-Arab was Iraq's key economic lifeline. In 1975, distracted by Kurdish rebellion in the north, Saddam had agreed to share the crucial waterway with Iran, splitting control down the median line. Now, he wanted to bring the Shatt al-Arab fully back under his control.

Saddam reasoned that a spot of publicity for the Khuzestani Arab cause would serve his purpose well on the international stage. But how best to go about it? If he helped Khuzestanis stage a terrorist 'spectacular' of the kind the PLO, the PFLP and the IRA had inflicted on a horrified world in the 1970s – hijacking aircraft; bombing; assassinating and even, in the case of the Palestinian Black September movement, massacring eleven Israeli athletes at the 1972 Munich Olympic Games – how would that win him international approval and support?

Saddam's secret police kept a very close eye on Iranian dissidents of all stripes. So when he learned of Sheikh Hadi's plan to seize the Iranian Embassy in London and hold its Khomeini-appointed staff hostage, Saddam saw a golden opportunity. Whatever else might happen, the world would become aware that Khuzestan's Arab population was suffering under pitiless and brutal Iranian masters. Saddam calculated that when his 250,000-strong army invaded Iran later that same year, as he planned, they would be viewed in the Arab world – and perhaps even outside it – as liberators. Khuzestan's ethnic Arab majority, Saddam reasoned, would rise up and help his troops sweep the chaotic new Iranian regime aside – and into the dustbin of Islamic zealotry where he thought it belonged.

London, he saw at once, was the perfect choice. It had to be a Western capital, for maximum propaganda. And of all Western capitals, London had the biggest and best-informed Arab community and a thriving Arabic press. What's more, London's foreign embassies were poorly defended. In Saddam's view, the British were toothless liberals, and probably lily-livered. Even if it was discovered that he was behind the plot, Saddam believed there was no chance that the British government would take retaliatory action against Iraq.

On 4 November 1979, the Iranians had stormed the US Embassy in Tehran and taken fifty-three American citizens hostage. The diplomatic repercussions were still rumbling: President Carter had been made to look impotent. In London, Saddam reasoned, the Iranians would get a taste of their own medicine.

With his invasion of Iran planned for October, time was of the essence. Saddam instructed a senior officer in Iraqi intelligence, Sami Mohammed Ali, aka 'the Fox', to find, recruit and train suitable candidates for the operation. He was to help them get into Britain, wind them up like clockwork mice and set them running. With his first-hand knowledge of the British capital, the Fox was the perfect man for what Saddam had in mind. Dossiers on him compiled by the British Secret Intelligence Service (MI6) featured multiple incidents of aiding and abetting terrorist activity, both within and outside Iraq's borders, and they were aware, too, of his strong and consistent links to Iraq's London embassy.

Already the Fox had one recruit in his grasp: Sheikh Hadi's acolyte, the sweet-looking Nejad. Selecting five more like him from the teeming ranks of Khuzestani refugees in Iraq did not prove too difficult. Filling their heads with visions of everlasting glory, the Fox saw his six eager new charges through basic military training at an Iraqi army base near Baghdad. They underwent elementary instruction in handling explosives, firearms and hand grenades. Then the Fox set about making preparations for his squad's secret infiltration into the UK.

Despite their background in revolutionary politics, all six were more or less innocents abroad. They were blissfully unaware of the way both Hadi and Saddam viewed them as utterly expendable pawns in a much bigger game.

Before they knew it, the six shining young hopefuls had been recruited and trained for an act of terrorism. They'd become the Group of the Martyr. And here was their chance to strike a blow for their homeland.

As the spooks and Fleet Street journalists vied to be first to piece the story together, they began to realise how audacious – and simple – the operation was. The Fox had travelled on a diplomatic passport. Under cover as a senior official of Iraq's Ministry of Industry, he sat separately, studiously ignoring the young men under his charge for the whole duration of the flight. Pretending to be excited young tourists on their first visit to London, the four men of the advance group had sailed through Heathrow Airport's immigration controls. Once outside, they'd hailed a black taxi cab and headed straight for the centre of town. The Fox had already taken a short-let, self-catering apartment at 20 Nevern Place in Earl's Court. The area was teeming with cheap hotels and bed-sits, and had long been indifferent to the comings and goings of a transient population.

The Fox had chosen the busy neighbourhood for its bewildering mix of nationalities, among which a well-established Arabic community figured prominently. The Group of the Martyr told the caretaker Zuhair Jawad – a young Iraqi student earning a bit of money to support his post-graduate studies – that they were English language students from Baghdad. Jawad was so pleased to be showing the flats to compatriots that he didn't register their names, much less take their passport details. Instead he asked them for a £20 deposit and then showed them two flats, each with three sparsely furnished bedrooms, a tiny bathroom and a lounge with an extra fold-out bed and a kitchen at one end.

The unit opted for the flat with an extra little alcove off the living room, where Makki dossed down on a makeshift bed. A few days later they were joined by Faisal and Nejad, who had arrived at Heathrow with a different cover story – letters informing the British authorities they were there for private medical treatment. The four became six. A tight group, they set their minds on having some serious fun before the fireworks began. Dazzled by the incredible array of shops and services now on their doorstep, not least the rowdy pubs, the six men took to their buzzy, cosmopolitan new surroundings like frogs to a lily pond.

Saddam's master plan was to whip up hatred of Iran. Sheikh Hadi's was to win autonomy for Khuzestan. But all these little tadpoles wanted to do right now was party – all night long. The siege nearly ended before it had a chance to begin. Let off the leash for the first time in a non-Islamic capital, with £750 each and no restrictions on their behaviour, the six did what a lot of young men from stricter cultures might have done in similar circumstances: they ran riot.

With money to burn, they went on a frenzy of shopping. They wanted Western goods – plenty of them – for themselves and for their friends and relatives back in the Middle East. Salim bought himself some expensive red-and-white leather trainers: 'These will bring me luck,' he predicted. 'I will not take them off the whole time we are inside the embassy.' They saved the evenings for drink and prostitutes. The men partied hard through the night to the early hours, enjoying this free and – so far – easy time in London.

Their activities did not go unnoticed. After nights of noise and disturbance, the other tenants got together and complained to the landlord. With many expressions of polite regret, the young caretaker asked them to leave.

The upshot was that on 7 April 1980, the six men moved down the road to 105 Lexham Gardens, a property that was owned and managed by a Jordanian citizen, Arafat Alsamhouri. Once again, the men were asked no questions: like their previous landlord, Alsamhouri was in the business of renting out properties and rarely bothered to find out why visitors were in town. As soon as Salim pressed a £350 wodge of cash into his hands, covering a week's rent, the deposit and his 'finder's fee', Alsamhouri handed over the keys to a spacious and infinitely more up-market apartment than their previous one. Even the lobby, with its gold-embossed wallpaper, blood-red carpet and proper reception area where the Egyptian caretaker made sweet-smelling tea, breathed luxury, Middle Eastern-style.

The Fox, too, liked his entertainment, and had been busily sampling the charms of certain Western women. But he knew the group had to cool it, for if their activities came to the attention of the British police it would compromise the whole operation. Had their partying resulted in the plot being exposed and the team deported, Saddam Hussein would not have been best pleased. And those who displeased Saddam had a tendency to end up in prison watching their relatives get raped and beaten to death, before suffering the same fate.

Once he'd put them in the picture about all this, Salim and friends reined in their behaviour. They stopped drinking and hiring call-girls and settled down to a thoroughly British way of life – takeaway food, beer and rented videos. One, Abbas, had fallen in love. He had struck up a relationship with Rashida, a Moroccan girl who lived in the neighbourhood, telling her his name was Hameed, and that he was a respectable student. He even visited her aunt to discuss marriage. The Fox soon put a stop to it – this was no time for a holiday romance. Though banned from seeing Rashida, the lovestruck Abbas still kept a photograph of her in his shirt pocket. Every day, whenever he could, he'd take it out and gaze at it longingly.

With the planned attack drawing steadily closer, by day Lexham Gardens saw a lot of visitors. Senior members of the DRMLA came to stiffen the group's morale and, more sinisterly, to ensure the six recruits went through with their mission. The mysterious visitors also gave advice, practical training and pep talks.

During the last days of April, the six went about in twos and threes, carrying out a number of covert surveillance missions. They rather enjoyed the walks through Hyde Park Gardens to Princes Gate. For several days they watched the early-morning comings and goings outside No. 16. Their reconnaissance alerted them to a worrying fact: the Iranian Embassy had a uniformed member of the Metropolitan Police Diplomatic Protection Group stationed outside its front entrance at all times.

'Don't worry, my sons,' the Fox reassured them. 'The police in Britain do not carry weapons. Their main function is to help the elderly cross the streets. They will not attack you.'

Since they had never seen any sign of a visible weapon on any of the DPG officers, the six assumed that he was telling the truth.

They were wrong.

On their way back from detailing the Iranian Embassy's Sunday rota one day, they were drawn to the crowds at Speaker's Corner in nearby Hyde Park. They hurried away when fighting broke out between pro- and anti-Khomeini protesters.

As April neared its end, the men had taken in all they needed. In addition to noting the times of their shifts, they had made an effort to note the faces of the different policemen who stood sentry duty outside the embassy. 'The trouble with British policemen,' Faisal joked, 'is that they all look the same.'

Finally, it was time. On the afternoon of Tuesday, 29 April, the Fox told Alsamhouri they would all be heading off in the morning to visit a friend in Bristol for a few days. Slipping him a sizeable sum in cash, the Fox asked him to airfreight their baggage – 100 kilos' worth of expensive suits, shirts, shoes, dresses and children's toys – to a PO Box number in Baghdad. They also left him a telephone number in case of problems: Baghdad 27461.

Later that evening, the Fox called his men together for a final briefing. He arrived at the flat with a sports bag containing the weapons they would use for the assault: two Polish-manufactured Skorpion sub-machine guns; three semi-automatic 9mm Browning pistols; one .38 Smith & Wesson revolver; and a clutch of Soviet-pattern RGD-5 hand grenades. By any standards, it was a lot of firepower. Using the skills they'd learned in Iraq, the team gave the firearms a thorough cleaning. The Fox then astonished the men by producing floor plans of the Iranian Embassy.

'Where did you get those from?' asked Salim.

'None of your business,' the Fox snapped. 'Just make sure you know where every room is by memory. Now, let's get our demands down on paper.'

For the next three hours, the group worked on the statement of demands they intended to broadcast once they'd occupied the Iranian Embassy and grabbed the full attention of the world's media. Salim translated the document from Arabic to English and Farsi, typing everything out laboriously on an old machine they'd bought for a song at a nearby junk shop. By the end of the night, following many discarded drafts that lay scrunched up in heaps around the room, they had copies of the statement ready to go.

The six were up early the next morning. They seemed calm. The Fox gave them last-minute instructions: 'Wait until all the staff and as many visitors as possible have arrived for the day. Don't attack before 1100 hours. You are well prepared. Stay focused. Good luck.

Your brothers and sisters back home are counting on you.' With that he kissed each man on the cheek in turn, took their passports for safekeeping and left. They would never see him again.

Salim, Faisal, Abbas, Makki, Hassan and Nejad – who now assumed the cover name Ali – were as ready as they would ever be. Salim took command as agreed. Pointing at Abbas, he said: 'Go now to check the workers are arriving at the embassy. We will come to the Memorial to meet you.'

Solemnly Faisal handed Abbas one of the three Browning 9mm semi-automatic pistols. The weapon was loaded with thirteen rounds of hollow-point ammunition, and the pockets of his anorak and jeans were bulging with extra bullets. At the door Abbas turned, smiled and saluted his friends: 'See you at eleven o'clock.'

Keeping one of the Skorpion machine-pistols for himself, Faisal gave the other to Salim. Ali and Makki took the remaining two Brownings. Hassan thumbed out the cylinder of the .38 Smith & Wesson revolver, checked it was fully loaded and then snapped it back into the body of the gun. Once he'd given out the firearms, Faisal handed round the hand grenades. He kept the last grenade for himself.

With the handguns and ammunition concealed in their pockets and the two Skorpion machine-pistols underneath their jackets, the rest of the gun-team quit the Lexham Gardens flat for good.

■ ■ ■

For the hostages, Day Two of the siege began at 0520 hrs. The Iranians said their morning prayers, the devout Abbas Lavasani reciting louder than anyone else. A post-revolutionary appointee, he spent most of his time reading his own personal copy of the Koran. The handsome young press officer with the neat beard was also distinguished by his odd taste in clothes; for some reason he liked to keep his trouser bottoms tucked in his socks, and he was still wearing the rather feminine-looking yellow cardigan he'd had on when the gunmen stormed in.

When prayers were over, the male and female hostages were all brought together in Room 9. Two of the women volunteered to go down to the basement kitchen and make breakfast. Lock had spent the entire night on his Queen Anne chair. Everyone else had crashed where they could on the green carpet. For a moment, as the teacups rattled and Morris came round with a tray of biscuits, the atmosphere seemed almost normal. The hostages might not have been so calm if they'd known about the noon deadline now hanging over them.

Drawing Mustapha Karkouti to one side, Salim asked if the Syrian journalist would telephone the BBC again and deliver a message on the group's behalf. Karkouti agreed; the sooner these maniacs got what they wanted, the sooner they might all be able to go home. In his own case, a loving wife and family were waiting anxiously for his return.

At 0702 hrs, using a landline in the embassy that was still working, Karkouti got through to Colin Thatcher, the BBC's duty deputy news editor. When a man with a Middle Eastern accent announced that he was a hostage in the Iranian Embassy and he wanted to deliver a message on behalf of the gunmen, Thatcher sat bolt upright in his chair. Like Hooper at the *Guardian* the day before, for Thatcher this was the kind of career-changing moment most journalists only dream of.

Switching on his recording equipment, Thatcher told Karkouti: 'Go ahead.'

In a slow, measured voice, Karkouti said: 'The group occupying the Iranian Embassy would like to assure the British public opinion [sic] that the British hostages, as well as all other non-Iranian hostages, will not be harmed. But the deadline for the safety of the other hostages and the others as well – which is twelve o'clock noon – is still valid. That's all.'

Thatcher was still stunned – but it didn't sound like a hoax. With the whole world desperate to know what was happening inside the embassy, he grabbed the opportunity that had been presented to him with both hands, and said: 'May we ask you a question about conditions inside the embassy at the moment?'

Salim shook his head. Karkouti said: 'The gentleman here doesn't want me to answer any questions.'

It was obvious the speaker was about to put down the phone. Thatcher knew that he had to come up with something that would keep the conversation going. 'No more questions?' he echoed. And then as the silence stretched out: 'Hello?'

Salim, in turn, realised that he had the very opportunity he had hoped for: the chance to broadcast his case to the outside world. He took the phone from Karkouti. 'Good morning,' he began.

'What are the conditions in the embassy at the moment?' asked Thatcher. 'Are all the hostages well?'

'All well. And everything all right,' Salim replied.

Thatcher then asked why the group had called for a doctor the previous day. Salim told him: 'We have an injured man.'

'Can you tell me what is wrong with this injured man?'

'Not exactly – but I think he's badly sick.'

'He's not suffering from gunshot wounds?'

His tone polite but resolute, Salim responded: 'He's not injured. But I think it's not important how.'

With the gunman apparently willing to keep up the conversation, Thatcher decided to push a little further. 'Do you have any food in the embassy?'

It was the wrong question. In fact, like the majority of hostage-takers, the gunmen had given no consideration to the need for food once they were on the inside. Salim said: 'I think I can't answer this question. I think there's water.'

Thatcher pressed on: 'When were you last speaking to the police?'

'I was last speaking, I think about twelve o'clock or eleven. I am not sure exactly.'

'You are not in communication with the police at the moment?'

'No.'

'Have you received a telephone call during the night from the Iranian Foreign Minister, Mr Qotbzadeh?' asked Thatcher. 'What was his message?'

'The message I think he says: "We will not yield to the demands of the group,"' replied Salim.

'And what is your reaction to that message?'

'Just a minute,' said Salim. Then, after a few moments' pause, he said, 'I think he will regret this statement.'

'Can you go into details? What do you mean, he will regret it?'

Calmly, but with evident intent, Salim said: 'I mean – after the deadline – I will kill everybody here. All the hostages.'

Thatcher found it hard to keep his voice on the same even keel: 'And the deadline is twelve noon today?'

'Twelve noon today,' Salim confirmed. 'This is what Qotbzadeh wants – because they are nothing to him. He don't care for the Iranian hostages.'

Thatcher then had some news for Salim: 'Do you know Mr Qotbzadeh has issued a warning that if anyone in the Iranian Embassy in London is harmed, then the people in Arabistan will be harmed?'

If this caused Salim any anxiety, he didn't betray it: 'OK. That doesn't matter.'

'That doesn't matter?' Thatcher pressed.

'Yes.'

Salim's matter-of-fact tone was chilling. Thatcher said: 'You are not concerned about that? I thought you wanted the release of these people?'

'We're concerned.'

Thatcher decided to push his luck. He already had a world-beating interview: 'Can you tell me exactly how many hostages you are holding in the embassy . . .?'

'No, sorry.'

'Are they being held in one room? Or are they tied up? Are they allowed to move about?'

Salim was beginning to run out of patience. 'Sorry. I can't answer that question.'

Thatcher asked if he could speak with one of his BBC colleagues – Cramer or Harris. 'No, sorry. We are very sorry.'

The same odd politeness. Anyone would think Salim was a Sunday school teacher, not a terrorist holding twenty-six hostages at gunpoint.

'Is it possible to speak to one of the English people there?' Thatcher asked.

'No. But they are all right. And will be all right,' replied Salim.

Thatcher asked then if Salim would guarantee that the non-English hostages would remain unharmed.

'Of course,' said Salim.

'Will they be released soon?'

'We will see.'

'Will they be released before the deadline at midday?'

'No.'

Thatcher asked the logical question: 'Then how can you guarantee that they will be unharmed?'

In a heavy voice, Salim replied: 'I will think about that.'

Then there was a long pause. Thatcher wanted to keep Salim talking, so he changed tack, asking him to specify the exact name of his group.

'The exact name is Muhydedden Al Nasser Martyr.'

'And this is the Movement of the Martyr?'

'Yes.'

'We have heard from Beirut, Lebanon, that three separate Arab ethnic groups have claimed responsibility. Is that right? Are you connected with any other Arab groups based in Lebanon?' Thatcher was referring to statements issued in Beirut by three hitherto obscure groups – the Arab Masses Movement, the Political Organisation of the Arab People and the Moslem Arab People's Strugglers Movement – claiming responsibility for the London operation.

Salim was more comfortable answering questions along this line: 'They aren't based in Lebanon – they are based in Arabistan.'

'But do you accept that these other groups are involved in this action of yours?'

'Yes,' Salim replied.

To this day, no one knows exactly what he meant. But that aside, Colin Thatcher had a world-beating exclusive to broadcast. 'Thank you,' he said.

'Thank you very much. Goodbye.'

The line to the Iranian Embassy went dead.

Listening in to the conversation between Thatcher and Salim had given Karkouti an idea: 'Will you release the non-Iranians before or after the twelve noon deadline?' he asked.

'I will think about it,' said Salim.

'Why don't you let the British out one at a time at half-hourly intervals?' Karkouti suggested. 'Let them go sometime between ten and twelve ...'

When he got back to the room where the other hostages were waiting, Cramer looked up and said: 'I'm going to live off this story in the bar for years. I'm never going to buy a drink again.'

Laughter rippled round the room. When some wag piped up: 'I'll go out and fetch us all some hamburgers,' there was more laughter. The two women came back in with breakfast: oranges, bananas, hard-boiled eggs, pitta bread, butter, jam – and raw carrots.

PC Lock, who still had the revolver concealed under his tunic, refused all offers of food. He was worried that if he ate, he would have to go to the toilet. And if one of the gunmen decided to escort him, then he might glimpse the gun concealed under his tunic. Lock sat on his chair in solitary splendour, trying to ignore the hunger pangs brought on by the sight and smell of food.

Cramer's stomach was beginning to ache for an entirely different reason. All of a sudden, the idea of eating anything sickened him. There was a nasty, queasy feeling in his gut he thought he recognised: a recurrence of the bowel disease he'd picked up on a job in Africa. His stomach rumbled and he began to sweat. One moment he was hot, the next, shivering with cold. He needed the toilet – fast. Climbing unsteadily to his feet, he got permission to visit the first-floor WC. The trip didn't appear to have succeeded in alleviating the symptoms. If anything, he told Harris as he stumbled back into Room 9, he felt worse.

Harris and Mustapha Karkouti fussed over Cramer, but there seemed little they could do to help. Cramer slumped down on the floor, put his hands on his stomach and let out a load groan.

Just then, Makki relieved the gunman on guard duty at the door. Nursing a broken jaw and feeling very unwell, Dr Afrouz made a move towards the nearest radiator. The central heating came on twice a day on the embassy timer, but he still felt cold. Makki misinterpreted the move as an attempt to reach the window with a view to another escape attempt. He told the Chargé d'Affaires to move and sit near him by the door where he could keep a closer eye on him. Outraged, Afrouz said: 'Why are you talking to me like that? If you want to kill me, then kill me and let the rest of the hostages go. I am the senior official here. They're simply innocent victims.'

Makki eyed him coldly, motioning him with the pistol to move. Slowly the Chargé d'Affaires hauled himself across the room. Makki shouted: 'Fast! Fast!' When Afrouz continued moving at a snail's pace, he raised his pistol and fired a shot into the ceiling. Some of the women began to scream. Two of the Iranians ran to Afrouz and helped him move over to the door.

Cramer stared at the five-centimetre hole that had appeared in the ceiling above his head. Tiny flakes of white plaster drifted slowly towards him, like snowflakes on a still winter's day. The whole incident, he decided, was bizarre beyond belief: like starring in his own personal horror movie, one that kept getting worse all the time. Looking to the side, he saw the brass cartridge case that had been ejected from the gunman's pistol when he'd fired. Reaching out, Cramer picked it up and put it in his pocket. The metal was still warm to the touch. It was also evidence.

To the hostages, the shooting incident came as a hard lesson: however friendly and polite their captors might be most of the time, their individual and collective mood could change in a moment. Dealing with them was like handling live ammunition: the only way to stay safe was to remember they were dangerous.

Huddling together, the Iranian hostages started praying again: the communal chanting seemed to help them cope in moments of extreme stress.

■ ■ ■

At 0900 hrs and with the police snapping hard at their heels, Post Office engineers finally detected the last surviving embassy phone link and cut it off. Now, for Salim and his little band, their only remaining contact with the outside world was through the green police field telephone.

Salim had gone off for another wander round the embassy. He came back into Room 9 clutching a poster-sized map of Iran. It showed where the country's various ethnic groups lived, with pictures of their respective traditional clothing. Handing it to Abbas Lavasani, Salim ordered him to read through the listed communities, translating the Farsi into English as he went. When Lavasani got to the end, an irate Salim shouted: 'There's one large group missing! The Iranian government manage to ignore four and a half million Arabs! Now do you see why we're here?'

By 1000 hrs, everyone including Salim could see that Cramer was in acute distress. Doubled up in pain, he looked pasty and the sweat was running down his face in rivulets. 'What medicine does he need?' said Salim. 'I've asked the police to send a doctor, but they won't.'

Harris, who was taking it in turns with Morris and Karkouti to comfort his BBC colleague, scribbled the brand name of the anti-diarrhoea medicine 'Lomotil' on a piece of paper. He volunteered to explain to the police what was needed. As Salim led him down to the field telephone on the ground floor, Harris, in turn, began to sweat. He was acutely aware of the man's sub-machine gun pointing at the small of his back. The stairwell was dark. There was a second gunman right behind him. A third lurked in the shadows at the back of the hall.

Leading him through into the small room behind the waiting room, Salim showed Harris the police-supplied telephone and explained how it worked. When the negotiator answered, Harris explained how ill Cramer was and asked for a doctor.

'It's gone upstairs to a higher authority,' the negotiator told him blandly. 'They say they're trying to get some drugs for him.' It was the usual stalling tactic.

When Harris got back to Room 9, he found the smallest gunman, Hassan, trying to give Cramer a glass of milk. If anything, Cramer looked worse: doubled up in pain, the milk dribbling down his chin as he tried and failed to swallow it. Karkouti, kneeling beside him, was openly weeping in concern. The tears splashed on to Cramer's face: 'It's going to be OK,' Karkouti kept saying. 'Hang on, hang on!'

Harris told Salim: 'He's too ill for a doctor. He needs to get to a hospital. Prove to us that you don't mean us any harm. Let him go now.'

Several of the gunmen got into a huddle. After some discussion, Salim came back. 'OK, we take him.' Harris, Karkouti and Morris lifted Cramer up and carried him out and down the stairs to the library on the rear ground floor. They laid the newsman on a mattress and covered him up with a blue woollen blanket. Cramer – curled up in agony, clutching his stomach and sweating profusely – gave every impression of being at death's door.

Salim told Harris to call the police again, and listened in to the conversation. This time, the negotiator said that no doctor was prepared to enter the embassy: Harris should try and persuade the terrorist leader to release his colleague. Harris swore softly under his breath. It was clear to him that the police were systematically stalling everything, but he wasn't about to let Salim know.

When Harris got back to the library, he saw a strange scene: tears streaming down his face, Hassan was thumping Cramer softly on the chest with both hands. At the same time he was shouting in Arabic: 'I'm sorry, Mr Chris, we didn't mean to hurt you!'

Even when Karkouti translated, it did nothing to lessen the bizarre drama of the moment.

The gunmen held another discussion, this one more animated than the first. When it broke up, Salim told Harris: 'OK, we release him. But he must not say anything to the police. Get him to promise.'

'Of course he won't say anything. Anyway, you released the woman yesterday, didn't you?'

'She knew nothing,' Salim retorted. 'Mr Chris is different. He can tell them everything.'

Two of the gunmen marched Harris and Karkouti back to Room 9. There, with PC Lock, they were made to kneel facing the curtains. The gunmen stood behind them, weapons steady on the backs of their necks.

Salim opened the embassy's monumental front door a crack and peered out. The street outside was empty. Leaning forward, he told Cramer: 'You walk straight ahead. You turn left or right, I kill you.' To make sure the BBC man did as he was told, Salim noisily cocked the Skorpion machine-pistol. At 1115 hrs, almost exactly twenty-four hours after the siege had started, he shoved Chris Cramer out of the embassy to freedom.

■ ■ ■

Two Anti-Terrorist branch officers helped the newsman into an ambulance. And got right in after him. A paramedic tried to place an oxygen mask on his face, but Cramer pushed it away. 'I'm not as ill as they think I am,' he told the policemen. 'You mustn't storm the building: there are six gunmen in there with machine guns and hand grenades. But PC Lock still has his gun.'

In one breath, he'd given the police, COBRA and the SAS some of the most vital information they needed.

At St Stephen's Hospital, a doctor came and gave Cramer the once-over. There was nothing seriously wrong with him – but when the doctor showed a smidgen of empathy, the BBC man suddenly found the tears rolling down his cheeks. 'That's all right,' the doctor said kindly. 'Let it all out – it's perfectly natural.'

Now they realised Cramer wasn't really ill, the detectives set about pumping him for everything he had. At first, he started telling the policemen, who said their names were 'John' and 'Ray', everything he knew. But when John asked him: 'Are you prepared to make a state-ment?' Cramer grew more cautious.

'No. Not if it will get back to the gunmen. I made a pact that I wouldn't tell you anything. If they find out I've spoken to you, they'll kill Sim and the others. I couldn't ever forgive myself.' The detectives shot one another a charged look.

'Look, Chris,' John said, 'there's no way anything you tell us will get back. But you've got to tell us everything. Otherwise the hostages might die anyway.'

They promised that absolutely everything he said would be confidential. Only the most senior police officers would be told. Nothing – *nada* – would be released to the press. And nothing would be broadcast or printed hinting that Cramer had cooperated in any way.

It was a long ten minutes before Cramer agreed to make a statement. And he insisted he wouldn't sign it until the siege was over. His interrogators agreed and left the room to get a supply of statement forms. 'I'm afraid you can't talk to anyone while you're in here,' John told him. 'A policeman is outside the door all the time, and he has strict instructions not to allow anybody in unless our bosses clear it. You can see your relatives, but only if the constable sits in the room while they're here.'

A short while later, forgetting what he'd already told the police, Cramer rang the bell by the side of the bed to summon the policeman outside. The constable brought the two Special Branch men back into the room.

'Did I tell you that Trevor Lock still had his gun?' Cramer said.

'You did. But we thought you might have been confused,' Ray said. 'Are you sure about that? It seems very unlikely.'

'Typical bloody police,' Cramer thought. 'They never believe a word anyone says.'

'I'm absolutely sure,' he insisted. 'Lock told me so himself, several times. He couldn't go to sleep because he was frightened they might find it. Anyway, he told me how to use it in case of trouble. Oh, and there's something else.' He reached out of bed and picked up his jacket. It was still damp with sweat. Reaching into one of the pockets, he felt the bits and pieces of pitta bread and broken biscuits he'd hoarded there. Delving deeper, his hand hit what he'd been looking for – the spent cartridge case from Makki's automatic pistol. He handed it to Ray.

The policeman did a double-take. 'Where did you get this? Whose gun is it from?'

'From the guy who fired above our heads this morning. I think his name's "Makki". I picked it up from the carpet.'

'Didn't he see you take it?'

Cramer shrugged. 'Yes. He just smiled.'

'Our very first exhibit,' Ray said, licking his lips like a cat that had just got the cream. He took a small plastic bag from his pocket and lovingly placed the brass cylinder inside, then took out a pen and labelled it carefully.

By the time the policemen left, Cramer was completely exhausted. 'Get a good night's sleep and we'll see you in the morning,' said one of them. 'If you want anything, the policeman outside will get it.'

What Cramer wanted most in the world was a cigarette. Like everybody else in the embassy, he'd spent most of the time trying to smoke himself to death. He was completely out of 'coffin nails'. A nurse took pity on him, and gave him a couple of her own. Back in the dawn of time, nurses smoked.

At 0400 hrs a wide-awake Cramer rang the bell by the bed. The policeman on night duty poked his head around the door. 'Please pass a message to the police at the embassy,' Cramer said. 'Get them to tell everyone inside that I'm recovering. And thank them for letting me go.' Suffering from classic 'survivor guilt', his conscience was playing him up.

■ ■ ■

A few minutes before the noon deadline was set to expire, Superintendent Luff of Special Branch made his way to the front of the embassy. He was an improbable sight. A voluptuous Farsi–English interpreter stood behind him, her arms wrapped tightly around his waist, as if she was so mad about Luff she couldn't let go of him. In fact, the intimate body contact was for additional safety. Additional, that is, to the heavy plates of body armour that hung over her stylish designer clothes. Darkly glamorous despite the bulky plates, the wide-eyed interpreter looked a bit like the Italian actress Sophia Loren, somehow miscast in a crime movie. She snuggled into Luff, glancing nervously around.

When Salim showed his face at the window, Luff shouted an appeal for the gunmen to extend the midday deadline, promising that if Salim agreed to the extension, Luff would make a statement on the group's behalf. After a lot of argy-bargy, Salim agreed to an extension of two hours.

All the while the two men had been talking, the police and SAS observers in the respective sniper teams had been snapping away furiously with their long-range cameras, trying to get a clear shot of Salim's face. Others, equipped with high-powered binoculars and telescopes, had been gathering whatever details they could regarding his appearance. Their efforts were hindered by the fact that Salim had pulled the hood of his anorak up around his head, and put on a big pair of dark glasses.

Right from the start, the SAS and police sniper teams had been systematically logging the gunmen's appearances at the windows and doors. The idea was to identify them and to find ways to differentiate between one gunman and another, and in the process hopefully develop the ability to tell them apart from the hostages. Assigning each gunman a codename – X-ray One, X-ray Two and so on – sniper observers recorded everything from their clothing ('X-ray Three always wears a green combat jacket and a black-and-white kaffiyeh') to what weapons they had, how they handled them, whether they smoked and if so, what. They noted jewellery, hairstyles and any physical features that made the gunmen stand out, like big ears or a prominent nose. They also tried to see if any of the hostage-takers had identifying marks such as tattoos.

The teams made the same detailed notes about any of the hostages who came into sight. The more the police and SAS knew about the people inside the embassy, the less chance there was of targeting someone innocent by mistake.

The SAS called the gunmen 'X-rays' because, whenever one of the bad guys got killed, they marked a thick, felt pen 'X' through his mug-shot.

All the various intelligence agencies were in overdrive, scrabbling to trawl up and collect every scrap of information about both the gunmen and the political context of the siege: anything that might shed light on their motivation, appearance and likely behaviour.

To help with the identification process, the SAS put the surveillance data 'green slime' provided on a big briefing board set up on the wall in the Doctors' House. The board gradually began to fill up with a detailed photographic and annotated list of all persons known to be in the embassy, weapons, floor plans, numbers of hostages and terrorists, together with any other useful snippets of intelligence that emerged. Pride of place was given to the rogue's gallery of gunmen rash enough to show their faces.

Someone suggested getting a model of No. 16 Princes Gate made up, so that the embassy could be studied in depth, room by room and floor by floor. The model turned out to be an excellent training aid for the operation.

Individual SAS men were also expected to compile their own portable intelligence boards, in notebooks or on pads, and study these in order to learn which faces were friendly, which hostile. In particular, they made notes of the gunmen's general behaviour and demeanour, looking for any indication as to how hardened and professional – or incompetent – they were. Was their body language nervous, or assured? Did they look and sound anxious or confident when they were dealing with the negotiators? Did they always wear the same thing, leaving them open to easier identification, or did they regularly swap clothes with one another – or with the hostages – in an effort to confuse the watchers? What about their weapons handling? Did this show signs of military training, or was it amateurish and/or dangerous?

At the same time, Met Police C7 and MI5 surveillance experts were looking to gain real-time intelligence about what was going on inside the embassy. Ideally, they wanted to know where the gunmen were; what they were saying; where the hostages were; and what plans, if any, the gunmen had when it came to defending themselves in the case of a rescue attempt. To this end, surveillance technicians began drilling through the embassy's walls from the adjoining buildings: not just the Doctors' House, but also No. 17, the Ethiopian Embassy, on the other side. The technicians used hand-drills with very slim bits, but even so it was impossible to cover up the noise of the drilling.

In an attempt to mask the high-pitched squeaking, C7 asked the gas utility representative on COBRA to have workmen start drilling

Salim Towfigh, the leader of the gunmen.

105 Lexham Gardens, Earl's Court, where the gunmen lived for three weeks before the siege. (*Observer*)

Smith & Wesson .38 Model 10 revolver of the type PC Lock carried.

Three of the hostages: Haydeh Kanji, embassy secretary; Chris Cramer, Producer BBC TV News; and Sim Harris, BBC sound recordist. (*Press Association*)

COBRA in part session. Lieutenant-Colonel Rose in the jacket with back towards camera.

Regent's Park barracks main gate.

Pro-Khomeini demonstrators.

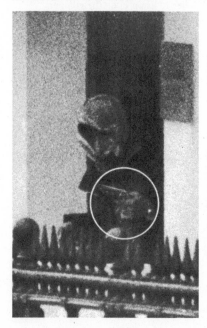

A masked gunman at the first floor 'talking window'. (*Sunday Times*)

Police Negotiator Supt Luff and interpreter talking to the gunmen. (*Sunday Times*)

On the Embassy roof, a bug is lowered down a chimney. It was one of a range of high-tech surveillance devices that allowed police to listen in on the gunmen. (*Sunday Times*)

Gunman at the window with Mustapha Karkouti to his right. (*Observer*)

Sim Harris and PC Trevor Lock on the Embassy balcony during the siege. (*Press Assocation*)

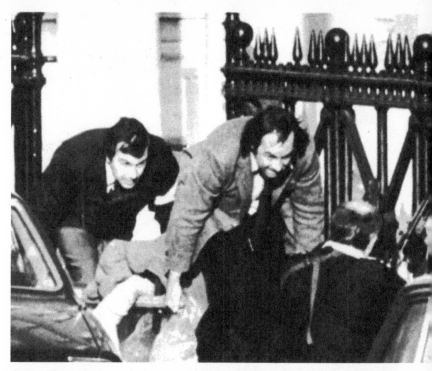

Covered by marksmen, police recover the body of Abbas Lavasani on Day Six.
(*Press Association*)

Abbas Lavasani. (*Sunday Times*)

Anti-Iranian graffiti written by the gunmen.

British Army L9A1 Browning High Power semi-automatic pistol 9mm as used by the SAS.

Rusty Firmin's S6 respirator

SAS assault kit and weaponry circa 1980.

Eight-man rear abseil team – final preparations for descent.

First, two-man abseil unit awaiting final order to start descent. Other six men rigged up.

Abseil in progress – Tommy Palmer on right. The broken window pane that semi-compromised the assault is visible.

Second-floor balcony. Red Team leader hung up on rope. Other assaulters make entry. The fire in the office beyond has just started.

Still trying to free Red Team leader. Fire has now taken firm hold.

a hole in the road near the embassy. The police told Salim the work had to be done in order to repair an emergency gas leak. The one they had just made up. The gas board's drilling certainly achieved its objective – inside the embassy, while it lasted, you could hardly hear yourself speak. But the noise was so great and so intrusive for police and gunmen alike it was quickly abandoned.

When the gas leak distraction failed, Lt-Col Rose suggested that Heathrow's air traffic controllers reroute incoming aircraft low over the embassy's roof. An unprecedented risk to central London's citizens, not to mention an infernal nuisance, the aircraft ploy nonetheless proved more successful when it came to masking the drilling.

The surveillance experts were looking to insert fine fibre-optic cables with embedded microphones and tiny cameras through the embassy walls. With the technology still relatively new in 1980, the immediate results of the bugging operation were mixed. Other technicians took to the roof: if its chimneys were still clear, then they would provide a set of perfect listening tubes that penetrated directly down into the rooms below. By lowering microphones until they dangled just above the embassy's fireplaces, they might be able to hear what was being said inside.

Workmen also started stripping the plaster and removing bricks in a section of wall between No. 17 and No. 16. The idea was to leave nothing but the plaster on the Ethiopian Embassy side standing, which would give the SAS another option if it came to a rescue.

At 2000 hrs that evening, the police tape machines that were now going twenty-four hours a day recorded a very suspicious Salim complaining about the 'high-pitched squeaking noises' he could hear coming from behind an electrical point on the second floor. He asked Lock and Harris to investigate. Although he knew perfectly well the noise was being produced by his colleagues trying to drill through the wall, Lock removed the cover plate, pressed his ear to the skirting and then made a show of inspecting the socket.

'Are they trying to listen?' Salim demanded.

'No,' Lock assured him with a perfectly straight face, 'that's not the way the British operate.' Then, as he lifted the edge of the carpet,

Lock got lucky: there was a small hole in the floorboards nearby. Pointing to it, he told the terrorist leader: 'This building's more than a hundred years old. Perhaps it's got mice.' Salim joined in the general laughter.

Several of the gunmen then went back to Room 9. Ordering all the Iranian hostages to put their hands on their heads, they herded them out and up to the third-floor front room – the press office. The sixth gunman kept watch over the non-Iranians. Then they, too, were pushed into the press room. After a while, Salim came in. 'Don't touch anything,' he told the hostages. 'We're all bombed up. We're all set.' The captives took him to mean that the gunmen had placed explosive devices around the embassy – booby traps in case of a rescue attempt. As if to confirm that, Salim said: 'If your police attack, we will kill you.'

Lock said: 'The police will not attack, please believe me. You're in England, we don't do things like that. If you don't hurt us, the police won't hurt you. All they want is for this to end peacefully.'

That might have been true, but preparations for an armed rescue were going forward at top speed. The Blue Team at Regent's Park Barracks had spent the morning of Day Two studying detailed plans of the embassy provided by Scotland Yard's Architectural Division. The Met's specialist carpenters had also been busy building a detailed and accurate scale model of the embassy's first and second floors, allowing the SAS to familiarise themselves with its interior. At the same time, Irish Guards' Pioneers began constructing walk-through replicas of the embassy's rooms out of hessian and plywood. The mock-up's doors opened and closed the correct way: if it came down to a rescue assault, little things like that made all the difference. In any operation where time allowed, for the SAS, God was in the detail.

■ ■ ■

At 1240 hrs, Salim picked up the field telephone and thumbed the red 'transmit' button. Ignoring the unctuous tones of the voice on the other end, he said: 'We are giving the Iranian government until

2 p.m. today. After 2 p.m., all responsibility falls upon the Iranian government. If the Iranian government will acknowledge that they are negotiating with the British government, that will extend the time.' He put the phone down and told the hostages: 'We have given them till 2 p.m.'

While some of the hostages sampled the press room's super-annuated collection of magazines to take their minds off their predicament, Karkouti chatted with the gunmen in Arabic, translating the discussion into English for the benefit of the Brits. One of the gunmen said: 'I have nothing to live for. They killed my whole family. They were martyrs.' The conversation branched out, involving more of the people in the room. When he'd listened to what some of the gunmen had said, Muhammad Faruqi said he thought the gunmen's basic demands – that Khuzestan enjoy a measure of autonomy; that the Iranian government stop harrying its Arab population and release political prisoners; and that the province reap some reasonable economic reward for its oil – were fair and just. Most of the other hostages agreed.

They all expressed their admiration for Salim. Karkouti said: 'Salim was tremendous. He can discuss politics with the hostages, supervise and keep a constant check on security, answer all the telephone calls from the police and listen to the news. He is capable of doing five or six things at the same time, all really well.'

Stockholm Syndrome, the psychological phenomenon whereby hostages and their captors in siege conditions form mutual bonds of admiration and respect, was setting in nicely. Salim told Karkouti: 'When you get out, please assure the world that we are not criminals. We released a woman on the first day; we released a man who was in pain on the second day. We cannot stand the idea of anyone being in pain.'

Karkouti said later: 'I realised that, like me, they loved life and did not want it to end.' Events were soon to prove whether or not he was right.

As part of the new-found chumminess, the hostages got together and decided to draft their own appeal on behalf of the gunmen, and send it to the Iranian Foreign Ministry in Tehran.

While the hostages were busy doing that, Salim tried one of the office telephones. It was dead. They were all dead. He rounded on the British hostages: 'Why have the police cut off the phones? What are they trying to do?'

Harris said: 'Maybe it's just a fault on the line.' Lock, too, tried to assure the gunman there was nothing to worry about. In fact, there was still one phone link working: the direct internal line to the Iranian Consular section in nearby Kensington Court. Salim told Issa Nagh-izadeh, the embassy's First Secretary, to get on it and order the Iranian staff on the other end to speed up negotiations with Tehran. Salim still seemed to believe that he would be able to force the Iranian government to release the ninety-one Arab political detainees.

At 1430 hrs, Salim told the police he would extend the new deadline to 1630 hrs if they reconnected the embassy's telex and telephone lines. 'If not,' he warned, 'the responsibility will be with the police.' He came back up and told the hostages that all he wanted now was the Jordanian, Iraqi and Algerian ambassadors to broker the gunmen's safe passage out of Britain. That and a bus to take the hostages, the gunmen and a representative from the Red Crescent as a guarantor of safe passage to Heathrow Airport. If those two things happened, he would release everyone. The hostages took him to mean the deal had already been agreed. They erupted in cheers and smiles and tears of joy.

Then came a crushing disappointment. They had misunderstood Salim: he was expressing a wish list, not a done deal. He hadn't actually told the police yet what he wanted. The prisoners relapsed into a deep gloom.

By mid-afternoon of Day Two, everyone inside the embassy was getting hungry. Salim got on the blower to the police again. 'I want twenty-five burgers,' he announced and put the phone down. When the burgers hadn't materialised half an hour later, he gave the police a fifteen-minute deadline for their arrival. The deadlines were piling up. But they kept slipping past unfulfilled.

Some minutes later, the police sent in trays of freshly cooked food, the first the hostages had enjoyed since the siege began. It included the much-anticipated burgers in long white bridge rolls, and the remaining half of a two-foot square steak pie that looked as if it had been prepared for – and then attacked by – the police. Lock, as before, refused to eat anything.

While the hostages ate, Salim and the other gunmen listened to news bulletins on the embassy's two portable radios. What they heard seemed to make them angry and nervous: LBC had broadcast another inaccurate report, claiming that the British Embassy in Tehran had been occupied. The demonstrators across the road in Hyde Park were listening, too. Fighting broke out between the two sides. In the fracas, PC Michael Perkin suffered a broken leg, and a seventy-five-year-old British woman was arrested and bailed to appear at Horseferry Road Magistrates' Court on a charge of breach of the peace.

As if that wasn't enough to keep them occupied, the police then had to deal with the crowds arriving for a Johnny Mathis concert at the Royal Albert Hall.

Shortly before 1700 hrs Salim phoned the police with a new set of demands:

- **An aircraft to fly both gunmen and hostages to the Middle East.**
- **The crew to consist mainly of females.**
- **A coach with curtained windows to take them out to Heathrow Airport, where all non-Iranians would be released.**
- **The ambassadors of Jordan, Iraq and Algeria to be waiting at the airport.**

The police released most of this new statement to the press, but sat on the request for mediation by Arab ambassadors. That was a thorny one. It needed careful handling.

Slowly beginning to realise that siege negotiations were the art of the possible, Salim had quietly dropped his demand for the Iranians to release ninety-one Khuzestani political prisoners. Even he knew the British government couldn't deliver on that. But he insisted the new set of demands he'd just made was final: if he didn't get what he wanted by 1900 hrs, then all the hostages would be killed. Promising to do everything they could, the police immediately negotiated an extension of the deadline to 2000 hrs.

At 1815 hrs, Metropolitan Police Commissioner Sir David McNee gave a press conference:

> The gunmen ... must know that it is not in our power to meet all of their demands, whatever the rights and wrongs of their cause. I appeal to them to remain calm. Hasty action may cause even more suffering to their own people in Iran ...
>
> All my officers engaged in this incident are concerned to do what we always try to do: resolve the situation without loss of life and uphold the law ... We must show patience and perseverance. That is what we intend to do.

There was no mention of Salim's request for the Arab ambassadors in McNee's statement, nor any suggestion the group's demands might be met. Bitterly disappointed, Salim complained: 'The police are treating us like children.' He was 100 per cent right about that.

A short while later, the hostages released the statement they'd written in support of the gunmen. It urged the Khomeini regime to concede to at least some of the gunmen's demands:

> This should reach Iran from all of the hostages at 16 Princes Gate, dictated by the First Secretary, Iranian Embassy.
>
> In order that world imperialism, meaning the US and all its supporters, do not benefit from the act of holding these hostages by a number of our Iranian/Arab brothers attached to the martyr group of Muhieddin al Nassir and lest they have a chance to take another step against weak nations. Therefore all of us who have signed this letter wish to represent our request to the Revolutionary Council and Minister of Foreign Affairs of Iran as follows, hoping that they will immediately investigate our request and announce a positive result.

1. We wish them to investigate and take necessary action regarding the requests of our brothers, the members of the Group of the Martyr Muhieddin al Nassir.

2. The request of our brothers is particularly to stress the point of our disagreement over the basic nature of independence which is both lawful and reasonable and is definitely worthy of investigation.

3. Not only do we have no hostility towards them but they have been very fair in the majority of affairs and we are well aware of their humanitarian attitude.

4. In the name of Mighty God, in whom we believe, in order to achieve this goal we will do our best and in our efforts we expect speedy cooperation and assistance from the officials of our beloved government.

From all the hostages and dictated by Mr Naghizadeh, First Secretary of the Iranian Embassy, London.

■ ■ ■

At around ten o'clock that evening, Lock suggested he try and find out what was going on by shouting down to his colleagues in the street outside. 'They might tell me more than they'll tell you,' he told Salim craftily. To the same purpose, Harris suggested he try and make contact with a BBC colleague. With the 8 p.m. deadline long since passed and nothing to show for it, Salim agreed to both ideas.

While three of the other gunmen stood guard, he led Lock and Harris down to the small first-floor accounting room. Lock put on his uniform cap. Leaning out of the window, he shouted: 'This is PC Trevor Lock. Is anybody there?'

His words echoed down the empty street. There was no one in sight, no sound from the street, just the darkness and an eerie silence. Lock tried again. Then a voice called back: 'Yes, Trevor?' A solitary figure loomed up out of the darkness and came to stand below the window.

'Sir, it's very difficult in here ... Would you please request the BBC to send a journalist who is personally known to Sim Harris as soon as possible?'

The shadowy figure below spoke into a walkie-talkie radio. Suspecting more police prevarication, Harris leaned out and shouted the direct telephone numbers of his boss, Tony Crabb, and one or two other BBC staff members. Salim said he would give the police one hour to find someone.

An hour later, at 2320 hrs, the two hostages and gunmen trooped back down to what they now called 'the talking window'. Lock asked if the police had succeeded in finding a BBC staff member. There was more walkie-talkie stalling, then the police officer called back: 'We made the request. But there is no one available.'

Harris knew this was a bare-faced lie. Any number of BBC colleagues would have jumped at the chance to help him and be part of what was shaping up to be the major British news story of the year. With customary guile, the police suggested it would be better to wait until morning. Daylight would bring the gunmen better publicity. Furious, Salim threatened to throw the green field telephone out of the first-floor window. But eventually, soothed by Karkouti, Harris and Lock, he agreed. When Salim had calmed down, they all went back up to the press room on the third floor.

In their absence, some of the women had rustled up a second meal of meat stew, rice and pitta bread. Lock had a glass of water and a biscuit.

■ ■ ■

The siege was now top of most international news agendas. Press City continued to grow, threatening to overflow the crush barriers. Journalists were resorting to all sorts of ruses in order to get access to – or failing that, direct line of sight on – the embassy. John Hemming, the Director of the Royal Geographical Society, rented a top-floor room in the building to the *Sunday Times* team and was appalled when the photographers started clambering over the antique furniture in order to gain the best angle of vantage.

In New York, UN Secretary-General Kurt Waldheim condemned the embassy seizure as an act of terrorism, and appealed for restraint and the safe release of the hostages.

The official Iraqi news agency expressed sympathy for the London embassy seizure, adding that it was time to 'aim a knock-out blow at the Persian racists' occupying Iran's oil-producing region of Khuzestan.

An Iranian Foreign Ministry spokesman said he had information that 'certain people' were planning to occupy the British Embassy in Tehran, warning the citizens of Tehran that threats of this kind were the work of 'the world-devouring USA and the traitorous Ba'athist regime of Iraq'. Fearing just such an attack, the British Ambassador had already closed the embassy and stepped up security patrols.

If the siege could be compared to a game of chess between the two sides, then in releasing Cramer and allowing two major deadlines to pass without any positive result in their favour, by close of play on Day Two the gunmen were at least a rook and a bishop down.

Not only that, but with the new demand for Arab ambassadors to mediate, a horrible mismatch of expectations between the British government and the hostage-takers was now in place. The chances of a peaceful resolution to the embassy siege were fast diminishing.

# DAY THREE: Friday, 2 May 1980

Blue Team were still in Regent's Park Barracks – and they were getting impatient. They'd been told they'd be moving into the holding area to relieve Red Team, who by now had been at the Forward Holding Area nearly twenty-four hours. Everything was packed and everyone was ready to move. All the Blue Team needed was the command. They'd spent the last twenty-four hours preparing equipment, carrying out final checks on weapons and ammo. There was only so much they could do; but as usual, they found things to do. Finally they got the nod to move. This was it.

For the move to Princes Gate, Blue Team split down into teams known by call signs: Bravo One, Bravo Two, and so on. Once again, they were using the hire vans; despite feeling naked without them, they had to leave the trusty Range Rovers behind. Firmin climbed into a van with three other men, plus personal bags. Hardly a word was spoken as the police driver took off and they slowly made their way across town. Firmin reflected that if they'd been called out to rescue the hostages and driven this route, there probably wouldn't have been any hostages left alive to rescue by the time they got to the embassy. Even in the early hours of the morning it seemed to take a long time. But by 0330 hrs, both Red and Blue Teams were finally together at the holding area. They even left off the inter-team rivalry for a while.

The first thing Blue Team had to do on arrival was change into the operational black kit. Then, when they'd loaded and prepared the weapons, Red Team's commander brought everyone up to speed on the current situation. As Day Two had worn on and new intelligence had come in, and as the team had familiarised themselves with the ground, some more meat had been added to the skeleton initial IA plan. Now more controlled and much more detailed, it was no longer a Wild West show.

With the briefing over, and following a few questions from the guys, Blue Team went to acquaint themselves with the chosen entry points on the roof. At that stage, they were the *only* entry points the SP team planned on using if they had to go in and rescue the hostages.

■ ■ ■

Early on Friday morning, the President of Iran's press officer woke Sir John Graham, the British Ambassador in Tehran, to complain about the way in which the police were treating pro-Iranian demonstrators in Hyde Park. Bani Sadr's office moaned that no food or blankets had been provided for the poor souls who'd been left shivering in the open air overnight. The general British response to this was: 'Tough.' Demonstrators were free to leave the compound if they wanted food and water, but the police weren't allowing them back in.

At 0700 hrs the gunmen woke the hostages. Many were already awake, following an uncomfortable night on the floor, made worse by Ghanzafar's world-class snoring. He was still making a noise like a boat going aground on a coral reef when the gunmen came in. Salim stopped in surprise: 'What is that terrible noise?' The others pointed at Gul. Salim went over and shook him awake. Never one to miss an opportunity, Gul sat bolt upright, shook his plane ticket at Salim and said: 'Right. I really must go now. I have a plane to catch on Monday, you know.'

A large man, with a vast black beard and a slight stammer, Gul had amused the others the night before when he'd introduced himself as 'an agriculturalist'.

'Does that mean you're a farmer?' one of the Iranians asked mischievously.

'No!' Gul said indignantly. 'I am a Bachelor of Science!'

Morris said: 'You look like Fidel Castro.'

'No – Fidel Castro looks like me,' Gul said.

In his mid-thirties and from a relatively well-to-do Punjabi family,

Gul had graduated from the LSE. Within minutes of meeting the other hostages, he was spouting gnomic truisms like: 'If you have mangoes to eat, then there must be trees.' Devoutly religious, Gul had accepted Lavasani's invitation to join the Iranians at their regular prayers. Now, realising Salim was not about to let him depart for Heathrow to catch his flight, he got up and stumbled over to begin his morning worship.

On a visit to the toilet, Harris noticed that the gunmen had done their laundry during the night and spread the washing out over the radiators to dry. They might be terrorists, but they were clean terrorists. Harris, on the other hand, felt distinctly shabby. Perhaps a stand-up wash might be in order? He'd have to ask.

Ahmed Dadgar was also keen to spruce himself up, but his request for permission to retrieve his shaving-kit from a desk drawer was refused. The desk had been shoved back against a wall, and the gunmen wouldn't let him move it.

Salim and the rest of the gunmen were edgy. They had been listening to the early morning news and were annoyed that none of the bulletins had mentioned the group's demands. Salim picked up the field telephone and shouted: 'Now we are going to kill the hostages. We have given you enough time – since Wednesday, you didn't do anything!'

Back in Room 9, he told the hostages he might have to kill one of them in order to show that he meant business. Eyeing the scared crowd, he told them angrily: 'You can choose who it will be.' But then, before they could make any response, he told his men to grab Abdul Ezzati and take him down to the first floor with Lock and Karkouti.

Ezzati had irritated the gunmen by lecturing them on the un-Islamic nature of their actions. Now, it looked as if he might be about to pay the price for his temerity. They dragged him to the 'talking window'. Three other gunmen stood round him, weapons trained on his back. Pressing the muzzle of his Skorpion into the side of Ezzati's head, Salim commanded Lock and Karkouti: 'Tell them – the police – we've got a senior diplomat here and we'll kill him and throw his body out unless the phones and telex machines are reconnected.' Ezzati came forward. He had a trim beard, a big bruise under his right eye and thinning hair. Ezzati said: 'They are our brothers. We are all Moslems.'

Donning his cap, Lock took Ezzati's place in the hot seat and passed the message. A voice from below shouted back: 'Impossible!'

Salim shoved the gun barrel harder into Ezzati's skull. The diplomat collapsed, convulsing, to the floor. Salim stared down at him in disgust and fear; he didn't want the Iranian to die – at least, not of natural causes. 'Take him back up,' he told Abbas. Clearly unwell, Ezzati had to be helped back to the second floor. Here, he fell to the floor, convulsing and foaming at the mouth. Clutching his chest, he moaned: 'They are going to kill me, they are going to kill me. I am going to die!' Several of the Iranian hostages rushed to help him, covering him with coats, massaging his chest and arms. A few minutes later, he started having a fit. Lock stuck his fingers down the stricken man's throat and made him vomit. 'We need a doctor!' shouted Morris. The gunmen had helped Cramer when he was ill – why not Ezzati?

'Never! Police must send doctor,' Faisal shouted.

Salim, was still at the talking window. Standing out of sight as before, he said, 'Mr Sim has told us to ask for his bosses to come.' As luck would have it, one of the three senior BBC executives who'd been taking it in turns to sleep on the floor at Television House in case of just such a request was Tony Crabb, the Managing Editor of BBC News and a personal friend of Harris's. The police were able to defuse the latest crisis by truthfully assuring Salim that Crabb was already on his way, and would arrive shortly. Salim went upstairs, excited. 'Mr Chris, Mr Mustapha, Mr Lock! You must all come now. A man from the BBC is coming! You must talk to him. Afrouz, you come too. You must demand in front of him that police put back the telex and phone.'

Morris helped Afrouz to his feet. The Chargé d'Affaires seemed slightly better, though he was shaky and his jaw was still painfully swollen. As they walked down the corridor, Harris told Lock he was nervous about speaking to someone he knew from the BBC. It made him think of the outside world, his wife Helen and small daughters Eleanor and Victoria. He was unsettled, almost tearful. 'Hey, look, Sim,' said Lock, at his calm and reassuring best, 'you've been bloody marvellous. Just keep calm. Tell him how it is. He will see how well you're doing, how you're holding up. Don't lose yourself now.'

At 0930 hrs, Harris peered out of the window. 'It's Tony Crabb,' he told Salim. 'He is one of the top men at the BBC. He will make sure your demands are broadcast.'

Salim was pleased: 'This is very good, Mr Sim. But I will be behind you, listening. You must not tell him anything about my group – or where we hold the hostages.' He swung the gun into view. 'If you do, it will be bad for you all.'

Superintendent Ray Tucker led Crabb forward to the talking window. Staying back behind a curtain, Salim kept his weapon trained on Harris. 'Ask him why the police aren't doing anything,' he urged.

'Why the hell haven't you broadcast these people's demands?' Harris shouted down to his colleague. To his consternation, Crabb called back: 'What demands?'

'What the hell are they playing at out there?' Harris said.

Salim told Harris that Crabb should take down what he was about to say. Rising to the occasion, Crabb whipped out a notebook and pen and made a flourish of taking notes. Through Harris, Salim outlined his demands for the Algerian, Jordanian and Iraqi ambassadors and a representative of the Red Cross to mediate. 'There must also be a coach to take the gunmen, the hostages and the ambassadors to Heathrow.' If that happened, he promised, he would release all the non-Iranian hostages at the airport. An aircraft 'piloted mostly by females', Salim stipulated, would then take the lucky diplomats and everyone else to a Middle Eastern country, again unnamed, where he would release the Iranians.

Crabb made his own note of the encounter:

There was movement at the ground-floor window, to the right of the front door. The heavy curtains moved and somebody looked out through the crack. I couldn't tell who that was. Then the curtains were parted by the man who eventually acted as interpreter: an Arab, approximately mid-forties and of medium height. He opened the sash window about two to three feet to allow us to talk. Sim Harris then came forward to the window and I was aware of another man (possibly 5'3") and of small build. He had in front of him what I thought was an automatic weapon. It certainly wasn't a rifle or hand gun. Sim said: 'You've got to get it over to the government how the police are acting. They've cut off the phones and telex so the Iranians can't communicate. There were two statements yesterday about mediation.'

I asked, what was the mediation proposal? Harris and the man acting as an interpreter explained: the ambassadors would go in the plane with the Iranian hostages leaving the non-Iranians at the airport. Sim said, 'I honestly believe these people are sincere. They're not stupid. They're highly intelligent: university educated. The tension has built up too high. They want to drop the tension. We have formed very good relationships with our captors but the police are determined to upset things by opening doubts. During a quiet period last night they heard sounds like drilling. That disturbed them. This morning one of the hostages (an Iranian) was told by the group that if the police did not cooperate they would shoot him. At this the hostage suffered what appeared to be a mild heart attack . . .'

PC Lock came to the window and explained that the hostage had apparently had a nervous convulsion and that he had a heart condition. All of this took time.

Sim came back to the window and said that he understood that the policy of the police was non-violent, but that they were showing psychological aggression.

Harris was angry with the official stalling. 'Your tactics are creating the most terrible problems for us in here. Please, you must understand that.' Supt Tucker replied: 'Keep calm, Sim. We are doing all we can to ensure your safe release.'

Crabb just stared at the ground. He felt useless. After all, it was the police who had the real power here, not the BBC. He wished he could just pull Harris and the other hostages out of the window and lead them to safety. It seemed ridiculous, surreal even, that Harris was only a few metres from him and yet so completely trapped.

'Tony,' said Sim, 'before you go, share this with as much of the media as possible. This is not a BBC exclusive. I need your assurance of this.'

Clearly moved, Crabb said: 'Sim, I will do my best to get you – all of you – out of there safely.'

Salim jabbed Afrouz to the window with a gun in his back. 'Please, sir,' he said to Crabb, 'you have to tell them we must have telex and telephone connected again. I must be able to get through to my government in Tehran to put an end to this.'

Once Crabb and Tucker had gone, the negotiators called Salim on the field telephone asking for a hostage to be released. Either a British or female one. Salim was firm. Not until the ambassadors arrived. And then all the British and female hostages would be released – at Heathrow.

He warned the police not to storm the embassy: 'Because we can kill the hostages, no matter how quick you think you are. We have no intention staying here two or three months. We will decide to finish this one day.' Then he changed tack: 'We are all hungry. We want food. Please send in lunch now. Include some cans of soft drink like Pepsi. Thank you.'

Salim raced up the stairs. He seemed satisfied with the morning's work. In Room 9, the mood lightened. 'Well done, mate. You were brilliant,' Lock congratulated Harris.

'I don't know about that,' Harris said, 'but at least Tony will be able to tell Helen I'm OK.'

The police delivered lunch to the front door. Hostages and gunmen alike tucked in gratefully. There were chops and steaks, peas and chips for the British and lamb kebabs, rice and salad for the non-Brits. Morris bustled around, butler-like, making sure everyone had enough to eat and drink. There was a strange, almost party-like feeling and for a while everything calmed down. Even Lock, who had so far refused all food, nibbled at the cheese and biscuits.

Abbas had found a camera in someone's desk. The gunmen wanted pictures of the hostages. They themselves refused to pose for any photos. Faruqi asked if, instead, the gunmen would sign his lunch carton. Faisal agreed and, flattening it out, wrote: *We have great hope that the world will understand our aim in this operation, which we consider is a kind of struggle against tyranny and enslavement directed against our Arab people in Arabistan. Long live the people's struggle against imperialism.* He signed it *The Warrior, Faisal.*

In her own scribbled inscription on the lunch box, Roya Kaghachi summed up the sadness she felt: *May we meet again in a happier future.*

Taking encouragement from the relaxed atmosphere, Karkouti, Harris, Lock and Faruqi asked to speak to Salim. He led them to the first-floor landing where they sat ranged out in front of him like small children. Faisal sat on the stairs, listening impassively like an emperor's bodyguard. Anxious to impress upon Salim that patience was essential when dealing with the British, Harris warned: 'British diplomacy is really the best in the world. But everything takes time. There are diplomatic channels to go through. You can't just get an ambassador at short notice. It's a question of meetings, many meetings. One thing is for sure – everyone will be working as hard as they can to get you what you want. But you can't rush it. We must all be patient.'

Karkouti was fiddling with the radio. A four o'clock news bulletin began. What he heard nearly gave him a heart attack: LBC radio news was reporting that the Iranians had executed two young Arab men for helping foment anti-Khomeini demonstrations. This was not what the gunmen wanted to hear. Luckily, he was listening in with the sound turned low. He signalled for Faruqi to keep the conversation rolling. (Other IRN radio news stations repeated the report about the executions five times, until the Home Office requested that they stop endangering the lives of the embassy captives.)

Faruqi took up the question of the group's aims and the global publicity the siege would be bringing. He warned Salim: 'If this continues as a peaceful demonstration then you will have made your point. If there is any violence you will have lost everything.'

Picking up on that, Lock made one more attempt for a non-violent end to the siege: 'Why don't you release us all and give yourselves up? I can get a coach to the front door and then drive you all to the nearest police station. No one will harm you. The British police do not torture or harm. They will treat you with decency. You have done very well to get publicity for your group. You will have got loads of coverage all over the world. Do the honourable thing now.'

'No!' thundered Salim. 'This would be the same as surrender.'

The meeting was over. He ushered the four men back to Room 9.

Here, too, the atmosphere had shifted. Lavasani was busy holding forth. Ezzati's ordeal had deeply affected the embassy's young press officer. Setting down his Koran, he told the other hostages: 'Next time they want a victim, I will volunteer. I have only my mother and father alive. It would save others' lives, and I've nothing to lose.' He then wrote out a will and went round the male hostages, hugging and kissing them goodbye. After that, he went to a corner of the room, knelt down and began to pray. He was announcing his readiness to die a martyr. And he obviously meant it.

Karkouti was appalled. He rushed over and told Lavasani: 'It will never happen! It will never happen!' But in his heart, he knew that it might.

The rest of the afternoon passed slowly. The camaraderie following the meal had gone and the grim reality of their situation bore in on the hostages. Salim was talking to the police on the field telephone: when would his demands be broadcast? Just after 1800 hrs, he returned to announce that the telex machine had been restored. The Iranians gathered together to write another message to their government. When Salim had approved the wording, he told Aboutaleb Moghaddam, the embassy's telex operator, to transmit it.

By this time the women were back in Room 9A. Earlier in the day they had complained to their guard, Ali, about 'noises from next door'. Now they told him how scared they were. Salim told Lock to go and investigate. Harris leaned and whispered to Issa Naghizadeh. 'Tell the girls to stop drawing attention to the noises. It's the police trying to listen in. They're just fitting in devices that will help them. They aren't going to burst through the walls. Can you calm the women down?'

Embassy secretary Roya Kaghachi had become the unofficial leader of the female hostages. She was not only beautiful but also fluent in English and extremely articulate. Throughout the siege, the gunmen treated all the women with the utmost respect. The women were developing a close relationship with Ali, talking to him about his homeland, his family and his dreams for the future. Later, this was to save a life.

The hours passed, evening stretched into night and still no broadcast. At 2300 hrs, an angry Salim ordered all the hostages into the second-floor telex room at the front of the embassy. It was more cramped and uncomfortable, but that wasn't what the captives were worried about. With Salim in a vile mood and the BBC apparently struck dumb, they feared the worst.

At 2330 hrs, the BBC finally made a passing reference to the siege in a short bulletin. But it missed out some of the group's key demands. Even worse, as far as Salim was concerned, the report said he wanted negotiations to take place between the Arab ambassadors and the Iranian regime, not the British government as he had stipulated. He stamped around the embassy, shouting and swearing. The hostages were very scared. In an effort to calm things down, the police sent in a carton of 200 cigarettes.

After a smoke, Salim relaxed a little. Dr Afrouz had ripped his trousers badly when he jumped from the window, and now Salim presented him with a new pair. But they were chequered blue and white – chef's trousers. As Afrouz pulled them on, his staff tried and failed to hide their amusement.

■ ■ ■

While negotiations with the terrorists dragged on at the embassy, at COBRA, Douglas Hurd and his Foreign Office team had been busy trying to sound out London's Arab ambassadors as to whether they might be prepared to help resolve the crisis. But although one or two – in particular the UK's old friend and ally, Jordan – were initially helpful, as soon as it became clear that the British government had resolved not to let any of the terrorists go free under any circumstances, they all drew back. As the Syrian Ambassador, Adnan Omran, pointed out at a joint meeting to discuss tactics, if the British had already made up their minds and there was no room for manoeuvre in the siege negotiations, then what positive – and for that matter, diplomatically sensible – role could the Arab ambassadors play? Omran was widely respected for his diplomatic skill and experience. The other ambassadors agreed: they would not allow themselves to be used simply as one more means of stalling the gunmen and wearing them down.

Only the Iraqi Ambassador agreed to help, provided he could talk personally to the terrorists. In reality, the last thing COBRA and the police wanted was any outside agent playing a direct role in the game of cat-and-mouse with the gunmen. And least of all, the Iraqi government. They politely declined the Iraqi offer.

In a sense, the British government's hands were tied – not just because the notably intransigent Mrs Thatcher was in power, but as a result of the widespread condemnation that had followed Prime Minister Edward Heath's decision to release PFLP member Leila Khaled after she led a hijacking attempt on an El Al airliner in September 1970. In return for Khaled's freedom, the PFLP released 160 hostages it was holding on board two hijacked airliners in Jordan. Many Western governments, and some from outside the West, subsequently agreed that any concession to terrorism only encouraged it. From then on, they decided, there would be no truck with terrorists. Jordan, which was now being asked to mediate in the Iranian Embassy siege, was a signatory to that agreement.

Given the background political radiation, it was no surprise that in a telephone conversation with the Prime Minister, Home Secretary William Whitelaw reaffirmed the policy of denying the gunmen safe passage out of Britain *under any circumstances*. Whitelaw agreed to keep Mrs Thatcher informed of important developments. If major decisions had to be taken, and there was time, he would consult her. If not, Thatcher gave the Home Secretary full authority to act as he saw fit.

Both COBRA and the police took the Movement of the Martyr's mounting threats to kill one or more of the embassy hostages very seriously. The SAS might soon need to break the siege. In which case, Whitelaw and Thatcher agreed, the SAS must be given the freedom to decide how that was done. The only rider the Prime Minister added was that she did not want the kind of debacle that had marked the recent American failure to rescue their hostages in Tehran. If the SAS went in, then they had better succeed.

■ ■ ■

There were faint snores and snuffles from the rest of Blue Team as they stretched out in their sleeping bags. Rusty Firmin was half-asleep, trying to pretend that getting any kind of rest dressed from head-to-toe in assault kit was possible. He could definitely do with a kip: as the days and the nights passed without any positive action, the first signs of fatigue were beginning to tell on them all. He was snoozing and dreaming of home when he felt a large hand on his shoulder. The hand gave him a gentle shake. Firmin opened his eyes and sat up to find two men crouching by his side: Staff Sergeant Roy T, Blue Team's 2i/c, and Captain Dave J. 'Rusty? You awake? A quick word.'

Firmin clambered out of the sleeping bag and followed Capt J and Roy T into an empty room. The big sergeant turned to him. 'There's been a slight change of plan, Rusty. They've asked me to build the top distraction charge, and make sure it goes off when we need that to happen. Frank Collins and a couple of the other lads are going to help me.'

Firmin realised the implications immediately but waited for Roy T to finish: 'It means I won't be leading Blue Team into the embassy as it stands if the IA goes in. And that means everyone in the team has to move up one. So you'll now be 3i/c of Blue Team and you are call sign Bravo One along with Bob.'

Capt J said: 'You'll be leading the ground- and basement-floor teams in through the rear. Make entry as planned with a frame charge through the library's French windows.'

Roy T added: 'I've set down some notes – personnel in the two teams, timings, and so on.' He held out a small sheaf of notes, written on both sides of pages torn from his notebook. 'Here, you take them.'

Firmin took the notes and glanced through them. They detailed the Red/Blue Team groupings, call signs, floor responsibilities, sniper groups and individual tasks. He was still only a lance corporal. But rank, as always in the SAS, mattered less than ability. He said, 'OK, Roy. Thanks for the heads-up. I'm good for it.' Then he went back to try and sleep with the rest of the duty team. But he was no longer dreaming of home. He was wide awake and thinking about the added responsibility.

■ ■ ■

Day Three drew to a close with one more positive development for the British authorities, albeit a minor one. On clear orders from Tehran, Dr Seyf Ehdaie, the Iranian Consul-General in London, told the pro-Khomeini demonstrators in Hyde Park that President Bani Sadr wanted them to abandon their protest and go home. To the astonishment and delight of the Met Police, they did. Later Ehdaie told the press that the British government had brought pressure to bear on Tehran.

The gunmen had ended another day on the back foot. The British authorities felt sure that now, more than anything, the Group of the Martyr were looking to save their own skins.

As the hostages settled down, Sim Harris made a note in the diary he had been keeping of the siege: *The Iranians pray before going to sleep. So do I.*

# DAY FOUR: Saturday, 3 May 1980

Thanks to the assortment of large brown corduroy-and-satin floor cushions they had found and were now allowed to drag to whichever room they were being held in, the hostages had managed to get a slightly better night's sleep. The gunmen woke them at 0730 hrs. As he handed round the morning tea with Harris's help, Ron Morris joked: 'We look like a bunch of squatters.' It wasn't just the makeshift sleeping arrangements: most of the hostages hadn't been near a bar of soap since the siege broke out, and some of them were scratching, itchy and uncomfortable. Lock worried that he'd started to smell – he'd kept both his overcoat and tunic on for four days. When one of the gunmen suggested he remove them, Lock said: 'No – I am still on duty.'

The Iranians set small pieces of paper down on the floor as usual, touching their foreheads to them as they bent in prayer. Harris, meanwhile, volunteered to go and fix the toilet on the second floor, which had become blocked. After he'd dealt with the problem, the BBC sound man treated himself to a good wash. He needed it. On his return, Lock said: 'You've got yourself a job for life, there, Sim.' The weak joke betrayed the slight air of boredom that had now settled over the embassy. There was a feeling of normality that morning, as if the siege were becoming almost routine.

Up on the third floor, Salim was listening to a Tehran Radio broadcast. It stated that any Arab ambassadors who agreed to intervene would be negotiating with the Iranian, and not the British government. While he knew that Tehran Radio routinely misrepresented the facts, the claim angered Salim. When the police negotiator came on the line at 0910 hrs, he flatly refused the offer of breakfast, and reiterated his annoyance at the police's failure to ensure the BBC broadcast the message Harris had dictated to Crabb the day before. He seemed to have forgotten about his request for the Arab ambassadors, concentrating instead on the need to make sure the statement went to air as soon as possible.

Tony Crabb, who'd been trying to catch up on some sleep at home in Sunbury, had just called the police at Zulu Control to ask if he would be needed that day. The police had told him no.

It was a mistake. Refusing to talk further on the field telephone, Salim said that, from then on, he would only conduct face-to-face negotiations through the talking window.

■ ■ ■

Surveying the mess in Room 9, Ron Morris asked the gunmen if he could clear up. Harris helped him. They picked up the litter of empty food cartons and drinks cans, emptied the overflowing ashtrays and bagged the mess.

The hostages leafed through the various magazines they'd pillaged from the embassy press office. The *Diplomatist*, with its glowing accounts of diplomatic life in exotic locations, was a favourite. It did not say how diplomats might cope when held at gunpoint, but its blithe optimism did provide a little light relief. Harris particularly liked the advice on how to move priceless antiques safely from country to country. He'd have to remember all that the next time he moved the piano.

Ahmed Dadgar had found a copy of *The Day of the Jackal* and promised to pass it on when he'd finished. There was a long list of people waiting to read the thriller, but he proved a very slow reader. There were lots of letters and memos scattered all over the place from when the gunmen had first seized the building, and while these were mostly tedious, there were some fascinating insights into top-level intergovernmental dealings. One letter confirmed payment of £5 million for a new Iranian Navy gunboat currently under construction in a Tyneside shipyard. Only a week before, there had been a report on the ITN news stating that Britain had decided to block the ship's final delivery to Iran. Somebody was lying.

Mustapha Karkouti was showing signs of strain. Spending every moment he could with the gunmen, he pleaded with them constantly to end the siege. They often hugged him, apologising for the fact that, as a fellow Arab, he had been in the embassy when they'd seized it.

The natural divide between the Iranian and other hostages was intensified by the gunmen's harsher treatment of their countrymen. But there was still an element of shared camaraderie between the two groups. Fluent in English and moving effortlessly between the groups, the banker Ali Tabatabai worked to bridge the gap. Known affectionately as 'Ali the Bank', his strong sense of humour helped maintain morale. Along with an endless stream of quips and jokes, Tabatabai devised puzzles for the hostages to solve: he offered £100 to anyone who could solve the riddle of the businessman who sold ten eggs for £100 and thirty for the same price. And Ezzati, who had by this time recovered some of his sang-froid, told Harris: 'Even if we get out of here, I can't give you a visa. But I do promise you one thing, Mr Harris: if we get out of here alive, I'll give you an Iranian residence permit instead!'

At 1130 hrs the morning's cosy domestic atmosphere evaporated in an instant when Salim charged into Room 9. He had been brooding on the failure to broadcast his statement, and now wanted immediate action. 'Why are your media not broadcasting our statement?' he shouted at Harris. 'What is going wrong?'

Harris suggested the British government might have put a D Notice, or blocking order, on the broadcast. It did nothing to calm the thwarted terrorist. Ordering Lock to take out his notebook, he dictated a new message. Lock was told to get up and come with Karkouti and Afrouz to the talking window. As always, the hostages chosen as go-betweens were held at gunpoint.

Swallowing hard, Lock called down and made contact with an officer in Princes Gate. He said Salim was very angry at the failure to broadcast the group's latest statement. And that the gunmen were anxious the police did not force them to take any action they were desperate to avoid – like killing a hostage. He relayed Salim's demand that Arab ambassadors be produced as a guarantee of safety for both gunmen and hostages, and that the police provide safe passage for them out of the UK.

Karkouti came to the window next. His statement on behalf of the hostages was telling. He said the police delaying tactics were lowering morale: 'I believe that tension is being built on us. They suspect that you have invoked a D Notice on the interview yesterday. They are intelligent and educated men and are aware of this procedure. As far as they are concerned, they have completed their mission and now wish to leave, but it has been delayed by your response.'

Karkouti went on to say that no one inside the embassy gave a damn for the reaction of the Iranian government, 'which is inhuman. So we are seeking the humanity of the British because it seems it is the only way out.'

To the police, Karkouti's use of the pronoun 'we' was a striking indication of the extent to which captors and captives had apparently bonded under stress. Dr Afrouz now stepped forward. His glowing testimonial – delivered with a machine-pistol at his head – did nothing to dispel the police view: 'Our relationship with those around us [the gunmen] is not of oppressor and oppressed. Whatever I'm telling is not at gunpoint. I am saying this willingly. They have been treating us very nicely and I shall never forget their kindness ... Please allow the newscaster [Crabb] to pay us a visit so that we can be heard ...

'But the group and the hostages, our aim is to finalise the affair peacefully ... We have also accepted that if the police have chosen other ambassadors, we will accept. Because at the moment we have only the police to talk to.'

The sting was in the tail: Salim brought the exchange to a terse close by setting a deadline of one hour for Tony Crabb's appearance at the scene. Since Crabb had just gone out shopping with his wife in Sunbury, that was going to be a tough ask. But unless it happened, and Crabb ensured the BBC put the message to air, then one of the hostages would be killed.

The police gave the impression they agreed to everything Salim wanted, and even suggested the gunmen and hostages hold a press conference on the embassy steps. They repeated their call for calm. If no harm were done to the hostages, they promised, no direct action would be taken to free them. Salim was pleased to hear this. But he did not agree to a press conference. And he was less than pleased when he learned that Crabb was out shopping.

When Crabb still hadn't turned up by two o'clock, the atmosphere deteriorated at top speed. The constant tension wore on the nerves, so that even those with the most equable temperaments found themselves breaking down in tears or shaking in fear. Ali the Bank was a case in point. The normally ebullient mainstay of the captives' morale wept quietly, wanting only for the siege to end. Karkouti, too, was now showing signs of stress – pale and sweating, he was complaining of sharp pains in his stomach, much like Cramer before him. Harris asked Lock: 'Do you think the police are tampering with the food, to make us ill and more able to get out?'

'No,' Lock said. 'It would not be a tactic they could safely employ in this situation.'

At 1530 hrs, an unmarked police car finally delivered Crabb to Princes Gate. Crabb had come straight from home. An angry Harris came to the talking window. 'Why,' he demanded, 'hasn't that statement you took down been broadcast? Don't you realise lives have been put at risk by the delay?'

Crabb was taken aback: 'I think there's been a misunderstanding. I didn't know it was supposed to be broadcast. I thought it was just a statement of demands. Anyway, Sim, you know I don't decide what the BBC broadcasts.'

This angered Harris even further. 'But you're powerful enough in the BBC to do *something*,' he retorted. 'You must put out the right statement – otherwise everyone could be killed.'

Salim and Karkouti, who'd been listening to the exchange, now came forward. Slowly, word for word, Karkouti translated the new statement into English. This time, one of the police officers at the scene wrote it down. As Salim spoke, the police transmitted his words directly to COBRA for assessment. Despite its slightly mangled English, it was the group's definitive and final message:

1. We swear to God and to the British people and government that no danger whatsoever would be inflicted on the British and the non-Iranian hostages as well as the Iranian hostages if the British government and the British police don't kid the group and don't subject the life of the hostages and the group to any danger, and if things work to the contradictory direction everyone in this building will be harmed.

2. We demand the three ambassadors, Algerian, Jordanian and Iraqi and a representative of the Red Cross to start their jobs in negotiating between us and the British government to secure the safety of the hostages as well as the group's members and to terminate the whole operation peacefully. If any of the three ambassadors is not available they could be substituted first by the Libyan or the Syrian or the Kuwaiti Ambassador.

3. The reason for us to come to Britain to carry out this operation is because of the pressure and oppression which is being practised by the Iranian government in Arabistan and to convey our voice through the outside world to your country. Once again we apologise to the people and government for this inconvenience.

Just then, Afrouz appeared and threw two sheets of screwed-up paper down into the street. When the police picked them up and flattened them out, they saw they were further messages from the hostages in support of the gunmen. The key paragraph read: *They state and assure us that they are struggling for their legitimate rights as 'Arab-IRANIANS' and they are not against Islam. They do not want to break away from Iran and their demand is only for [Khuzestani] self-rule within the Islamic Republic of Islam.*

Harris was shaking and sweating. 'Tony, just promise me that the statement will be read out on air,' he implored.

Seeing the distress etched on his colleague's face, Crabb shouted up: 'How are you, mate?'

'Oh, bloody marvellous,' Harris said. 'It's terrific in here, having a machine gun pointed at your head the whole time.' As he turned away from the window, seeing he was shaking, one of the gunmen handed him a coat to put on.

Upset by his colleague's distress, Crabb now appealed directly to Salim. 'If we broadcast your demands, will you show some goodwill in return?'

'Goodwill? Do you mean we release hostages?' asked Salim.

The police nodded at Crabb to continue. 'Yes. Are you prepared to do that?'

Salim nodded. He said that if they broadcast the statement, then there would be a 'positive response'.

Crabb promised he would do his level best to get it to air.

'Right,' said the policeman next to Crabb, 'let's talk about that now on the phone.'

Inside, Salim picked up the field telephone. A negotiator and translator were waiting. The two sides got straight down to business: 'How many hostages will you free in return for the broadcast?' the police negotiator asked.

Salim replied, 'One.'

'We need more,' the negotiator haggled.

'Two.'

The police closed the deal.

After some discussion with Faisal, Salim decided to release Hiyech Kanji and Ali Guil Ghanzafar. Kanji was an obvious choice because she was pregnant. Ghanzafar was an equally obvious choice because his supernatural snoring kept all the other hostages awake and annoyed the gunmen on sentry duty. The gunmen were pleased. They wanted rid of Ghanzafar for another reason: he'd been pestering them relentlessly for four days about the fact that he had a plane to catch to Pakistan. As a hostage, making a bloody nuisance of yourself is a risky strategy – but Ghanzafar was living proof that it can work.

Not wishing to fail his friend for a second time, Crabb was already over at BBC Television Centre in Shepherd's Bush, arranging for transmission of the group's latest communiqué. As far as Crabb was concerned, he had never had a more important mission. And he doubted if he ever would.

. . .

At seven o'clock, Salim heard a broadcast on Tehran Radio. The report claimed that British police were only awaiting permission from Iran before storming the embassy. The newsreader also said that 'the Iranians in the embassy have volunteered to die for Islam'. Several of the Iranian hostages burst into tears and implored Afrouz to contact Tehran Radio, and assure them they were not looking forward to martyrdom.

Salim lost his temper again. Karkouti pleaded: 'You say Tehran Radio tells lies, so why believe them now?'

'That is not how the British work,' said Lock. 'They don't take instructions from anyone.'

Salim said he had also heard a BBC report stating there were six gunmen inside the embassy, not three as had previously been believed. Flying into a rage, he said: 'Mr Chris has been telling police things he shouldn't have done.' Ever the peacemaker, Karkouti insisted the police must have gleaned the information from elsewhere.

But Salim was beside himself. Pulling his kaffiyeh over his face, he ran downstairs to the field telephone, ordering his men to bring Karkouti and Lock. Why, Salim demanded, had the police failed to broadcast his statement? The police replied that they would only put the statement out if the gunmen released two hostages beforehand. The response infuriated Salim. He shouted that he would only release one. The police countered with a flat refusal to play ball unless one of the hostages came out alive first. Salim screamed down the phone: 'You obviously don't care. You don't mind if we start shooting people. I am going back upstairs to kill a hostage.'

Realising he meant business, Karkouti sank to his knees, grabbed Salim by the legs and begged him not to carry out the threat. 'I implore you not to kill anyone. Please. You will gain nothing by killing. Release Mrs Kanji and she can instruct the police to broadcast the message on the nine o'clock news.'

Salim ignored him. Lock took the gunmen's leader by the shoulders, but Salim shook himself free, shouting: 'What can we do? We treat you well, we like you, we agree with what you say. But the police do not keep their word.'

Lock came back into the hostage room utterly dejected; head down, he told the others it had all gone horribly wrong. Karkouti came in behind him, tears running down his face.

Salim ran in yelling that he would not talk to the police again until the BBC had made the broadcast. Karkouti tried in vain to calm him down: Salim was beyond advice. 'If nothing comes out on the nine o'clock news,' he railed, 'I'll kill a hostage. And I'll send out the body.'

Ordering them to put their hands in the air, the gunmen forced the hostages upstairs to the 'tension room', the embassy telex office. The captives looked at one another, white-faced. There were few who were not trembling. Worried sick there'd be another misunderstanding, and that this one might cost him his life, Harris asked permission to speak to the police by phone. He was afraid that the BBC would either fail to put the statement out in time, or that, without knowing which station was broadcasting the message, the gunmen would miss it. Salim let him talk. Harris was desperate: how was his wife, how were his two young children? He told the police that if the statement wasn't broadcast this time without fail, then the gunmen would shoot one or more of the hostages.

A short while later, the police called back: the gunmen were to listen out on BBC Radio 1, Radio 2 or the BBC World Service.

Salim was ready to snap. He came back up to Karkouti. 'You say I should not kill a hostage. What should I do?'

Karkouti snatched at the opportunity. 'Show a goodwill gesture. Release a hostage.'

Salim turned away without a word. He told his men to fetch Hiyech Kanji from Room 9A and take her downstairs. Lock said: 'They are going to kill her.' Karkouti once again burst into tears. But his plea had worked: at 2021 hrs that same evening, Mrs Hiyech Kanji walked free from the Iranian Embassy. Another of the hostages – and her unborn baby – had been saved.

Following the conversation with the police, Harris and Salim went into Room 9 and tuned the radios to the BBC. The minutes ticked by slowly, creeping ever closer to the witching-hour of nine o'clock.

In the attic at Zulu Control, duty hostage negotiator Max Vernon was on edge. The reality of what he faced held him in a cold grip. Salim had some two dozen people at his mercy. There were armed police everywhere outside the embassy. And he knew the SAS had been on the scene from the word go. If he made a mistake, Vernon was only too keenly aware that something terrible could happen. And in his arcane trade, mistakes were only too easy to make.

Nine o'clock came round – and it seemed to Vernon that there'd been a catastrophic mistake: 'It was the BBC. They were in an awkward spot, the terrorists: they weren't getting what they wanted. We were in an even worse spot, because we couldn't offer them what they wanted. Eventually, we agreed the BBC would broadcast a statement from them, word for word.

'If we did it, we'd have a hostage. If we didn't, we'd have a dead one. It was agreed this statement be broadcast on the nine o'clock news. Which was the end of my shift. So I'm sitting there in the negotiator's chair. The night-duty staff had arrived as well. We sat there waiting for the nine o'clock news. It came. The newsreader spoke about all sorts of things: football, tennis, snooker, weather – and eventually gave a short version of the script.

'I sat there horrified. I'd agreed with Salim that it would be verbatim – that's what they'd been told. I was now waiting for a dead body to come out.

'I looked at my co-negotiator. He looked at me. The phone rang. I said: "You can bloody answer that – I'm not talking to him. I just can't do it."

'He said: "I'm not talking to him, either." So the two main negotiators refused to answer that call. One of the night-duty staff eventually picked it up. He spoke briefly and then looked daggers at us.

'"Salim is delighted," he said.

'"How the bloody hell can he be delighted?"

'The night officer said: "The BBC have put it out on another programme – verbatim."'

Salim had listened to the BBC World Service. The negotiators were all in complete agreement: it was a bloody good thing he hadn't listened to Radio 2.

■ ■ ■

Joy and jubilation erupted inside the embassy. Still in the third-floor 'tension room', the hostages started screaming in delight. The gunmen were weeping openly. It was clear they'd been preparing to kill hostages. Everyone was on their feet, hugging and kissing: hostages and gunmen celebrating together until eventually Salim intervened and told his men to pull themselves together.

Now that the broadcast had been aired, Salim could fulfil his own part of the bargain. At 2120 hrs, he took Ali Guil Ghanzafar down to the front door and ushered him to freedom. As he left, Ghanzafar sweetly said: 'You are all my friends. Everybody in here is my brother. I will never say anything.' For several hours after his release, this was literally true: the shock of being released resulted in Ghanzafar developing lockjaw. To the intense frustration of his Special Branch interrogators, he was unable to say a word until the affliction wore off.

As Gul left the embassy, the hostages speculated as to who might be the next lucky candidate for release. 'Sim, it will be you,' predicted Ali the Bank. 'Please take this note for my boss with you.' He handed Harris a tiny scrap of paper. On it, he'd written: *My name is Ali Tabatabai. Please phone David at the Midland Bank and tell him I am OK.*

Salim and the other gunmen were so delighted with what they had achieved that they listened to the statement again on the ten o'clock news.

Thanking him fulsomely for releasing the two hostages, the police negotiators agreed to Salim's request for a celebratory meal: the Persian food they were so missing for the Iranians, and those non-Iranians like Ron Morris who counted themselves Iranian anyway. The food came from Pars, a nearby Persian restaurant, arriving just before one in the morning. Delicate Persian starters, deliciously heavy on the herbs; kebabs and rice with all the trimmings; and a nifty sweet to follow. The Brits got cottage pie with extra potatoes, carrots and French beans, followed by cheese and crackers, bananas and sweet biscuits. Nothing too adventurous there, then. Two large insulated urns containing tea and coffee also put in an appearance. Muhammad Faruqi flew a gastronomic solo by asking for – and getting – a vegetarian meal.

Cans of Tango and Pepsi arrived in a large orange crate. Emptying it and distributing the drinks, Morris turned the crate upside down, covered it with a cloth and Hey Presto! – they had a table. Morris was a bit of a Jeeves like that: resourceful. His resilience was good for morale.

Pale and shaky, Karkouti ate a little and then sat back. He was feeling terrible. What he wanted most in the world was a bowl of soup – but there was none on the menu. When they'd eaten, he went and sat close to Harris and Morris. In a low voice, he told them the gunmen were worried about his health. They wanted to release him. But as the only fluent English and Arabic speaker, he felt he should stay in the embassy. He might be needed to continue the negotiations – and help calm Salim when he lost his temper. Urgently he whispered that Abbas Lavasani had reiterated his readiness to die as a martyr.

Incongruously, Salim appeared with an extra treat: a large box of Bandit chocolate biscuits. Morris said: 'Trust the police – we've got highwaymen holding us up, and they go and send in bloody Bandit biscuits.'

Harris agreed: 'Someone out there has an effing terrible sense of humour.'

The euphoric atmosphere persisted into the small hours. Hostages and gunmen alike signed their autographs and wrote messages on the empty food boxes. Salim was on such a high, he agreed to be interviewed by Karkouti and Faruqi, both journalists with an eye for an eventual scoop. Delighted to be the centre of attention again, Salim held forth at some length. Among the many things he told Karkouti, some in particular stood out:

'During the sixties and the first half of the seventies, there were two organisations – the Arabistan Liberation Front and the Al-Ahvaz Liberation Front – which called for complete separation from Iran and wanted to join Iraq. These two organisations were dissolved shortly before the Islamic Revolution, and our political programmes were re-formulated. After the Islamic Revolution failed to secure our demands and grant Khuzestan autonomy, we formed a new structure, the Arabistan People's Political Organisation [APPO].'

Before becoming part of the APPO, Salim had been one of a thirty-member committee representing Khuzestan's persecuted Arabs. The committee had met several times with Mehdi Bazargan, the former Iranian Prime Minister and his deputy, Amir Indizam. It had also met with the governor of Arabistan, Ahmed Madani. In addition, several delegates had visited Qom to meet Ayatollah Khomeini. But all these talks, Salim told Karkouti, had been fruitless. Any demonstrations were met by shootings.

The breaking point in relations between the two sides was the 'Al-Muhammara City Incident' on 29 May 1979, or 'Black Wednesday', as the Arab population knew it.

Salim said he realised that the embassy operation wouldn't necessarily force the Iranian government to grant Arabistan its autonomy. But it would at least make the Khuzestani Arab voice heard.

As a special concession, Salim allowed the hostages to move down to Dr Afrouz's large office on the first floor, overlooking Princes Gate. The plush Persian carpets and the solid antique furniture made them feel more secure. Arranging the big floor cushions wherever there was space, everyone settled down to rest. The hostages slept well that night. They thought the worst was over.

It wasn't.

■ ■ ■

While the hostages made merry, the SAS was busy making other plans. Fully aware that the festivities below would help mask their movements, at 2300 hrs a small team slipped out on to the roof of

No. 14. Clambering carefully through the forest of radio and television aerials that cluttered their path, they crossed on to the embassy roof. One wasn't careful enough: slipping slightly in the darkness, he broke a slate with his boot. The noise rang out like a pistol shot on the still night air. The team froze: it was just as well the gunmen were off-guard below. Otherwise, they would almost certainly have been up to investigate.

Signing to the surrounding snipers that all was still well, the SAS men ghosted forward. Their lead man, Snapper, gave the signal to stop. He had seen a glint from the roof below: a pale edge of moonlight reflecting on a sheet of what he took to be glass. Snapper and the man next to him knelt to investigate. The embassy skylight. Snapper tested it by pulling up on the lip. It was locked. Looking closer, he saw that the lead flashing around the panes of glass was old and unstable. He began to pick at the lead, lifting it and peeling it back. Catching on at once, the other call signs knelt around the skylight to help.

After fifteen minutes' work, they had freed a large panel of glass. Carefully, they lifted it out. Reaching in, Snapper removed the lock, and then pulled the skylight wide open. He stuck his head inside. He was looking down into a small bathroom. An enamel bath lay directly below, gleaming white in the near-dark. A wash-basin stood in the left-hand corner. Opposite that was a door. Immediately, Snapper realised it must lead out on to the top landing of the embassy – and from there to the terrorists. A small team with silenced weapons could go right in and finish them off.

Except that would be extra-judicial murder.

Snapper felt a rush of excitement: 'I had to stifle the urge to become the first SAS man into the embassy. It would have been quite easy to grip the wooden surround of the skylight base and lower myself down on to the edge of the bath. But thoughts of immortality were interrupted by a hand on my shoulder and Roy T's voice whispering, "Come on. Let's get back to the holding area. We can tell the boss we've got a guaranteed entry point."'

They all knew one guaranteed entry point wasn't ideal – what if they got in at that one point and the door was barricaded and/or locked? But it was a start.

Leaving the pane of glass loose but looking as if it was still securely fixed in place, the team moved across to the rear rooftop. Working quickly and deftly, they secured abseiling ropes around a number of the embassy chimney breasts. With the ropes fixed, abseil teams could make a rapid descent down the rear of the building. And smash in through the windows on the second floor.

The SAS team stole back to the Doctors' House the same way they'd come. The Deliberate Assault plan was taking shape. The SAS now had all kinds of options: it was a matter of choosing which one and refining the plan down to the finest detail. But with peace and love breaking out on all sides, it looked for the moment as if the very special services the Regiment offered might not be wanted.

But they had to behave as if they were. Well into a routine now, Red and Blue Teams alternated back and forth between the Doctors' House and the MBS. They went through the room-clearance drills endlessly: who goes where; the 'what ifs'; constantly looking at what things might go wrong and working out how to fix them. The Pioneers who'd built the room mock-ups in the gymnasium had excelled: it was only wood and hessian scaled down in size, but they'd done it with great skill and imagination. The only thing the teams couldn't do was practise any live firing. That took the edge off things – slightly.

The teams were also contingency planning in case the terrorists/ hostages were permitted to move by coach from the embassy to an unknown destination.

John McAleese had some clear ideas on how the SAS might deal with that: 'There were only three ways to take out the baddies: in the embassy, between the embassy and them getting on to the coach; or on the coach itself. The third option was the one everyone preferred. We couldn't attempt a rescue directly outside the embassy as there were too many people around, especially if the shooting started. The coach would have to be ambushed somewhere safe between the embassy and the airport. So now, not only did we have to train and plan for the stronghold assault in the mock-up of the embassy at

Regent's Park Barracks, but we had to start training to rescue the hostages from a bus.

'So this forty-seater bus turned up and we started training with that inside a large garage. Gonzo got chosen to be the driver because he was thin and wiry. The reason his size and shape mattered was because, when the rescue started, he had to get out of the bus's side window, which was only nine by eighteen inches wide. The baddies had asked for a police driver so we had to give Gonzo a bit of a haircut to make him look more like a copper, which he wasn't happy about. The basic plan was to stop at a prearranged point somewhere along the route to the airport. Gonzo would slam on the brakes and then we would attack the bus from the front and rear.

'Attacking a bus from both sides is difficult because it's thin-skinned: there was a strong risk we'd end up shooting each other, never mind the terrorists. Gonzo was our main consideration. We knew the moment we attacked, the terrorists would probably start killing the hostages and that Gonzo would be the first to get it. He was going bare-buff: no body armour, no gun, so we'd have to be quick. The attack teams were briefed to get Gonzo out as a priority even if it meant dragging him out through that small window. Gonzo got knocked about a bit as we practised getting him out over and over, but that was better than having his brains spread all over the bus. This doesn't mean we'd forgotten about the poor hostages, we hadn't. But Gonzo was first in the line of fire. In the end we got it down to three seconds, from the moment the bus stopped to the moment we got him out. Not bad, eh?'

Rusty Firmin has a slightly different take on the coach option: 'A lot of our time on days Three and Four of the siege was spent looking at how to release the hostages and rehearsing how we would assault the coach. For example, we needed to plan where the coach would be stopped, and it needed to be in a position that suited the assault team, not the terrorists.

'We had to work out how many assault team members we'd need, what weapons, and how many; we needed to have cut-offs to kill or capture any fleeing terrorists if that happened. Plus we needed a hostage reception party to cater for both male and female hostages after the assault. But one thing was certain, whatever happened, there would be total panic. Whatever rescue method we practised, the mission never changed: to rescue the hostages, no matter what.

'The second we stopped the coach, assaulters carrying small ladders, sledge-hammers and other equipment would surround and go at it: smash the windows, throw in flash-bangs to disorientate both terrorists and hostages, and pump in CS gas. At the same time, team members would gain entry through as many broken windows as possible. That way they could try and release the hostages and neutralise terrorists as required. Snipers concealed on nearby vantage points would look for opportunity targets, and be on hand to update any intelligence that would be of use to team members.

'My job was simplified to some extent as I was supposed to gain entry from the door almost opposite to where the coach driver was. I would be the first man into the coach, backed by the Mink, Gerry, Snapper and the rest of the lads. As soon as I gained entry, the coach driver was to escape through his window. We would work our way through the coach and try to release hostages and kill or capture the terrorists if required. In training it took about sixty seconds to enter and clear the coach. The evacuation of the coach would take a little longer, depending on numbers of casualties taken on our side.'

With the coach assault plan finalised, the teams began rehearsing for its use in live action.

# DAY FIVE: Sunday, 4 May 1980

In the early hours of Sunday morning, a wakeful Trevor Lock decided to have his first wash in five days. Pretending he had terrible wind, he managed to get the gunmen who came with him as far as the bathroom to let him go in and wash alone. That way, the terrorists wouldn't spot his service revolver. When he came back out, Lock both felt and looked much better.

At 0730 hrs the gunmen told the hostages to pick up their beds and return to Room 9 on the second floor. As usual, Harris and Morris did the rounds with the tea. Morris rustled up what breakfast he could from the preceding night's leftovers, supplementing those with the dwindling supplies of Garibaldi and Rich Tea biscuits.

At 0900 hrs Salim came into the room with a fresh box of Bandit chocolate wafers. He was still in a good mood – triumphant about the global airing that his statement had now enjoyed. Finally, the cause of Arabistan was on the international map. He told his men the hostages could take baths, starting with the women, as it would not be right for them to follow the men. A number of the hostages took advantage of a hot dip.

One of the women had managed to find some toothpaste, which also came as a blessing on the hygiene front. Dadgar spotted his upturned desk and retrieved his razor. Alarmed when he saw himself in the mirror, he rapidly scraped off his five-day beard. Catching scent of his aftershave, the gunmen took the bottle and splashed themselves with it liberally. Everyone felt much better for cleaning up.

And there was good news on the radio that morning: it seemed that some of the Arab ambassadors had expressed a willingness to cooperate. Harris told Salim: 'You should be really pleased. If the

BBC is reporting that news, then it means the government are happy for them to broadcast it.'

At 1000 hrs the police made a routine call on the field telephone. They had nothing concrete to report, and offered no compromise – but they wanted to keep the mellow atmosphere going for as long as they could.

In the embassy, things were quiet, much as they'd been on the morning of Day Four. The hostages were scrounging desperately for something to read, or talking in small groups. There was a feeling of drift, of nothing happening. But beneath that, Harris, for one, sensed an ever-growing current of unease. The more time that slid by without news, the more likely another of Salim's explosions became.

To allay the boredom, Salim commenced his now familiar lecture about the plight of the Arabs in Iran and Arabistan and how the Group of the Martyr was fighting for APPO, the Arabistan People's Political Organisation. The hostages were unmoved by the information. It did nothing to break the tedium, and if anything, made it worse. Why should they die for the APPO?

Ever-anxious to keep up the pressure for a peaceful resolution, Karkouti, Faruqi, Lock and Harris steered Salim round to the subject of surrender. In getting his message across to a global audience he had, they assured him, achieved a great and resounding success: surely as much, if not more than he had hoped for.

It might be a good time to quit now, while he was ahead of the game. 'You've made your point,' Faruqi said: 'Now let's try to think of a way out of this.'

Karkouti resurrected his pet solution: 'You hold a press conference *inside* the embassy. You get two representatives of at least two news agencies – say Reuters and Agence France-Presse [AFP]. You get the cameramen and reporters and they come inside the embassy. They talk to you, they talk to representatives of the hostages. After half an hour, whatever, they leave. They broadcast the press conference. Immediately afterwards, you release the hostages. Trevor Lock will stay behind and collect your guns in a box and then come out with you.'

Salim grunted. Surrender was not in his game plan. But he began asking Lock about British law: what offences had the Group of the Martyr committed? How long were they likely to spend in prison?

Lock told him the only offence they had committed outside the embassy was illegal possession of a firearm, which might carry with it a sentence of 'two, three, or four years'.

'But with good conduct, that would be reduced,' he said reassuringly. 'And remember, we're civilised – there's no capital punishment in Britain.' He neglected to mention that, inside the embassy itself, the gunmen were guilty of kidnap and false imprisonment, not to mention offences against the Terrorism Act.

'You are only twenty-seven years old,' added Karkouti. 'You'll be out by the time you're thirty. You'll still have at least thirty or forty years ahead of you for the struggle. Anyway, the British government will almost certainly deport you in two months' time.'

The last statement was unwelcome. If Britain deported him to Iran, he could just imagine the warm and loving welcome he would receive. He told the men urging him to capitulate he'd think about it. To them, it seemed as if there were times he wasn't listening.

Back in Tehran, Qotbzadeh was ratcheting up the rhetoric with an extraordinary and inflammatory statement:

You, the revolutionary members of the Iranian Embassy in London. We admire your steadfastness and forbearance against the criminal actions of the Ba'athist Iraq as well as those of the agents of Imperialism and international Zionism. But we want you to know that in these critical moments in which you have been placed under heavy pressure by these criminal agents, the nation and the government of Iran are intimately standing beside you. Since it is a fact that the whole of the Iranian nation is prepared for martyrdom for continuity in our glorious revolution, and will under no circumstances yield to any kind of force and pressure exerted by imperialism and international Zionism, we feel certain that you are also ready for martyrdom alongside your nation and do not accept that Iranian nation pay ransom to the agents of world imperialists. You must rest assured that we shall save no effort for your release and should you so wish and if need be, tens of thousands of Iranians are just ready to enter the premises of the embassy not with weapons but with cries of 'Allah-uh-Akbar' [God is Great] and thus bring punishment upon those mercenaries of the Ba'athist Iraq in a manner they deserve.

Qotbzadeh was good at volunteering other people for martyrdom.

The business about sending in an army of zealots was probably nothing more than sound and fury. But it was one more scenario for the Met Police to add to their growing contingency list. The proximity of the Household Cavalry units just up the road in Knightsbridge barracks might prove useful in the event of a mass, ayatollah-inspired embassy invasion.

In the early afternoon Salim left off tub-thumping to speak to the police negotiators again, but by 1330 hrs he was back on the second floor. He asked Harris: 'When we finish the operation – will they make some programme about it?'

Harris said: 'Too right they will – there'll be documentary crews all over the place.'

Salim nodded gravely. 'Very well. We will give them something to film.'

With nothing much else to do, his men had been poking around the embassy. They'd found the stationery cupboard, and with it a stock of marker pens. Salim and two of the other gunmen now began scrawling anti-Iranian slogans on the walls in Farsi, Arabic and English with the coloured pens. At one point, Faisal stopped to ask Karkouti: 'How do you spell "fundamentalist"?'

Jumping angrily to his feet when he saw the slogan *Death to Khomeini* in the corridor just outside the toilet, Dr Afrouz began shouting in Farsi. Alarmed, Faruqi tried to stop him: 'No. Don't do anything silly. Don't say things we will regret! Please, my friend, sit down!'

To make things worse, Lavasani got up and stood next to Afrouz in a show of solidarity. Some of the other Iranians begged their two compatriots to sit down and be quiet. But if anything, Afrouz was working up a head of steam. 'It's very bad,' he raged. 'Have you seen the slogans these people have written against Khomeini?'

'Ignore it,' said Faruqi, trying to calm the Chargé d'Affaires. 'The Ayatollah will not die because someone writes a slogan against him – we will.'

But Afrouz wouldn't let it go: 'No, no, no, we can't take this any more! We have to fight these people.' Lavasani shouted his agreement. Terrified and appalled, the other Iranians flapped around the two men, hushing them and imploring them to calm down. Slouched on guard duty at the door, Hassan started to shout back. When Afrouz and Lavasani kept on protesting, he took a hand grenade from his pocket. Brandishing it at the two outraged Iranians, he shouted: 'Shut up!' Disturbed by the commotion, three of the other terrorists came in and pointed their weapons at the hostages.

Salim was with Karkouti on the first floor when he heard the racket from overhead. 'OK, OK,' Salim said. 'Don't worry. Don't worry.' But in reality, the argument was getting out of hand. When the shouting flared up again, Karkouti and Salim returned to Room 9. The atmosphere in the room was now verging on the hysterical: one of the Iranians had thrown himself to the ground, weeping and chanting in high-pitched prayer. Several more were on their knees, making emotional appeals to the gunmen, Afrouz and Lavasani in turn.

Then Abbas Lavasani charged across the room and threw himself at Faisal. Faisal cocked his machine gun and forced the press officer to the floor, screaming at him all the while and giving every indication that he was about to shoot. Several of the Iranians rushed forward. Grabbing Lavasani by the arms, they tried to restrain him. Abbas the doorman kicked him. Lock went across and, staring Lavasani in the face, barked: 'Just bloody cool it. You – shut up now! And keep still.' Turning to Harris, he said: 'Smash him in the face.' But Harris didn't want to use violence against anyone.

In an effort to shield him, Karkouti sat down in front of Lavasani. 'If you want to hit someone,' he told him, 'then hit me. I don't mind.'

The words calmed Lavasani. Reaching up, he hugged Karkouti, pressed his face into the older man's chest and then kissed him on both cheeks.

Salim quit the room, perhaps hoping to defuse the situation. But Faisal was up for the argument. He kept coming in and out of the hostage room, taunting Afrouz and Lavasani and shouting anti-Khomeini insults. Two of the Iranians told Lavasani that if the gunmen wrote more slogans, then he wasn't to get angry. Right on cue, Faisal came back into the room with a felt tip and started scribbling more anti-Khomeini graffiti on the walls.

Struggling against the Iranians holding him down, Lavasani yelled: 'Stop! Do not dishonour the Ayatollah's name!'

Faisal stalked across the room and glared at the young press officer. 'If you want to die,' he shouted, 'we will kill you!' Then, his angry gaze sweeping the hostages as one, he told them all further talking was forbidden until he permitted it. And with that he turned and marched out of the room.

In the pin-drop silence that now took hold, the hostages heard Salim and the other gunmen start to argue outside. It was the first real sign of disagreement between them. It quickly became clear that Faisal, the most hardline of the gunmen, wanted to make an example of Lavasani.

Eventually, when the argument had died down, Faisal came back into Room 9. The hostages were allowed to talk – but only in whispers. And from now on, he added, the Iranians had to pray individually and in silence.

■ ■ ■

At the Foreign Office in Whitehall, Hurd and his team were still playing footsie with a whole raft of Arab ambassadors. First in to see him were the Kuwaiti Ambassador, Sheikh Saud Nasir Al-Sabah, and the Jordanian Chargé d'Affaires Zaid Kasim Ghazzawi. Then came Algeria's Abdelkrim Benmahmoud, and Adnan Omran. Hurd told them that, thus far, the gunmen had seen only the police at the embassy. Would their Excellencies consider going to the embassy and talking with the Group of the Martyr?

Omran asked the obvious question: to what effect? Hurd made it plain the only option for the gunmen was surrender. And not on their terms. Omran saw at once that the position of the British government hadn't changed since it had made its first approach to the Arab diplomatic community, and he also sensed that it would never change. 'Why,' he wondered, 'should I or any of my colleagues act as go-betweens and glorified messengers?' He, like his Arab counterparts, feared unforeseen consequences for their states if they agreed to mediate: this siege had already inflamed tempers in the corridors of power in both Iran and Iraq.

Omran, however, had a suggestion. In his opinion, the best person to mediate was Nabil Ramlawi, the PLO representative in London. Salim would certainly listen to him. Maybe Ramlawi could help engineer a peaceful climbdown?

Hurd demurred: asking a member of what the government already considered a terrorist organisation to intervene in an act of terrorism was hardly the British way.

One by one, the doors to a peaceful solution were closing.

■ ■ ■

The police shared the gunmen's frustration. It wasn't that they didn't want to help, simply that they couldn't. International agreements and the laws of the land forbade concession when it came to granting the gunmen safe passage out of the UK.

At Zulu Control, Professor Gunn noted: 'We got the impression that there was a very genuine attempt by the government to save life. But it takes time. Diplomatic things didn't just happen. All we could tell the terrorists was: "We have told the government what you want, and they will tell us the minute they have some definite answers." All that was honoured, and there was no jiggery-pokery in the police HQ...'

The various surveillance devices picked up little sound from the embassy that afternoon. Following the bitter morning row, the atmosphere inside was still extremely tense with the gunmen and hostages no longer talking. The gunmen were hardly even talking among themselves.

At 1706 hrs, negotiators called Salim to tell him the bad news: so far, the British government had not been able to persuade a single Arab ambassador to mediate. But the Foreign Office was still trying. In response, an angry Salim threatened to kill the hostages.

An hour later, the listeners heard Lock trying to explain to Salim why it was so difficult to get any of the Arab ambassadors to come. Salim's response was a furious: 'Shut up!' Lock duly subsided.

Hoping to ease the fraught atmosphere, the negotiators offered to send in more food. Exhausted, embittered and increasingly at his wits' end, Salim refused.

Over the course of the day, Mustapha Karkouti's condition seemed to have deteriorated. He was now having stomach pains and frequent bouts of diarrhoea and running a high fever. As the evening drew in, he began to complain of numbness in his arms and legs, and said he was finding it painful to pass water. In an effort to cool his fever, some of the hostages bathed his face. Karkouti's illness seemed to be a re-run of Cramer's. But were the symptoms real, imagined or fabricated? Several of the other hostages were complaining of stomach upsets. A new rumour ran through the group – had the police spiked the food they'd sent in?

Whether or not that was the case, at 1900 hrs, Salim requested that the police send in pills for the sick man. The medicine arrived twenty-five minutes later, but did not appear to alleviate Karkouti's symptoms. He was sitting hunched in what appeared to be severe pain, weeping silently from time to time as if the whole situation had simply become too much for him. In truth, it had become too much for everyone concerned.

Shortly before 2000 hrs, Salim spoke with Karkouti alone in the telex room, asking the journalist how he was feeling. Karkouti hardly needed to reply: still sweating, he looked very poorly. 'We've seen you in too much pain,' Salim told him, 'and you need medical attention. We will let you go.'

'If you are in the mood to release a hostage,' Karkouti asked, 'will you let a woman go instead?'

Salim shook his head. 'No. It's you or nobody.'

'Now?'

'Now.'

'Can I go back upstairs and say goodbye to my friends?' Karkouti meant Lock, Harris, Faruqi and the other hostages.

'No. They will be upset, and I'm not having that. I will say goodbye to them for you. Go right now, or not at all.'

Karkouti didn't need telling again.

Salim picked up the field telephone and warned the police a hostage was coming out. The gunmen helped Karkouti down to the front door. There, Salim turned to Karkouti for the last time: 'Tell the police to get in touch with the Arab ambassadors,' he said. 'Or something bad will happen.'

Karkouti looked him in the eye. 'Don't get yourselves killed,' he said.

At 2020 hrs, Karkouti stumbled out on to the embassy porch. He was bent almost double, clutching his stomach, but the police shouted: 'Stop! Put your hands above your head!' They came forward and escorted the bewildered journalist to Zulu Control. A doctor gave him a quick check-up. Like Cramer before him, the journalist seemed to have made a remarkable recovery. His stomach cramps had eased and he had stopped shaking. The police asked him about the mood inside the embassy. Karkouti made it clear the gunmen were angry and dangerous, very near the end of their rope. He repeated Salim's threat that 'something bad will happen' unless an Arab ambassador came forward to help them escape. It could only mean killing one or more of the hostages.

From Princes Gate, the police drove him out to Hendon Police College, in the far reaches of north-west London. Following a more thorough medical examination, Karkouti was pronounced fit to undergo further questioning.

Two plain-clothes men started the interrogation: Who had eaten the food that had been sent in the night before? Had the gunmen

Rusty Firmin leading the rear assault team. Bob C going in, Firmin (no gloves) no. 2; The Mink (Pete Morrison) no. 3 with MP5, torch attached.

First-floor front balcony. Bravo Four make entry.

Reserve Team outside back door. Trooper with silenced MP5-SD on left. Red Team signaller with radio pack on right.

First-floor front balcony after frame-charge explosion.

Sim Harris escaping from the burning embassy. (*Press Association*)

Salim in the Chargé d'Affaires' office.

Embassy telex room with bodies of terrorists Makki and Hassan. Murdered hostage Ali Samadzadeh in foreground on left.

The Russian pattern RGD-5 hand-grenade that Faisal dropped on the stairs. Rusty Firmin later handed it back to the authorities.

Faisal dead in ground-floor hallway at foot of main stairs. Note bullet holes in table to right.

Firmin's view of library from rear-entry point post-assault.

Hostages face down on lawn.

Hostage and reception rear gardens. Sim Harris in jacket and glasses at right identifying gunman 'Ali', real name Fowzi Nejad.

Fowzi Nejad immediately after identification. The SAS hostage reception team are about to plasticuff him and hand him over to the police.

Fowzi Nejad under arrest post-assault. (*Sunday Times*)

Fire and scene of crime police officers removing Faisal's body from crime scene. Note SOC Polaroid camera in foreground.

Aftermath – ground-floor hallway.

Police guarding front door of the Embassy after the siege.

PC Trevor Lock and his wife Doreen, after the siege. (*Keystone*)

Sami Muhammed Ali, aka The Fox. Still wanted. (*Sunday Times*)

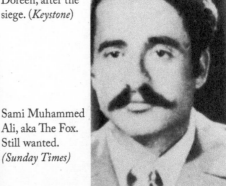

eaten any of it? Karkouti shook his head. No one had ever seen any of the gunmen eat the food the police had supplied. Why did they want to know that? The police ignored him, and moved on to the next question: Where were the food containers? Where exactly were they positioned inside the embassy?

The questions made Karkouti very suspicious. Was it true the police had spiked the food? In some ways, it made sense: a terrorist with diarrhoea probably wasn't going to be able to maintain his focus. But it seemed a haphazard way of going about things: what if only one or two of the gunmen had eaten the doctored meal? Karkouti found it hard to believe the police would have done that. Or was it that the food had simply been sitting around for too long before it came in?

But then, why were the police interested in the precise location of the food containers? Had they been fitted with tiny listening devices?

The police made it clear that it was they, and not Karkouti, who were asking the questions. In the end, his answers provided them with a very insightful debrief. They showed him photographs of the hostages that had been supplied by their relatives and friends. Karkouti was able to identify most of them, give a quick estimate of their general state of health and morale, and confirm that each and every one was a hostage. So now the police – and the SAS – knew for certain that anyone else was a terrorist.

■ ■ ■

Back in the embassy, the same sombre atmosphere prevailed. For the most part, hostages and gunmen sat in silence. As yet, they did not know of Karkouti's release. Then, shortly before 2100 hrs, Salim told Harris and Lock to follow him to the second floor. When he switched on the radio the two Brits were astonished to hear the newsreader report the release of another hostage 'within the last few minutes'. Still very grave, Salim told the two men not to tell anyone else. A little later, Salim also took Morris down to the front hall and told him of Karkouti's release.

The British hostages had pleaded for Karkouti's freedom, and on one level they were glad that it had happened. But at the same time, they were worried: had the gunmen released Karkouti, a fellow Arab, because they were going to kill everyone else?

A few minutes later, the duty police negotiator thanked Salim for releasing another hostage, and repeated the offer of food. Salim retorted that he wanted neither thanks nor food, just a meeting with the ambassadors to 'find a peaceful solution to all this'.

With no food sent in, the hostages had eaten little that day: only the 'siege tea' that Ron Morris and the women had been able to scrounge up. With his usual cheerful manner, the embassy manager shared out milk, biscuits and left-over rolls. Someone found a small supply of butter and some happily ate it – pasting it on to the rolls with their fingers. Other hostages refused to eat, on the grounds that the food must be stale. In an effort to boost the rock-bottom morale, Morris told everyone that he had recently re-stocked the embassy, so there was a good supply of basic provisions – toilet rolls, teabags, biscuits: great stores of stuff down in the basement.

One hour later, the negotiator called again: it was too late now to get an ambassador, but contacts were going on at a high level. Plainly dispirited but not surprised, Salim said very little in reply.

As the night crept on and the frightened hostages tried to get some sleep, the gunmen were once again disturbed – and annoyed – by what Lock had tried to pass off as the 'mice' noises: intermittent high-pitched squeaks mixed with low rumbling and the occasional knocking. Once again, Salim asked Lock to investigate.

Sticking to his story, Lock explained that mice come out at night and that the noise – which was, of course, caused by drilling to insert yet more surveillance equipment – was a combination of small furry animals burrowing and the heating system cooling down. Losing patience, Salim burst out: 'These noises are being made by the police.'

There was frenetic police activity back at Zulu Control, too, and in the headquarters of COBRA, the national crisis management team. With negotiations at stalemate they sat up late into the night plotting tactics for the following day.

# DAY SIX: Monday, 5 May 1980

The gunmen woke Lock at 0400 hrs. It was Bank Holiday Monday, a national day off work, and exceptionally quiet. Unless, that is, you happened to be dealing with an embassy siege. In the profound silence of the small hours, the gunmen said they'd heard noises from the ground floor. Wide-eyed and fingering their weapons, they were convinced an intruder had broken into the embassy. Shaking him into wakefulness, Salim told Lock: 'We think there is a stranger inside. Go and see, Mr Trevor.' The gunmen's leader didn't apparently see the irony in getting one of his captives to go and deal with a possible intruder. Perhaps he reasoned that if Lock flushed out anyone snooping around, it would give the Group of the Martyr time to take up defensive positions. And massacre the other hostages.

Scrambling to his feet, Lock donned his uniform cap and dutifully went off to investigate. Moving slowly down through the silent embassy, he called out repeatedly: 'This is PC Trevor Lock. Is there anybody there?' His shouts woke the other male hostages, who stared at one another owl-eyed in the dark. A few minutes later, Lock came back into the male hostage room shaking his head. No one was there.

After this alarm and excursion, Lock and the other hostages tried to get back to sleep. Everyone was dog-tired. The constant nervous pressure was taking its toll on them all, especially the gunmen, most of whom had hardly slept, and in Salim's case, hadn't slept properly at all.

In the attic at Zulu Control, the police negotiators, too, were feeling the strain. Although they were working in shifts, one had suffered a minor nervous collapse and had to be replaced.

The psychiatrist, Professor Gunn, found he was having to spend an increasing amount of time telling the negotiators they were doing a good job: 'By Monday, fatigue and tension had set in on both sides,' he said. 'I had to do a lot more talking to the police negotiators, sitting down with them, going over the tapes, reassuring them that they hadn't made any mistakes. They were beginning to wonder how long it was all going to last.'

If some among the authorities worried that push might be coming to shove, Gunn wasn't one of them. Fully expecting the siege to last a few more days, he called his office at the Maudsley Hospital and asked his secretary to rearrange his Tuesday and Wednesday appointments. Dellow, too, was upbeat: 'If they keep releasing two hostages every day, this will all be over in eleven days.'

At 0800 hrs, Salim woke Lock and the other hostages for the second time. He was visibly agitated: rocking from one foot to the other, his head going from side to side and his hands shaking. He led Lock down to the first-floor landing and along the corridor towards the toilet. Pointing at the wall dividing the Iranian Embassy from the Ethiopian Embassy, he stood back.

Lock stared. He could see what Salim was nervous about. In several places it bulged alarmingly. With a bit of a shove from the other side, it looked as if the whole wall would collapse into the embassy corridor. It was the same stretch of wall where the gunmen had scribbled their provocative political slogans the day before. The bulging plaster warped the coloured scrawls into weird shapes.

Lock knew it was going to take more than his mice story to explain away the bulges. His comments about 'building settlement' and 'blocked water pipes' weren't going to cut the mustard either. In the event, there was no need for him to make up any more white lies. Fingers on the cocking lever of his machine-pistol, Salim said: 'The police are going to attack. They are going to come in through the walls. The wall was flat when I wrote on it yesterday.'

Back in Room 9, Dr Ezzati was in a very bad way. He was taking the medication the gunmen had got from the police for his heart complaint, but he was still suffering. Harris was helping the Cultural Attaché take the pills at regular intervals – setting his watch alarm to buzz every four hours. But like Karkouti before him, Ezzati complained that his limbs felt increasingly numb.

At 1100 hrs, Salim jumped to his feet. He was pale and his long face was pinched tight. The hostages glanced at him fearfully, then looked away so as not to catch his eye. Salim was showing all the signs of a man at breaking point. He ordered Lock to go to the first-floor window: 'Tell the police we will shoot a hostage within thirty minutes if there is no news about an Arab ambassador.' Lock picked up his cap and did as he was told.

Harris wrote in his diary: 'I feel that things are starting to look grim. I have to do something. I really do think they mean business this time. The days for playing around are over.'

He was right.

Salim had his men move the male hostages from Room 9 to the telex room. They were made to sit against the walls, Iranians and non-Iranians in separate groups. The women were left in Room 9A. With its curtains tightly drawn and only a lamp on, the telex room was in near darkness. The gunmen had piled chairs and tables up against the window, intensifying the close, forbidding atmosphere in the room.

Salim was wound tight. A new note had crept into his voice: mockery. Sweeping the hostages with a contemptuous gaze, he told them: 'It's obvious the police don't care about you.' The strong implication in his words was: So why should I?

Harris and Lock persuaded him they should go to the window and tell the police that he was serious and intent on killing a hostage this time. Salim agreed. When they were ready at the talking window, Salim checked his large gilt digital watch. 'You have five minutes,' he hissed.

'Look,' said Harris, 'it will take longer than that to talk to the police. We need longer.' Salim conceded five more minutes.

Despite all that he had been through and was still enduring, Harris was still battling away. Seeing the street deserted, he shouted out through the window: 'What's going on out there? They're going to shoot one of us if we don't have news of an ambassador! Can you please ask the Foreign Office to speed things up.'

Superintendent Fred Luff and another officer came forward, arms wide and fingers spread to show they were unarmed. 'It's not in our hands. We have no way of speeding up talks at the Foreign Office. But the talks are still taking place. If you want confirmation, listen to the BBC World Service at midday.'

'Please get on to the FO and tell them to act quickly,' Harris pleaded. 'It's critical in here. They're playing with our bloody lives.' From Salim's manner, Harris really did feel that the bluffing was over and the gunmen were now ready to kill. Police prevarication, the everlasting stand-off and the lack of any real progress had driven him to desperation.

'We'll go off now and make contact,' the negotiator promised. 'But you must all understand that we don't control the political moves. Just try and keep calm.'

Listening from his post behind the curtain, Salim snapped: 'Getting the ambassadors is the only way out now.'

'Why don't you think about the alternatives?' said Lock, trying to make the gunman see reason. 'Why not give yourselves up in honourable surrender? You've made your point. Why not end it all now, without violence? You can't start shooting people. That makes you into a lot of common criminals. You'll just lose all public sympathy for your cause.'

Salim wasn't having any of it. 'No! I have had enough now. They are just messing me about. This operation was supposed to last twenty-eight hours and now it has lasted six days! Your police, they want this to go on forever. They don't care if it takes a week. They don't care you die. They make noises in the night to keep us awake. I had enough.' The angrier he grew, the more his English deteriorated.

He led Lock and Harris back to the telex room, where they listened to the midday news. The broadcast was bland, and from Salim's point of view, wholly inadequate. 'Talks are taking place,' the announcer said. 'Apart from that, all is quiet at the embassy.'

Harris reflected on how inappropriate the use of the word quiet was, 'while we were inside sweating it out on another deadline'.

At 1215 hrs, Salim prodded Lock and Harris out of the telex room again. As they reached the top of the stairs, they heard footsteps behind them and looked back. Abbas Lavasani had raised his hand: the signal he wanted to visit the toilet. Now, three of the gunmen had him at gunpoint. Lavasani looked nervous but defiant – perhaps even a little contemptuous. He did not lack for courage. But he did look strange: he was wearing his trousers tucked into his socks again, and the odd, old-fashioned yellow woman's cardigan with the two lowermost buttons done up. Lavasani had volunteered to die a martyr and it was beginning to look as if he might.

The gunmen forced the three hostages down two flights of stairs to the ground floor. The field telephone was in the small ante-room near the ground-floor toilet. Lavasani used the toilet. When he came back out, the three gunmen surrounded him, weapons levelled. Looking at their set, implacable expressions, Harris and Lock feared the worst.

Salim dictated a message to Lock. 'Mr Trevor, tell the police we have brought a hostage down here and we will shoot him in five minutes' time unless we get what we want.'

Lock looked at Salim. Now they had come down to it, the whole thing felt unreal, beyond the realms of nightmare. He found it hard to believe that Salim, this seemingly pleasant and earnest young man, could really be on the point of committing cold-blooded murder. But peering into the darkness of the hallway, he saw that two of the gunmen now had Lavasani fast by the arms. They were tying him to the hall banister with parcel string they'd found in the stationery cupboard. Lavasani made no attempt to struggle as they trussed him.

Slowly, Lock pressed the button on the field telephone. When the duty negotiator answered, he said: 'Please, sir, will you understand that they intend to shoot a hostage? They have brought one downstairs and he is standing next to us.'

In a low monotone, Lock went on to describe what was happening: 'They have one of the hostages. They have some brown string and they are tying the hostage to the banisters of the stairs, his hands behind his back. Sir, I implore you: they are trussing him up like a chicken.'

In a firm tone, the negotiator replied: 'Trevor, tell them this won't get them anywhere. Try and calm them down.'

Overhearing the negotiator's remark, Salim snatched the phone:

'You have had enough time. If you really cared, someone would be here already.'

If anything, Salim was only too composed. In everything he did, there was a new air of deadly intent. When the gunmen had finished trussing Abbas Lavasani, they stood back. Wrapped up in string with his hands tied behind his back, the young press officer looked absurdly vulnerable: a human parcel, ripe for martyrdom. His liquid dark brown eyes held the same mixture of defiance and contempt. But now he saw that he was nearing his last, there was a new expression in them: fear.

Two of the gunmen led Lock and Harris back up to the telex room. As they went, they passed close by Lavasani. It was hard to look at him. He was a man under sentence of death. On the way upstairs, they heard Lavasani's voice. Salim was holding the phone to his mouth and Lavasani was talking directly to the police negotiators – pleading for his very life: 'My name is Abbas Lavasani. I am tied up and they are going to kill me. Please help ...'

'You should not have told them your name!' Salim yelled, snatching the phone away.

Upstairs, the other hostages listened in silence as Salim ranted at the police for what felt like hours. Then the embassy fell silent again. There was a pause that seemed to last for an eternity. Followed by three deep, explosive coughs that echoed up through the stairwell. At the end of another short pause, the hostages heard a deep sigh. It was abruptly cut off. After that, there was a muffled thud – the sound a corpse might make if it had been cut down and let fall.

For long seconds, there was absolute shock in the telex room. Gradually, as the reality of what had just happened sank in, someone began to weep. More of the hostages joined in. For the most part, they cried silently; only one man, head slumped between his knees, heaved loud, dry, despairing sobs. No one spoke until Salim came to the door.

Morris confronted him: 'Have you really shot him?'

'Yes, we have,' Salim said. And then cruelly: 'Do you want to see the body?' He sounded like a perverted undertaker, eager to wave the shroud.

For the first time, Harris felt pure hatred welling up inside him. For Salim – and not just Salim. He hated all of the gunmen, their cause and everything to do with it. He shook his head. 'They were terrorists, animals, common criminals, who would kill us for the sake of it. I couldn't even look at him: I blocked out his bearded face as he stood in the doorway, offering to display Lavasani's corpse.'

'I don't want to see the body either,' Morris spat. 'But if you have shot him, it's pointless shooting any more of us. One more or twenty, it doesn't matter. You've done it now.'

Morris was right: with Lavasani's death the terrorists had crossed an invisible line. Seizing hostages was one thing. Murder was another. Abbas Lavasani might have been talking when he would have been better off listening – but that didn't justify killing him in cold blood.

'It doesn't matter,' Salim said in a flat voice. 'I am prepared to die.'

One or two of the other hostages tried to remonstrate with him, but Salim sneered: 'They don't care about you out there. The British government wants you to die. They would send an ambassador if they did not want you to die. We have told them we will shoot one of you every forty-five minutes until we get an answer about the ambassadors. It's in their hands now.'

Again the room descended into a shocked silence. After fifteen minutes, Issa Naghizadeh asked Lock to try and get one of the police negotiators up to the window so he could talk to him. Naghizadeh said emphatically: 'We have no more time to waste.'

At 1325 hrs, the terrorists took Lock back downstairs, his heavy footsteps echoing on the steps. Salim instructed him to relay the threat he had just made to the police. 'Make sure they will know we mean it. One hostage every forty-five minutes.'

Lock got on the field telephone as instructed. 'One man has been shot,' he confirmed. 'Another will be killed in half an hour.'

When Lock returned, Harris asked him: 'Do you reckon they did it? What could you see?'

'I don't know,' Lock replied. 'He's not there any longer and the floor is all wet, with a piece of loose carpet where we left him. I couldn't see any blood, but it's all dark down there.'

Morris intervened: 'Look,' he told Salim, 'diplomatic moves take a long time. You can't just drive a car round to an embassy and take an ambassador down to negotiate a siege.'

Salim thought about what the embassy manager had said. Then he announced: 'I will put back the deadline to five o'clock. But that is absolutely final. If they don't agree to give us safe passage, another of you will die.'

■ ■ ■

Outside in Princes Gate, at Zulu Control, in the hush of COBRA and in the great offices of state, the three gunshots resounded and reverberated long after the lethal bullets had been fired. At lunch in his grace-and-favour home in the Berkshire countryside some twenty-five miles outside London, Home Secretary William Whitelaw heard the news in a flash alert. Dropping his knife and fork, he ran for the door, shouting: 'Get the car! Get my driver!' With police motorcycle outriders clearing the way, and officers rushing to clear junctions along the route, Whitelaw's big supercharged Jaguar flew towards London at warp speed. The Home Secretary covered the twenty-five miles to COBRA in eighteen minutes.

On arrival, he took charge. When he'd heard out the short action briefing, he sat back and looked at the committee. There was hardly any need to say the words. But he spoke them anyway for the record: for the silent tape recorders running under the desks, and beyond that, for the long judgement of history: as soon as confirmation came that the gunmen had started killing hostages, he would pass control of the siege to the SAS. Then the highly trained men who had been standing by, poised for immediate action, would go in and break the deadlock.

Until that confirmation came through, however, it was worth exploring every avenue. Whitelaw asked Foreign Secretary Hurd to make one more round of calls to friendly Arab diplomats, in the last-ditch hope of getting one to agree to be a go-between. Hurd did his level best, but there was nothing doing.

The hostages were in despair. Many were still weeping. But, locked in their own private corridors of fear and despondency, they could not offer one another comfort. A negotiator called to say they would have confirmation within half an hour as to whether an Arab diplomat willing to speak with the gunmen could be found.

'Not half an hour,' Faisal said bitterly. 'Five minutes.'

Ahmed Dadgar asked: 'What will you achieve by killing?'

'I don't mind getting killed,' said Faisal. 'When I left home, I didn't think I was going to get back alive.'

To Faruqi the official delay was incomprehensible. 'We were unable to understand why it wasn't possible to bring in just one ambassador … it would have relieved the situation tremendously. It didn't even have to be an ambassador.' He was right. But the police couldn't budge.

At 1340 hrs, Salim allowed Issa Naghizadeh to use the field phone. Speaking in rapid Farsi, he pleaded with the police to break the impasse. He got the same 'we're trying our best/these things take time' response the police had been giving for six days. When he came back upstairs, Naghizadeh was in a rage. Glaring at the British hostages, he shouted: 'It's all the fault of your police and British government. They are causing all this trouble. It's their fault.' He slumped down against the wall. When he'd calmed down, he looked back at Morris, Lock and Harris and said, 'I am sorry. I did not mean to shout at you personally. I know you have done everything you can to help. It's your government I should be blaming, not you.'

Morris and Harris did what many British people tend to do in times of extreme stress – they went down to the embassy kitchen and made tea. By now, the gunmen were also on the verge of tears. They had relaxed their guard and were walking around in what looked to the hostages like an almost catatonic state. Salim, the only exception, was in the corridor. He had a large roll of Sellotape, which he was using to fix one Skorpion magazine upside-down to another. If it came to a firefight, he wanted to be able to change mags super-fast like they did in the movies.

Calling Harris over, he asked: 'What will your police do, now that I have shot one of you? Will they attack?'

Harris shook his head. 'I don't know. I really don't know.' Just then, his digital watch-alarm buzzed: it was time to give Dr Ezzati his pills. But as he searched around the room and through his pockets, Harris realised he couldn't find them. The hunt for the pills now became of paramount importance. They'd been in an envelope. Had anybody seen them? Ali the Bank piped up: 'I think maybe I accidentally threw them away in the wastepaper basket in Room 9. I thought it was waste paper – I'm sorry.' Makki went with Harris to Room 9. Fearing attack, the gunmen had locked it. Retrieving the key from beneath the doormat where it had been hidden, Makki took Harris inside and allowed him to the search the bin. Harris found the pills, still inside the envelope, half-buried in rubbish. The little drama was a welcome momentary escape from the crushing fear that had now gripped everyone inside the embassy.

Back in the telex room, Harris felt absolutely sure that, even if the SAS were coming in, they wouldn't storm the embassy in broad daylight: an assault would come when everyone was asleep and off-guard.

■ ■ ■

At 1420 hrs, Superintendent Bernard Hodgets of the Anti-Terrorist Squad asked to be put through to Dr Sayyed Darsh, the senior Imam at London's Central Mosque in Regent's Park. In a final and rather desperate attempt to end the siege without further violence, the police had come up with the idea of asking Darsh to appeal to the gunmen to renounce violence on the grounds of Islamic teaching; and, if he managed to establish a rapport with the terrorists, persuade them to give themselves up.

Hodgets already knew Darsh: only three weeks before, Libyan broadcaster Mohammad Mustafa Ramadan, a regular worshipper at the mosque, had been shot dead on its steps. Darsh and Ramadan had been friends, and the Libyan's murder had deeply affected him. In the course of the police investigation that followed, Hodgets had met with Darsh and come to respect him.

Darsh was out when Hodgets rang, but at 1500 hrs the Imam called back. Hodgets explained that Commander Peter Duffy, head of the

Anti-Terrorist Squad, was hoping Darsh might agree to go to Princes Gate and see what he could do, as London's top Moslem preacher, to talk the gunmen down.

Darsh was reluctant. His position was delicate: representing the vast spectrum of Moslem believers in the capital, who came from all kinds of ethnic, social, political and faith communities, he had to tread a fine – and demonstrably neutral – line. He could not see how talking to a bunch of what looked to everyone in the know like Iraqi-backed gunmen would help him stay on that line. On the contrary. The Iranians, for certain, would assume Darsh was taking sides.

But when Hodgets explained that the siege was reaching its desperate endgame, and the British authorities had run out of all other options bar him and the SAS, Darsh reluctantly agreed to help. Half an hour later, a police car drew up in front of the mosque. Darsh got in, and the squad car raced over to Hyde Park Central police station. Then, after all the hurry and scurry, the police left Darsh sitting in the grubby waiting room, wondering what on earth could be causing all the delay.

■ ■ ■

Half an hour before the latest deadline was due to expire, Met spokesman DAC Peter Nievens called a press conference. 'Earlier this afternoon,' he told the goggle-eyed journalists, 'what sounded like two or three shots were heard from the direction of the Iranian Embassy. The significance of these noises,' Nievens added, 'is being investigated.'

Even before he'd stopped speaking, journalists were racing for the bank of phones Post Office engineers had installed at the edge of their compound. At last! After six days of the most indescribable boredom and no information they could usefully print, something had happened in that damned embassy!

Inside the embassy, time had slowed down to a crawl. In keeping with their relatively favoured non-Iranian status, Harris, Morris and Lock were sitting on the only chairs in the telex room. The Iranian men were sitting on the floor. The Iranian women were in Room 9A.

But British or Iranian, every last one of the hostages was wondering the same thing: who among them would be shot next?

The gunmen kept coming back into the telex room asking for cigarettes. In exchange, they allowed the hostages to use the toilet or take some water from the nearby drinking fountain. Dr Ezzati was getting progressively weaker, complaining of pains in his chest. Dr Afrouz, on the other hand, had been steadily recovering from the injuries he'd sustained during his fall. He was now taking a leading role in the Iranian group.

At 1645 hrs, the buzzer sounded from the green field telephone. Salim listened impassively, then called Lock and Harris to the telephone. The negotiator told them that Metropolitan Police Commissioner Sir David McNee had written the gunmen, 'a very important letter. It has been translated into Farsi and it is vital that everyone understands its contents. You must come to the door to receive it. I would like a guarantee from Salim that the officer delivering the letter will not be shot down.'

Salim's reply was curt: 'If they do not play tricks, it will be OK. Put it through letter hole.' He decided that Harris would retrieve the letter while Lock was held at gunpoint. 'Any tricks and we shoot him,' Salim told Harris in an ominous tone.

They waited in the entrance hall. Once Salim was sure the letter had arrived, he ordered one of the other gunmen to unlock the inner security door. The lock had jammed, and it took several attempts before the key turned and the door swung open. Harris took the long brown envelope from the mat, tore it open and gave the Farsi version of the letter to Salim. Slowly and with increasing disbelief, he read the English version:

> I think it is right that I should explain to you clearly and in writing the way in which my police officers are dealing with the taking of hostages in the Iranian Embassy. I am responsible for preserving the peace and enforcing law in London and do this independently of politicians and government. I and my officers deeply wish to work toward the peaceful solution of what has occurred. We fully understand how both the

hostages and those who hold them feel threatened and frightened. You are cut off from your family and friends, but you need not be frightened or threatened by the police. It is not our way in Britain to resort to violence against those who are peaceful. You have nothing to fear from my officers provided you do not harm those in your care. I firmly hope that we can now bring this incident to a close peacefully and calmly.

Coming at the time it did, McNee's letter could hardly have been less helpful. A bland mish-mash of the usual police blather, far from being 'of vital importance' the letter was of absolutely no importance at all. Nor was it of any use.

Furious that a letter from the Met's most senior policeman offered nothing concrete, no tangible offer in response to his demands at the eleventh hour, Salim swept the hostages with an enraged eye: 'This letter is nothing. Nothing good at all. An ambassador must come, otherwise I will shoot one of you in forty-five minutes.'

While his leader was occupied elsewhere, Abbas came back into the telex room. Kneeling briefly next to the young Iranian student Vahid Khabaz, the gunman passed him a tiny scrap of paper. Khabaz concealed the note in his palm. When the gunman they all knew as 'Ugly' had moved away, he lifted it surreptitiously and read what Abbas had written. Astonished, he waited until he was certain none of the gunmen were watching him, then crossed the room and sat down next to PC Lock. 'Ugly says his name is Abbas and he wants to escape,' Khabaz told Lock. 'He wants you to write a note saying he had nothing to do with the shooting. He says it is all going wrong and he wants to run away.'

'What does it say, exactly?' Lock asked.

Khabaz looked sadly at the note and translated: 'I promised nothing would happen to you. I have fights with my friends. I beg you to look after me. I leave you for Allah. Do not forget I did give you your life. Pray for me.'

Lock looked upset. 'Please tell him that I can't write notes for him. Tell him to escape if he wants to. I can't give him safe custody. I just don't have the power to do that.'

Khabaz took back the note, went and sat down, took out a box of matches and set fire to it, slapping out the flames with his hands as it turned to ash.

For the first time, Lock was showing signs of worry on his own account. He told Morris: 'I reckon I'll be next. I'm their trump card, being a British policeman and all that. It's them against the police now.'

■ ■ ■

At the same time Salim was reading McNee's letter, the police were finally leading Dr Darsh in through the barricade at one end of Princes Gate. But once again, they parked the Imam – this time in a police van – with no explanation for the delay.

While the leading representative of the Moslem religious community in London sat kicking his heels, the diplomatic community were gathering at the offices of the Arab League in Green Street, Mayfair. All London's Arab ambassadors, with the exception of the representative from Oman, had come to discuss the hostage crisis for the final time. It took only an hour or so for them to reach agreement: they would help the British authorities only if certain conditions were met:

• there must be no use of force while they were attempting to negotiate;
• they must be permitted to release a press statement pointing out that it was the Foreign Office that had asked them to intervene, and not the other way round;
• as a last resort, they must be allowed to offer the gunmen safe passage out of the UK.

The conditions were not in any way acceptable to the British government.

At 1820 hrs, the police led Dr Darsh into Alpha Control. They told him they believed the gunmen had killed a hostage. They wanted him to impress upon them how morally wrong that was, and, if he could, reinforce the message with the full weight of his Islamic authority. Finally, the police said, Darsh should stress that no harm would come to the gunmen if they surrendered peacefully.

For Darsh, it was a tall order. Especially when he realised, like the Arab diplomats before him, that the police simply wanted to use him as a lever to obtain the terrorists' peaceful surrender.

Darsh had no sooner sat down in the cramped, smoke-filled attic with its briefing boards, telephones, reel-to-reel tape recorders and the bank of CCTV monitors showing the outside of the embassy, when the green handset on the desk in front of him started to buzz. One of the policemen made it clear Darsh should pick it up. He lifted the phone to his ear. It was Salim. Darsh introduced himself, in Arabic, as the Imam of the London Central Mosque. 'I have heard about the plight of Khuzestan from students in my mosque,' he told Salim. Then he did his best to appeal to Salim's conscience, reminding him that the Koran did not permit the shedding of blood, and there could be no justification for killing a hostage.

Angry and barely coherent, Salim retorted that he had already killed a hostage, and he'd kill another one unless he got what he wanted. With that, he slammed the phone down.

Darsh asked the police why Salim could not meet at least one of the Arab ambassadors as he wished. An officer replied: 'The ambassadors are in a meeting. They cannot be disturbed.'

Darsh lifted the phone and called Salim back. The ambassadors, he explained, were even then meeting to discuss what they could do to help. Still furious, Salim nevertheless said he would extend the deadline by half an hour to seven o'clock. After that, if there was no resolution, he would kill not one but two of the hostages.

'Killing is against our law,' said Darsh.

'We are not interested in such talk,' Salim replied, then severed the connection again. A few seconds later, he was back on the line. 'I have changed my mind. If they [the police] don't tell me something in *two* minutes, I will kill another hostage.'

'Please,' Darsh implored, 'I'll see what I can do.' But once again, Salim had disconnected. Darsh tried appealing to the gunmen's leader one last time: 'I will go personally to the Arab ambassadors – at least wait for me to do that,' he said. There was an ominous silence on the other end. Darsh broke it with a final plea: it was one of the Koran's best-known lines, where the Prophet Muhammad says: 'The destruction of the whole universe is much less in degree than the shedding of the blood of one person.'

In reply, Salim shouted in Arabic: *'Aa'demhoom colohom!'* – I'll kill them all! And rang off.

Then the phone buzzed again. The Imam and the police in Alpha Control listened, appalled, as three gunshots rang from the loudspeaker. Equally spaced, they sounded deliberate. The effect in the crowded room was chilling. An officer leaned forward and grabbed the handset: 'That's no answer!' he shouted. 'It's not going to help anyone!'

There was no reply. For the last time, the line had gone dead.

■ ■ ■

News of the gunshots went immediately to COBRA. Douglas Hurd rang the Arab League offices. He told Adnan Omran, the Syrian Ambassador, that three more shots had been fired inside the Iranian Embassy. Had he and his colleagues reached a conclusion? Omran said they had: they would only cooperate on the terms they had already stated. Hurd and the British authorities could not agree to them. The last avenue of hope had been blocked.

■ ■ ■

The hostages sat in silence, listening intently. They could hear Salim shouting in Arabic on the field telephone. He had lost his temper again, he was screaming what sounded like a name down the phone: 'Mustapha' or possibly 'Muhammad'. Harris, who thought it was the former, wondered if Karkouti had been brought back in to negotiate. There was no way of knowing. The shouting went on for a few more seconds and then stopped abruptly.

There was a sinister dragging sound, followed by the slow creak of the front door opening. Then they heard the steel security door clang back into place. It sounded like the door to a cell slamming shut.

Morris, who had exceptionally good hearing, heard Salim say: 'There's a body on the doorstep. You can come and collect it.'

Salim raced back up the stairs. Breathless and pale-faced, the gunmen's leader appeared in the doorway. The hostages knew what had happened even before he told them: 'I have given them one body. I am going to give them another one in forty-five minutes unless I hear something.' Then, after a pause and staring directly at Trevor Lock, he added: 'We shall kill you all before the police get to you. You cannot be saved.'

Some of the hostages, like Muhammad Faruqi and Kaujouri Taghi, the accountant, had tried to convince themselves that the supposed shooting of Lavasani was in fact just another example of Salim's bluster – another of his missed deadlines, but with an explosive attempt to turn the vice. Now, they knew otherwise. Salim was a killer, plain and simple.

Faruqi had already turned to face Mecca and pray when Salim's appearance interrupted him. His response to Salim's threat was simply: 'Please let me finish my prayer.'

Taghi was thinking: 'I can't judge whether I'm a good man or a bad man. It is the others who must judge. But whether we live or die, that is up to God.'

Ron Morris was thinking: 'Now I'll never finish repairing the roof of my loft.'

Sim Harris was thinking: 'They'll be all right. I'm insured, and anyway, if I die in the line of duty, then the BBC will take care of them. Who knows, maybe they'll even count the Iranian Embassy as foreign soil. In which case, they'll get extra.' Worrying about his family's wellbeing in the event of his death was a way of fending off a much harder concept: that he might die, very soon. And never see his lovely family ever again.

■ ■ ■

On the monitors at Zulu Control, the police saw the front door of the embassy swing open. A human body thudded out on to the step. Then, as quickly as it had opened, the door slammed shut. The gunmen had dumped the body of a young man in a yellow cardigan on the step, as if he meant no more to them than a sack of stones.

With the police and SAS marksmen surrounding the embassy on full alert, two officers went forward with a stretcher to recover the corpse. They saw at once it was the young embassy press officer, Abbas Lavasani. He had been shot in the back of the head. Covering the dead man with a blanket, they picked him up and laid him gently on the stretcher. Lavasani's body was quite cold: he'd obviously been dead for several hours. The first set of shots heard had been the fatal ones. As the police carried him away, one of Lavasani's arms flopped out and dangled to the side, a bright canary yellow accent in the gathering dusk.

The police and COBRA now knew the gunmen had murdered at least one of the hostages. But what about the second series of shots? Could that be a bluff? The dilemma didn't occupy them for very long. The bald fact of Lavasani's death left them with no option: they had to assume that a second hostage had been killed.

Then, as if to confirm the need for action, a listening device picked up three of the gunmen discussing what to do next:

—'We do something before sunset.'
—'Kill two, or three, or four.'
—'Kill all by 10 p.m.'

At 1905 hrs, the switchboard operator at St Stephen's Hospital took a chilling call from one of the officers at Alpha Control: 'Prepare for casualties.'

With those three words he triggered the Major Accident Procedure, putting the doctors, nurses and anaesthetists on high alert for the night ahead.

■　■　■

ITN news director David Goldsmith was sitting in the outside broadcast vehicle in Kensington Gore, just behind the press barricades. He was keeping a beady eye on the monitors displaying ITN's rival channels. But where all the other media outfits had cameras on the front of the embassy, Goldsmith had a trump card: he had a crew filming the rear.

It had taken a lot of trouble to install that camera.

From the outset of the siege, the police had prevented journalists gaining access to the rear of the embassy. Some hacks had tried to bribe their way into the blocks of flats running down the western side of the shared rear gardens in Exhibition Road. The views from the rooms would have assured stellar views of the embassy's rear elevation – and of any rescue attempt that might be launched from that side. But in every case, the police had caught the ambitious journalists and escorted them away. One persistent hack had even been arrested.

Goldsmith was unwilling to accept the restrictions. He might have been more sensitive to official anxiety if he'd realised that the gunmen had access to a television set in Dr Afrouz's office. And if they were watching it, and if a rescue attempted to gain entry at the building's rear, then they'd have been able to see what the SAS were doing in real time and react accordingly. But like many newshounds at the scene, Goldsmith viewed the blanket denial of coverage as unnecessary police obstruction. From the moment the story had broken, he'd been scouting around for somewhere to position a camera overlooking the back of the embassy.

At the police change of shift in the early evening of the first day, Goldsmith had talked his way through to Exhibition Road. As he walked down past the large red-brick buildings, he caught sight of a night porter on duty just inside one of the luxury apartment blocks. Ten minutes later, he came away with the name of a resident who might just be willing to allow a camera into his flat. One phone call, early next morning, had secured the deal.

There remained one problem: how to smuggle the camera past the police. Even the new ENG (electronic news-gathering) cameras were large and unwieldy. But in the course of the job, the ITN man had learned to be resourceful. At eleven o'clock the next day, a taxi carrying two well-dressed businessmen drew up at the police cordon blocking off Exhibition Road. Pointing at their suitcases, which were liberally scattered with labels from all over the world, they explained that they had just arrived back from abroad and were staying with a friend who lived beyond the barrier. Convinced by the fine English manners of these two well-heeled travellers, the policeman redirected the taxi to the address in question via a side street. Ten minutes later, the two men got out. Another helpful policeman there carried their suitcases to the front door and buzzed up. Once the owner of the flat confirmed that his 'friends' were expected, the policeman gave them the go-ahead. Up on the top floor, the ITN camera crew unpacked. Within minutes, the camera was up on the tripod and ready to record.

Sitting in the OB vehicle press enclosure, Goldsmith wondered if his ruse had been worth all the effort and expense. With plenty of nothing happening yet again inside the embassy, it didn't look like it. Then he heard the first reports of shots fired inside the building. The efforts of the last few days were about to pay dividends. Big time.

■ ■ ■

Lt-Col Rose, Major Gullan and the other personnel involved in crafting it delivered the fully fledged detailed Deliberate Assault plan just before Whitelaw took the decision to hand control to the SAS. And it didn't involve smashing through the Ethiopian Embassy's walls.

The situation was simple. The mission was to rescue the hostages inside the Iranian embassy.

The assault teams were faced with a 'stronghold option' – the gunmen were holed up inside a fortified building with the hostages. The SAS had to blow their way into that redoubt, overcome the opposition and free all the innocent people without harming them. If they could arrest the gunmen instead of shooting them, so much the better.

The Deliberate Assault plan had five operational phases:

**Phase One** – Deployment: Snipers in position; assault teams and reserve to deploy on command; all personnel to await command initiation.

**Phase Two** – Initiation and Entry: On command initiation, assault groups to enter on stated timings covered by SP team snipers with pre-arranged deception ploys and distractions.

**Phase Three** – Stronghold Assault and Domination: Teams to clear and secure all allocated areas of responsibility, while maintaining their dedicated limits of exploitation.

**Phase Four** – Evacuation: On completion of Phase Three, teams to evacuate the hostages via a secure route to the secure hostage reception area in the embassy's rear garden.

**Phase Five** – Post Assault: Check and secure all hostages. Hold initially as prisoners, check identities for terrorist sleepers and then hand over to Met Police. SP team post-assault procedure and extraction as per SOPs [standard operating procedures].

There had been no official handover from police to military control. But the instant they heard that the gunmen had shot dead Abbas Lavasani and chucked his body out on to the porch, the whole SP team assumed the rescue was a goer. While they awaited the order: Red and Blue teams joined forces. All personnel moved up to their final assault positions. From now on, they would be operating as one unit. By now, every single man was poised to go. They knew both the building and the Deliberate Assault plan upside-down and arse-about-face. They'd rehearsed the outline assault plan until they were dreaming the actions and possible reactions in their sleep.

As each day had passed without a peaceful resolution, they had known SP intervention became ever more likely. With Lavasani's killing, it had become a racing certainty. Everyone was waiting on the order to go. They didn't have to wait long. They were just willing Hurricane Higgins to pot a long green when they heard Major Gullan's voice crackle in their earpieces: 'All stations, this is Sunray: I have control.' It was 1907 hrs.

The men exchanged glances. Responsibility for resolving the siege had passed from civilian to military hands. The rescue was on.

For their part, the six gunmen made ready for battle by pulling their kaffiyehs up and readying their weapons.

■ ■ ■

From the most up-to-date intelligence reports based on optical, audio and Mark One eyeball surveillance, this is how the SAS believed things stood inside the embassy immediately before the assault:

The instant they heard shots fired inside the embassy, Major Gullan and Cpl McVicar raced to the trigger point. 'Sunray' was a sixth-floor room in one of the private flats overlooking the rear of the Iranian Embassy. Its owner had gallantly agreed to loan it to the SAS for government purposes – at no expense to the British taxpayer. From its windows, Gullan could see the whole of the back of the embassy and monitor the rescue as the assault went in. He would trigger the rescue at the optimal moment and help fix any problems as and when they arose. Every single man in the rescue assault units hoped there weren't going to be any snags, but from long experience, they all knew that the most unexpected things could – and often did – go wrong.

Blue Team and Red Team would attack the embassy as one. Individual Blue Team sub-units, generally consisting of two assault team members, were given the call signs Bravo One, Bravo Two and so on. Red Teams were identified as Romeo One, Romeo Two, etc. Outside the embassy on both sides, the individual call signs Juliet One and Two – sniper and back-up units – stood ready to bolster the other assault teams by lending covering fire, taking on targets of opportunity and, if necessary, firing small quantities of gas through available windows with weapons known as 'Polecats'. Call sign Zero Delta's teams at the front and rear of the embassy would create covering smoke, as required, and cut off any gunmen who tried to make a run for it.

The basic plan was for Red Team to clear the top section of the building from the roof downwards, working through the fourth, third and second floors. Blue Team's job was to work upwards, clearing the

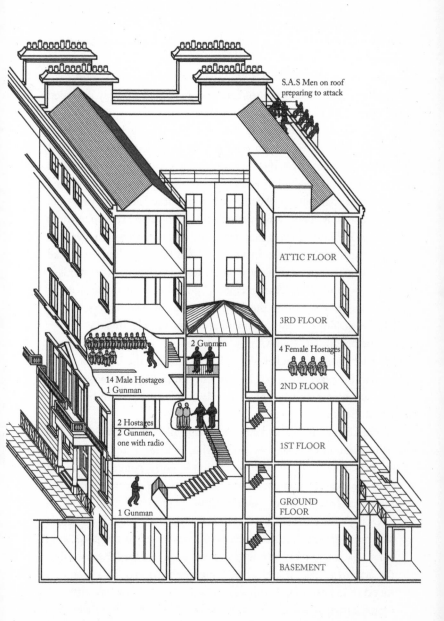

S.A.S Men on roof
preparing to attack

ATTIC FLOOR

3RD FLOOR

4 Female Hostages

2 Gunmen

2ND FLOOR

14 Male Hostages
1 Gunman

2 Hostages
2 Gunmen,
one with radio

1ST FLOOR

GROUND
FLOOR

1 Gunman

BASEMENT

basement, ground and first floors. The two teams would meet in the heart of the embassy.

Each individual sub-unit had strictly defined 'limits of exploitation': pre-planned areas of the embassy they had responsibility for clearing and securing. When they'd cleared their own area of exploitation, each team would then stop, consolidate and move forward only if needed or ordered up in support of another team.

The system minimises the risk of a 'blue on blue' – accidentally shooting one of your own side. It also helps with command and control of the situation. If you'd reached your own limits of exploitation but could see a neighbouring unit in need of help, or if they requested assistance, then, taking all due precautions not to harm your own side, you went for it. There was a natural and safe overlap between teams, a built-in flexibility born of experience and practice. To help individuals distinguish who was who in the confusion of battle, Red Team had small strips of red masking tape on the leading edges of their gas mask canisters, while Blue Team members sported corresponding strips of blue tape. In most cases, they also had strips of coloured tape on the MP5 magazines. They bore no other formal ID markings.

The final orders from General de la Billière and Lt-Col Rose gave the teams a simple and clear mission: 'To rescue the hostages in the Iranian Embassy.' That was it – but how much flexibility was there in that statement? To be on the safe side, the formal operational orders stated the mission twice.

The schematic of the deliberate assault plan on p.159 gives a fair representation of what they were trying to achieve and how. It was important to have simultaneous multiple entry points on different floors to guarantee entry. The more points you attack at once, the more chance you have of gaining entry.

Outside the embassy, the assault units were gathering. Every single man was intently focused; every mind was keyed to the purpose in hand. Each knew his own job, his team's job and, as far as possible, the actions to take if and when things went wrong. This was what they'd trained so long and hard to do. And unless the terrorists had rigged a massive suicide bomb, nothing was going to stop them. The

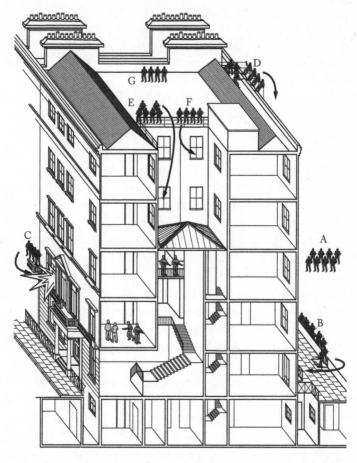

A: Eight-man hostage reception, smoke and reserve team on black [rear].

B: Firmin's ten-man assault team lined up, six men ground floor and four men basement on black. Bravo One, Two and Three.

C: Parry's four-man assault team Bravo Four, first-floor balcony. On white [front].

D: Two four-man assault teams, Romeo Two, ready to abseil to second-floor balcony. On black.

E: Six-man assault team ready to clear third floor.

F: Four-man assault team ready to clear the fourth floor.

G: Four-man roof security, distraction charge placement initiation team ...

Not shown: Six-man SAS sniper group. Two on white and four on black.

heavy ceramic plates inside the Bristol body armour felt as light as air. On the razor's-edge of action, every nerve and synapse felt alive. The same thought was flashing through every man's mind: rescue the hostages. Never lose track of the mission.

The tension built in the men waiting in the Doctors' House, poised to go. To break it, McAleese took the toy frog he'd used to amuse his infant son, Paul, held it up, pulled the string to work its limbs and made appropriate croaking noises. All the men around him started laughing.

Call sign Romeo Two, the two four-man abseil teams tasked to make entry through the embassy's rear second-floor balcony windows braced ready. According to the latest intelligence, the hostages were on that floor. The abseilers were leading the critical point of attack.

A further four-man roof unit had responsibility for the top distraction charge. Ray T, Blue Team 2i/c had built the charge and worked out how to lower it safely down into the light-well. Trooper Frank Collins had responsibility for actually lowering the device; positioning it just above the atrium skylight; and exploding it on cue to launch the rescue. A second pair of men would provide their security. The codeword for 'top charge ready' and 'begin abseil' was 'London Bridge'.

The distraction device was a lump of PE4 plastic explosive weighing about one pound. The amount of explosive used in that confined space was critical. A length of detonation, or 'det' cord ran from a primer which was initiated electrically by a 'clacker' or hand-powered dynamo. Confined in a Mini, a pound of PE is more than enough to blow the car apart. In the unconfined space of the light-well, the purpose of the distraction charge was different. It would make a massive amount of blast and noise and leave the gunmen inside the embassy sat back on their arses. This would give the assault teams crucial initiative and momentum.

Just below the distraction charge unit, on the parapet above the fourth floor, a further eight men of Red Team stood ready with caving ladders and abseil lines in hand. One four-man team would go in through the skylight Snapper had uncovered on Day Four, drop down to the bathroom floor below with the help of the caving ladders and clear the fourth floor. The second would make entry through the third-floor windows looking into the embassy's internal light-well and clear that level. If you liked action – and they did – then these two teams, along with the rear-garden support team, reserve team and hostage reception team had drawn the short straw. These guys were the least likely to see any action.

This was it. At 1914 hrs Major Gullan transmitted the codeword 'Road Accident'. The four-man distraction charge unit and the eight abseilers went forward as one. On their way across the flat section of roof, they bumped into the young policeman on duty. The constable stared. Twelve armed men were advancing towards him in a tight, black crocodile. He had never seen anything like it. With those weird things on their heads, they looked like creatures from the furthest reaches of outer space. There was an air of controlled menace about them, a purpose whose objective he was glad he didn't know. The blood left this face. He keyed the radio. His fingers were shaking so much he could barely work it. And it wasn't just because of the cold evening air. 'Er – are there supposed to be ten men on the roof with sub-machine guns, sir?' The pitch of his voice swooped wildly up and down as he spoke. Four of the men stopped. While the other three kept guard, one put down a small, sinister-looking object with wires sticking out of it on the parapet overlooking the embassy's inner light-well. Then, taking great care, he began to lower the bomb into the void.

Silently, the eight abseilers kept going until they reached the edge of the roof. The first four men lifted the abseil ropes lying there prepared and slipped loops of rope around the figure-of-eight abseil 'descenders' or braking devices attached to their climbing harnesses with Karabiners. Then, when the second four men were attached, the first wave threw the ropes out and down the back of the building.

Trooper Collins thought the policeman looked a little nervous. As the man who was about to cause a massive explosion, he felt it only right to say a word or two about what was presently going to happen – especially since no one seemed to have told the constable on roof duty anything. 'All right?' he asked quietly.

The bobby gulped and nodded.

'There's going to be a fucking big bang in a minute,' Collins said, glancing down at the distraction charge in front of him. 'Might be best if you get well back and take cover.' Keeping a careful eye on Collins, the policeman retreated slowly across the roof, having decided it was probably best to do what the frog-creatures said.

Collins picked up the distraction charge, manoeuvred it carefully over the edge of the parapet and lowered it on the rope until it was resting just above the apex of the glass pyramid below. Then he stood with the clacker in his hands, ready to initiate the explosion on the Go! command.

He looked round. The policeman had disappeared into cover. Everything was ready. All he had to do now was trigger the charge.

Less than one minute later, at 1923 hours, Gullan transmitted: 'Bank Robbery'. On that signal, the first pair in the abseil team turned to face the building, edged backwards out over the edge of the roof and stood ready to go. The second pair of men in the first wave and the four men in the second wave were right behind them, ready to descend and prepared for any option.

Figure-of-eight descenders have several advantages: they create less friction on the rope, and so create less heat; they're good for heavy loads, and the full assault kit adds a further 20–30 lbs to the normal weight of a big, hairy and fully armed SAS man; plus they're reasonably simple to use. But there are downsides, the two main ones being that 'eights' tend to put a twist in the rope you are descending. And if you accidentally put your braking hand too far out to one side, the chances of that happening increase exponentially. Any twisting in the rope severely increases the chances it will lock up and strand you on the rope.

At least one of the abseil ropes was brand new. Fresh from the drum, its long, snaking coils stood out stark white against the dark, blue-grey slates. Clambering over the low parapet, the abseilers turned and made ready to descend. There were three tall windows in a row at the second-floor balcony. In pairs and as close together as they could, the four Romeo call signs were going to drop to the balcony and punch through them at top speed. They wore special gloves, the

Figure-of-eight abseil device, or descender

palms reinforced with reverse calf leather to prevent friction burns. But since those were much too heavy-duty for firing a weapon, the abseilers wore a second pair of thin leather, olive-green Army Air Corps gloves beneath, discarding the first pair when they were down and off the rope.

They shook the long coils free and made sure they fell clear. The first man on each rope leaned outwards and backwards into empty space. Tied fast around the chimney breasts, the standing parts of the ropes they were attached to went bar-taut.

The abseilers started off a few seconds ahead of the other assault units – they needed the extra time to get down to the second-floor balcony and into their final assault position. There had been no change to the running intelligence picture. The gunmen were still holding the hostages on the second floor: the Iranian and non-Iranian men separated on either side of the general office, Room 9, the women in the cipher room, Room 9A, next door. So it was essential that the second-floor team be in position and ready to attack when the distraction charge exploded. They were critical to the rescue assault's success: they had to get to the hostages fast – otherwise, there could be a massacre.

But – and it was a big but – many of the SAS were asking: Why abseil? Why not use ladders, since they were available?

At Sunray, Major Gullan gave the codeword: 'London Bridge'. One to each rope, the first pair of abseilers launched off the rear roof.

Palmer was on the right-hand rope facing the rear of the building; Red Team leader was to his immediate left. As they plummeted down, their ropes buzzed softly through the abseil devices, breaking their fall.

A few seconds after beginning his descent, the leader's rope snagged. Frantically, he tried to free it. The rope refused to budge. He pulled and pushed at the jammed rope with every ounce of his strength, determined to get down to the balcony and get in. He was stuck fast. Stranded just above the second-floor windows. He gave the tangled mess at his waist another furious tug. What was the matter with the fucking thing? Had he held his arm out too far to the side on the descent, putting a twist in the rope and making it spring back up, curl in and jam the device? He didn't think so. He'd only abseiled a hundred times before with the figure-of-eight rig – and probably more. Perhaps they had simply failed to stretch the new rope sufficiently? But then, it was 'static', not 'dynamic' rope – especially designed for abseiling, with minimal built-in propensity to twist. Whatever the reason, the line had tangled itself up in a horrible, immovable mass: the dreaded 'lark's tongue'.

Triple fuck.

Next to his leader on the other rope, Tommy Palmer had his own problems. As he came off the edge of the roof at speed, he swayed involuntarily in towards the embassy. Not very much. Just enough so that a boot went in through the tall vertical window on the far right of the second-floor rear balcony. Even through his gas mask, balaclava and hood, the sharp, penetrating crack of the shattering glass shocked Palmer. He swore softly to himself. He had to assume the sound had alerted the terrorists. There was every possibility he had just compromised the whole operation.

■ ■ ■

In the attic at Zulu Control, the suave and outwardly calm hostage negotiator Max Vernon had a key part to play in the plan to rescue the hostages. His job was to deceive and distract Salim up until the SAS went in – and beyond, if possible. By now, the exhausted negotiators' shifts were down from twelve to eight hours: still too long to be under such sustained stress.

As the first abseilers started down the ropes, Vernon was doing well: he had the terrorist leader on the field telephone. The exchange had been carefully prepared in advance. His job now was to keep the courteous Salim talking for as long as he could, fixing him in time and place as the assault went in. And stop him leading any fight back.

Summoning all his nerve, Vernon kept his voice on the same calm, reassuring and conciliatory keel he'd adopted throughout the siege. On the inside, he was in torment: he had to do it right; keep Salim nibbling at the bait. Vernon kept up the soothing flow of words. From the length of telephone wire that had been paid out, he – and the SAS – knew exactly where Salim was: on the embassy's first floor, close to the main stairs.

Sweat trickled down Vernon's neck. If he blew it – if Salim lost patience, slammed down the phone and took command – the consequences didn't bear thinking about. If the gunman was able to lead an effective defence, then both the hostages and the rescuers would be at much greater risk.

'What sort of coach do you want? How many seats should there be, twenty-seven?'

'Yes,' Salim said and then immediately corrected himself. He didn't want Vernon to be sure how many hostages were left inside the building. 'No: make it for thirty-six.'

'OK, that's fine.'

'Mr Trevor must drive the coach to the airport.'

'Fine. Where do you want it parked?'

'Outside. And I want to search it first.' Without warning, he handed the phone to Lock. They were on the first-floor landing, peering at one another in the gloom. Lock knew what Salim wanted. He sensed also that he should, if he could, help keep the gunmen's leader pinned down. 'Sir, the group are very concerned that you are going to invade. Can you give me any sort of assurance that it's not going to happen?'

Like a fond uncle, Vernon said soothingly: 'Now come on, Trevor.

Let's forget about all that and work out the arrangements to get you all out of there. We have to arrange the coach. Give me back Salim.'

Salim took the line again. Vernon said: 'Are the Iranians happy with your plan to fly them to a Middle Eastern country?'

'Yes, yes, they are all happy about that.'

Vernon pushed his luck a little bit further: 'Can we talk to one of them to make sure?'

As Salim stayed on the line listening to his fairy tales, Vernon's nervousness transformed into a quiet, manic glee. He began to sing a rhyme in his head, like a nursery rhyme, in a made-up little sing-song. But the words of the song in Vernon's head were anything but childlike: 'You're all going to die-i, you're all going to die-i . . .'

Vernon was ready to promise Salim the world and all its riches: coaches to Heathrow; an Arab ambassador as escort; dancing girls; champagne and oysters – whatever Salim wanted, he need only ask. Vernon could promise the skies. The words were meaningless: a skein of lies to keep Salim tied to that critical line.

Then, when it all seemed to be going well, Salim asked Vernon to stop talking. For a cold-blooded killer, Salim was still bizarrely polite. He'd heard something. A distant sound, like breaking glass.

His own nemesis.

Salim said: 'I am listening to some suspicious movements.'

Vernon hurried to assure him otherwise: 'There is no suspicious movement.'

'There is suspicion. OK?'

Vernon tried his utmost to delay him that crucial second longer: 'Salim!'

But already, it was too late. 'Just a minute – I'll come back. I'm going to check.'

Major Gullan was listening in to the conversation. As soon as he overheard Salim say he'd heard something suspicious, Gullan knew the game was up. He'd have to trigger the rescue a few seconds early. Picking up the microphone, he said: 'Go! Go! Go!' It was 1924.

Every single SAS man waiting poised to rescue the hostages heard the command. With one mission fixed in their minds, they launched into action.

■ ■ ■

The other two men in the first-wave abseil unit threw a third rope over the edge of the embassy's rear elevation, zipped down it to the balcony and unclipped. They were looking up as well as in, unable to help the other two men in their call sign but willing them to stop fucking about on the ropes; get down to join them; and make entry.

That wasn't happening.

■ ■ ■

Bravo Four's final assault position was on 'white' at the front, next to the balcony on the first floor of the Doctors' House. The gunmen didn't know it yet, but Bravo Four were the neighbours from hell. When they were crouched ready inside the room, unit commander Trooper Mel Parry called the Desk: 'Sunray, this is Bravo Four: in position.' Gullan acknowledged. Now all he had to do was give the 'Go' command.

While the units waited, they went through their final preparations for the last time: gas respirators tight; flash-bangs at the ready. MP5s made ready, safety catch on, 9mm Browning semi-automatic pistols loaded, ready, and safety catch on. As always, McAleese made sure the masking tape he used to stop the pistol on his thigh falling out in action was in place. The holsters they'd been issued with were rubbish. If he drew the weapon, the little loop of tape would simply break. Until then, it was a much-needed extra safety measure. Most of the other men in the teams used the same trick.

All webbing tight, boots properly done up – it was basic, but they'd all learned the hard way: in a firefight, it's often the smallest things that can catch you out. They made the checks automatically, hands and eyes moving almost of their own accord, thoughts tightly focused on the job in hand. What was the mission? To rescue the hostages.

In his mind's eye, McAleese was placing the frame charge on the window over and over again. He'd rehearsed it dozens of times, but he was still going through the mental drills. The front balcony frame charge was the second opening shot in the short, sharp rescue war the SAS now meant to bring. McAleese had to trigger it as soon as the main distraction charge blew. It was crucial to get it right: make entry through that window at the first attempt. And it had to be exactly on time. The key to any hostage rescue is Speed Aggression Surprise and controlled firepower. The SAS had to seize the initiative from the very first moment – and keep it. The drills had to be slick and quick. Any delay risked disaster.

As McAleese stood ready with the frame charge, he was all too aware that the lives of twenty-odd hostages were at stake. Not to mention the reputation of the British.

Failure was not an option.

Next to McAleese, team leader Mel Parry was going through his own rehearsals: mentally reviewing Bravo Four's limits of exploitation, thinking through each step in the plan and their own role in it; listing the 'actions on' or back-up options if things went wrong. The other two – Lance Corporal Thomas 'Tommo' Macdonald and Trooper 'Deggs' – had inward routines of their own.

McAleese found it hard to believe, but apart from a quick adrenaline stab when the radio squawked in his ears, he wasn't really thinking about the danger that was waiting on the other side of the wall. Like the others, he'd done so much training for it, he'd reached the point where this kind of job was exactly that – a job, like any other, to be carried out as precisely and professionally as possible. The extraordinary was what the SAS did for its bread and butter. Even so, he could feel the door-knocker thump of his heart and the sharp buzz of every nerve. He might be calm, but he was wound tight and waiting to spring.

He picked up the frame charge from its resting place against the wall and checked it over for the umpteenth time. Detonator wires inserted fully, everything taped so it wouldn't fall off. Clacker securely attached and ready. As Bravo Four's demolitions expert, or 'dems man', McAleese had responsibility for placing and exploding the charge. He felt the weight of that responsibility, heavy in his mind.

The charge was a taped and nailed wooden rectangle like a picture frame, about three feet by two, that had been made to fit inside the target window. The frame had CLC – Charge Linear Cutting – taped all around it. CLC was plastic explosive enclosed in triangular section strips. The really clever bit was the small groove cut into the base of the strips. When it detonated, the explosive packed inside the strip took the path of least resistance: its apex blasted downwards and into the hollow space. In basic terms, the CLC was an enormously powerful explosive axe that could slice through a fair thickness of most metals, so armoured glass shouldn't really be a problem. It comes in varying degrees of explosive power per metre and McAleese had opted for the most powerful variant: 'P for Plenty', as the SAS call it.

With so much riding on it, he had also rigged the frame charge for triple initiation. Three sets of twisted brown-and-black initiation wires ran back from three separate detonators placed in the CLC, then came together as one and plugged into the clacker. If that massive sheet of armoured glass didn't atomise, Bravo Four's part in the siege would be over before it began.

The clacker, or electrical trigger, was adapted from a US-made Claymore anti-personnel mine. Frank Collins would be using the same thing. It consisted of twin hinged handles held in place by a U-shaped, spring-loaded safety catch. McAleese eased the clacker's safety catch free of the handles and handed the unit to Macdonald. He looked him in the eye. 'Whatever you do, Tommo,' he said in his Falkirk growl, 'don't squeeze the fucking handles together until Mel and me get back into cover. If you do, there'll be two fucking great big holes in us, not the window. Understood?'

Macdonald grinned: 'All right, man.'

■ ■ ■

Collins was expecting to hear the normal command to trigger the rescue: 'Standby ... Standby ... Go! Go! Go!' Instead, as Gullan saw the predicament of the first abseil pair from his upstairs eyrie, and heard Salim's words to Vernon, he realised that they'd already lost the element of surprise. His brain rapidly computed all the different bits of information he'd got from the teams. Unlike the other units, the rear abseil team had not reported it was in position. It no longer mattered: with Salim on his way to investigate the noise, the rescue would have to start that second. So 'Standby' fell by the wayside. He shouted: 'Go! Go! Go!'

Crouching back down behind the parapet, Collins gave the clacker's handles a firm squeeze. The distraction charge exploded. Twenty feet below, a terrifying wall of sound blasted out. The shock-wave shook the embassy, smashing windows, dazing hostages and gunmen alike. The big atrium skylight dissolved into splinters of wood and glass. The whole building trembled to its granite bones.

■ ■ ■

Already in position on the rear second-floor balcony, Cpl Pat G and Tpr Pete S ignored the two men stuck on the ropes above them: there was nothing they could do to help. The front first-floor window entry charge was their own cue to attack, but as yet they hadn't heard it. As they waited for the second explosion, the seconds seemed to go by in extreme slow motion. If they had to, they'd go in without their leader and Palmer, forming a team of six with the other four abseilers who were whizzing down the third rope and landing on the balcony next to them.

Then, for the second time in less than a minute, a massive explosion rocked the embassy. The front first-floor demolitions man had done his work.

They were in.

Smashing the windows in front of them, Pat G and Pete S posted stun grenades into Room 9. It was known in the trade as 'lighting-up time'. With only point five of a second fuse delay, the stun grenades explode almost as soon as they leave the hand. The magnesium powder inside creates a blinding flash, dazzling any gunmen in the room. But the flash-bangs carried with them the risk of fire.

Today, it was a real risk. The gunmen had piled furniture up against the windows of Room 9, then stuffed sheets of newspaper into the barricade and doused the whole lot in lighter fuel. The sparks and burning magnesium from the grenades ignited the fuel-soaked paper.

It went up now, with a loud whoomph. Fire raced across the barricade and leapt at the curtains. Sprinkled here and there with more of the accelerant, the heavy drapes caught light.

Setting fire to the curtains is one of the quickest ways to burn down a building. The embassy was no exception. Flames began to curl up the thick material. In seconds, the wooden window frames and shutters were on fire. Oxygen rushed in through the smashed glass and fed the blaze. On the second floor of the embassy, where the hostages were waiting, the rescue wasn't going entirely to plan.

■ ■ ■

As soon as he put his foot through the window Palmer braked to a stop. The curtains in front of him were drawn. The room beyond appeared to be in darkness. If a gunman came to investigate, he'd see SAS abseilers sailing down the ropes, all nicely outlined against the evening sky. Sitting ducks.

Palmer didn't even need to think what he should do. Booting the rest of the glass out of the pane, he grabbed a stun grenade, pulled the pin and threw it into the general office. Then he posted another. That ought to keep the X-rays busy long enough for the Romeo Two teams to get down and in.

Palmer looked round. Next to him, his leader was still floundering on the rope. Jesus Christ, he was stuck! He'd put a foot through the window and now this. He leaned over to help. But Red Team's leader was a big man and he was carrying a lot of weight. No matter how hard he and Palmer wrestled with the rope, it point-blank refused to budge. He hauled himself up with both hands, so that his weight – and the pressure – came off the jammed rope. Seeing this, Palmer hauled at the knot with renewed force. It was no use: the line was locked solid in the jaws of the metal device. It was like trying to drag a hook from the mouth of a Great White. Short of a knife, there was no way they were going to free it. Red Team's leader was trapped, with the lower half of his body dangling right in front of the tall second-floor windows.

Then Palmer saw the orange-yellow leap of fire from the window just below them. How had that started? It was probably the stun grenades. Could things get any worse? Already, smoke was beginning to pour through the shattered pane. A few seconds later, Palmer felt a searing wave of heat. Long fingers of flames followed the smoke. Another pane of glass popped, and in seconds the heat and flames were all around them. He gripped the rope trapped in the jaws of the stuck descender and pulled with every ounce of strength he possessed. Unless they got out of that blossoming inferno, both of them would be roasted alive.

Together they kept working at the jammed rope. It was no use: nothing would budge the knot. Palmer saw flames licking hungrily at his leader's lower legs. He felt the sharp sting of heat around his own feet. There was no point keeping on at the jammed rope. There was less than no point both of them burning alive. Dropping the remaining distance down to the balcony, Palmer pulled up the bottom of his face mask and drew deep, long breaths of cool air.

He looked back up. His leader was still twisting helplessly above him, still roasting: a human kebab on a rope spit. He kept kicking himself away from the flames, but every time he swung back in towards the window, they claimed him anew. The next two abseilers were poised to descend. This was supposed to be a silent mission, dammit. Still, there was nothing for it. 'Cut him down!' Palmer shouted. 'Cut him down before it's too late!'

Palmer was about to shout again when one of the roof men did just that: brought a knife up and sliced through the rope. The staff sergeant fell through space and crashed to the balcony. Palmer looked down at him, expecting the worst. His leader's lower legs had been badly roasted: Palmer could actually smell the burnt flesh. And now, on top of that, he'd just fallen a good twelve feet, weighed down by body armour, weapons and kit.

'You all right, mate?'

Red Team leader shook his head like a bear trying to ward off a swarm of bees, then climbed to his feet. He was furious about the fuck-up on the rope, but all he said was: 'Let's get in.' Palmer was in full agreement with that. The clock was ticking: already, more than thirty seconds had passed since the front entry charge had exploded. The whole plan depended on a coordinated attack. They were late. Best get motoring.

Palmer and the other three drove through the smashed general office windows as one. There were no gunmen – and no hostages. Two doors stood directly ahead of them on the far wall. The one on the right led into Room 9A, the small cipher room where they believed the four remaining female hostages were being held. Pat G and Pete S went right.

Pete S turned the doorknob and yanked it back. The door was locked. He lifted the nose of the MP5, pointed it at the lock and opened fire. The lock disintegrated. Booting the door open, he looked inside. No gunmen. But the four female hostages were in there, huddled together in a heap on the floor. Terrified by the sound of explosions and gunfire, two of them were screaming. One had her hands on her ears, as if she could stop it all happening if she just kept the sound out. When they saw the black-dressed frog-creatures bristling with weapons standing in the doorway, the two who'd been screaming yelled all the louder. The other two female captives were shaking and pale with fear, but otherwise composed and quiet. They instinctively understood that these guys were their rescuers.

Room 9's left-hand door led out on to the landing and stairwell. Palmer and Red Team leader were already trying to get through it. But, anticipating just such an attack route, the gunmen had locked that door as well. Raising his MP5, Palmer put a burst into the lock. It shattered, taking a large section of the solid oak panelling with it. The skin of his partner's lower legs was horribly blistered. Despite the searing, second-degree burns to his calves, Red Team leader raised a foot and booted the door. It budged a tiny bit, but then held fast. Using tables and chairs they'd dragged in from the adjoining rooms, the hostage-takers had piled another barricade on the other side. As the remaining abseilers joined them, they each took it in turns to kick, shoulder-charge and blast the door, desperate to get out on to the landing, reach the telex room and rescue the male hostages. If they were still in there.

The barricade was holding fast: they couldn't smash through it. Palmer realised he had to do something – and do it now. They were taking too much time. Time they didn't have. He remembered there was a third window leading off the rear balcony. It gave into the neighbouring room, another of the embassy's rear offices, Room 8. Suppose the door to that office wasn't locked and barricaded? Suppose he climbed back out on to the balcony and tried that route? There was just one tiny problem: the fire.

Behind him, the two windows to Room 9 were now well and truly ablaze. The paint on the wooden frames, the curtains and the barricades were burning fiercely. Gritting his teeth, Palmer chose the lesser of the two bonfires. He started to climb through. It was like stooping into the mouth of a furnace. Unable to grasp anything to help him for fear of burning his hands, he slipped and staggered in the blazing mass. A great ball of flame seized him, like a predator waiting for prey. 'Whatever happened to the 1974 Safety at Work Act?' he wondered.

He felt a sharp, searing pain. Apart from the black coveralls, which were standard British Army issue, almost everything he wore – from his lightweight Northern Ireland boots to his black respirator – was made of rubber. Rubber burns. This lot was no exception. The tank coveralls were flammable into the bargain, and under them Palmer simply wore a pair of jeans and a T shirt. There was no fire-resistant underwear available in 1980s Britain, even for the Special Forces. The heat was steaming up through the soles of his feet, and the hot stink of burning rubber was searing his lungs. Gathering himself, he half jumped, half threw himself out through the flames.

Out on the balcony, he ripped off the respirator and snatched the smouldering NBC hood back off his head. His hair felt as if it was still on fire and his neck was badly scorched. Palmer slapped at his head and shoulders, trying to put out the flames. Bits of his scalp were crisp to the touch and his head felt as if it had been par-boiled. He was carrying magnesium-filled grenades in leather canisters on his belt, along with five extra fully charged 9mm ammo. A few seconds longer and he'd have been a human firework.

The same mission kept repeating in his mind: 'rescue the hostages.' There was no time to lose. Stepping left, he took a quick glance in through the left-hand window. There was a figure crouched on the floor at the back of Room 8. Fuck! It was one of them.

■ ■ ■

Bravo Four were at their final assault positions. McAleese was standing just inside the window in the Doctors' House, holding the frame charge. Tommo Macdonald was right beside him holding the clacker. The wires stretched between them like some weird, multicoloured umbilical cord. They stood there, waiting for what felt like forever, with the explosive device held in front of them, as the seconds dragged by. Every second stretched a small age. Then at last, they heard Major Gullan's terse voice: 'London Bridge.'

The top distraction charge was ready. Then, with a slight added edge of urgency, the same voice gave the command: 'Go! Go! Go!'

There was a deafening explosion. The distraction charge blew in the atrium skylight, showering glass, dust and wood splinters down into the embassy's heart. Most of the debris ended up on the lower sets of stairs and in the embassy's hall. The whole building shook as the shock-wave slammed through it. A thunderous, resonating echo filled the air, followed by a moment of complete silence. The concussion blast had done its job: frightening the life out of everyone inside, but leaving the main structure of the building intact. Screams and shrieks rang out, and the police dogs in the Doctors' House started to bark and howl.

The explosion was meant to get Salim's attention and put the fear of God into him and his crew. Hopefully, some or all of the gunmen would run to the core of the building to find out what had happened – while the rescue teams smashed into the building from the sides.

The ruse succeeded on every count.

Already, Parry and McAleese were out and on to the RCGP's front balcony. Parry went first, MP5 at the ready to engage any gunmen who showed at the windows. McAleese was right behind him with the frame charge. He lifted it carefully over on to the embassy's first-floor balcony and propped it there for a moment. Running on pure adrenaline, he vaulted the stone balustrade, landed, whipped round and grabbed the charge again. He had to move at top speed – but at the same time, not knock or disturb the CLC. He'd helped make the device, so he knew just how flimsy it was. Parry was already at the embassy window, scoping the room they were about to hit.

McAleese stepped up to the embassy window and went to place the frame. He stopped dead. There was a face on the other side of the glass. The man was pressed close up to the panes, staring back at him. McAleese recognised him from a photograph on the briefing boards, but under the pressure of the moment he couldn't put a name to the face. In a flash, it came to him: Sim Harris, the BBC sound man. Harris looked like he'd just seen a Martian. A large section of the building had just blown in behind him, leaving him partially deaf. Now, two strange men dressed from head to toe in black, armed with machine guns and wearing weird masks were standing outside on the first-floor balcony. How had they got there?

One of the men kept making downward movements with a flat hand. He seemed to be ordering him to drop down and stay low. The other one was carrying something. At first glance, it seemed to Harris it was a window frame. But then, why would he be doing that? Harris watched them, goggle-eyed. The man holding the strange object was shouting something, the words muffled by the menacing rubber mask obscuring his face.

'Get back! Get away from the window! Get down!' The human eyes behind the weird, insect-eyes of the respirator glared back at him. Watching Harris, Parry thought: 'That's nothing. You should see Mac after a beer or ten.' Again, the insect person shouted at him through the mask: he sounded to Harris like a Glaswegian drunk with his head in a barrel of cotton wool. 'Get down!' For another long second or two, Harris just stared.

McAleese despaired. 'There's nothing else I can do,' he told himself. 'There's another nineteen hostages to rescue. So if that fucker doesn't take cover, too bad.'

Then Parry motioned and shouted at Harris to get down. This time the sound man got the message. He dropped to the left of the window and lay flat. They didn't look like the kind of men it was wise to argue with.

McAleese had a separate length of one and a half by three-quarter-inch wood with him. When he was happy the frame charge was correctly positioned, flush up against the glass, he jammed it in place with the strut. As he did so, he heard the whiplash *crack!* of a bullet passing close by. A puff of dust flew up at his feet. 'Fuck,' he thought, 'some bastard's shooting at me.' Then he realised: it must have been one of the watching snipers, firing at him by mistake when they'd seen him appear. Either that, or more likely still, someone had squeezed off a random shot in error. Just what he didn't need: death by negligent discharge.

After checking one last time to make sure the frame charge would stay put, McAleese spun round, put one foot up on the balcony rail and leapt back across to the Doctors' House. Parry had already taken cover. Even before he'd tucked in tight to the wall, McAleese was shouting at Macdonald: 'Fire! Fire!'

Tommo squeezed the clacker's handles. A weak electric current fizzed from the dynamo. Weak, but fast enough to travel instantaneously down the wires. And ignite the detonators.

A second deafening explosion shook the building. A billowing cloud of smoke covered the front. It rendered the snipers, poised to pick off any terrorists who appeared at the windows, completely useless.

A shock-wave of blast and heat thumped into McAleese. The blast-wave rushed past, pushing him into the wall and scouring the embassy's façade. In another moment, it was gone. McAleese whirled and leapt back on to the embassy balcony with Parry, Deggs and Macdonald. There was a huge, gaping hole where the window had been. It was smouldering at the edges, threatening to set fire to what was left of the curtains. A large chunk of the balcony was missing, and big lumps of masonry lay all around. McAleese took in the damage. It might be he'd overdone it just a bit with the CLC.

'Christ,' he thought, 'I've blown half the bloody embassy out.' But he also felt as if a huge weight had been lifted from his shoulders. There was now a fucking great hole in the front of the building – and sections of the balcony had fallen right off and crunched to the pavement below. No matter. It had worked. They had done it. They were in.

McAleese heard a heavy, metallic clunk. He looked down. A small egg-shaped object had just landed at his feet. 'Fuck!' he thought. 'First they take a pot-shot at me, and now it's raining grenades.' The metal egg sat looking at him. 'That's it,' he thought grimly. 'I'm done.' Then, as time slowed down to nothing, he saw the only thing you want to see when there's a grenade lying next to your size 10s. The pin was still in place. The gunman had forgotten to pull it.

Bravo Four team were now grouped on the first-floor balcony. Grabbing stun grenades from their belt kit, Parry and McAleese pulled the pins and lobbed them in through the smoking breach. The flash-bangs turned the Chargé d'Affaires' room beyond into a blinding, deafening cage. Ferret-quick, Parry was in through the gaping hole. McAleese was right on his heels. Macdonald and Deggs were up on their shoulders. Each man was responsible for his own room arc.

McAleese moved forward along the left-hand wall in the gloom, eyes sweeping ahead and right towards the opposite wall. A single door ahead opened out on to the landing. Parry cleared the inside right-hand corner, then moved forward down the right-hand wall, looking ahead and to his left. In that way they made sure the room was clear and they hadn't missed anything. Or anyone. As they advanced, Deggs covered them; Macdonald made sure no one jumped the team from behind. McAleese reached the door, turned his head and shouted 'Room clear!'

He looked round at the front, right-hand corner of the room. There was a body lying under a pile of plaster, glass and brick over there – he could tell by a pair of feet sticking out of the mound. It had to be that bloke he'd seen, the BBC sound man, Harris. 'Great start,' he thought. 'One hostage dead already. And I killed him.' Just then, the pile of rubble shifted. A cloud of dust billowed up in the air, mingling with the haze and smoke that was already making it difficult to see in the room. A head emerged from the mound, followed by the upper part of a man's body. Harris's hair was pale with dust and plaster and his glasses were cracked and wildly askew. His eyes were saucer wide and there was a mad, staring expression on his face. But he was alive. 'Christ,' McAleese thought, 'he survived the blast! Thank fuck for that.'

Parry went over and picked Harris up with one hand: 'Stay there and don't move. Someone will come and get you.' However much he now resembled a pile of human masonry, Harris must have been feeling reasonably perky: as Macdonald ghosted past him, the BBC man looked up and called: 'Go on, lads – get in there! Get the bastards!'

'Don't worry,' McAleese thought. 'We will.'

■ ■ ■

Outside the front of the embassy, two members of the SAS sniper team, L/Cpl N Kelly and L/Cpl J Thompson (who had been attached to B Squadron for the duration of the operation from A Squadron at little notice) stood up and took aim over the wall they'd been using as cover. They were about twenty or thirty metres away from the first-floor balcony. Dressed in jeans and casual clothes, only the balaclavas they wore marked them out as members of the SAS. Both were armed with Polecat grenade launchers and 9mm Brownings. The Polecat looks like a flare pistol, only it's longer and its barrel is wider in diameter. The weapons are fired from the shoulder, greatly enhancing their accuracy.

Taking careful aim, the sniper pair fired CS canisters in through the hole where the window had been. The canisters flew plumb through the gap, hurtled to the back of the Chargé d'Affaires' room and split open. A noxious, swirling fog of gas billowed out into the room and on to the landing. The idea was to disorient and slow down the terrorists. If the hostages suffered temporary discomfort in the process, that was too bad.

■ ■ ■

Call signs Bravo One, Two and Three had to make explosive entry into the embassy library via the rear French windows; clear and secure the embassy's ground floor, then continue clearing up the stairs to the first floor and hold at their limit of exploitation.

Once the whole building was cleared and the terrorists arrested, they'd help get the hostages down and out along the stairs to safety. Simple! Rusty Firmin had command of the six-man team. Snapper and the other two men under the command of Tak Takavesi in Bravo Five waited in line behind Firmin's team. They hunched forward over their weapons.

'Road Accident,' said Gullan's voice in their earpieces. As one, the ten men in the two teams came out of the Doctors' House and walked calmly round to their form-up point, facing the back of the embassy behind a low white wall.

As he came out into the back garden of No. 14, Firmin glanced round. He knew there were snipers everywhere on the flats overlooking the back of the embassy, but they were invisible. There wasn't a single rifle barrel to be seen: the marksmen were all in perfect cover, a fact that Firmin found somehow reassuring.

He looked down and realised his hands were bare: like everyone else, he'd been watching the snooker right up until the call to action. Normally, he'd have shoved his gloves down inside his body armour. He must have placed them on the table in front of him, and never picked them up when they all stood to. 'Christ,' he thought, 'I'm the only guy with no gloves on. Too late to worry about that now: I can't go back.'

The ten men got down behind a low wall about ten metres from the rear of the embassy. Firmin was trying to keep up his all-round visual checks, but the respirator kept steaming up on the inside. 'Bugger always does that at the wrong time,' he thought to himself. He was taking deep, controlled breaths inside the respirator, waiting, waiting, mentally rehearsing the mission: 'Make entry. Rescue the hostages. There are always "what ifs". But stay focused, keep the job at the front of your mind.'

A few seconds after they arrived at their final assault position, they heard the next code in the sequence: 'London Bridge' – the signal for the roof team to make the top distraction charge ready. It might only be seconds, but to the waiting men, the intervals between commands seemed to last an eternity. The next codeword, 'Bank Robbery', came over the airwaves. Then, almost immediately, and sooner than they'd all been expecting, Gullan's executive order: 'Go! Go! Go!'

A massive explosion rocked the building. As the others covered him, Steve U, Bravo Three's demolitions man ran forward across the short, intervening stretch of flagstone patio with the designated CLC charge.

Firmin looked up. A man was hanging horizontally from one of the abseil ropes – one of their own. Firmin couldn't be sure who it was, but it looked as if the abseiler was in trouble: he was wriggling furiously, kicking out against the stonework with his legs, obviously stuck and trying to free himself. A second man was alongside and just above the first, not caught up in the rope but apparently trying to help the first. 'Shit,' Firmin thought, 'we ain't even started yet, and already there's a problem.' After the head shed's initial Deliberate Action briefing, most of the team had thought that if anything was going to go wrong, then it might just involve the abseiling.

Sure enough.

At a glance, Firmin realised they couldn't use the frame charge to blow through the French windows now. If they did, the blast would very likely kill the men caught on the ropes directly above. Decision time.

Racing forward, he shouted: 'Steve! Pull the dets! Pull the charge!'

Steve U, having realised the danger for himself, was already pulling the detonators out of the frame charge and discarding them. Firmin joined him, yanking the remaining detonator out of the plastic explosive and rendering the device safe. Even as he was doing it, Firmin realised the decision might have serious consequences for him. A man's life was in danger if he blew the frame charge, but the assault couldn't be allowed to fail. In pulling it, he'd made the first major decision of the day. How costly would it be? Would the head shed back him up at the end of the operation?

Firmin asked the man next to him, Bob C, to take out the Equaliser he was carrying as a back-up. The Equaliser was a six-pound sledge hammer with a short wooden shaft. Firmin studied the back of the building with a fresh eye: the French windows looked sturdy; they might resist efforts to break through them manually for longer than the teams could afford to delay. But the small sash window to the right of the doors looked to be an easy and inviting entry point – leading directly into the library on the ground floor. Perfect.

By now, the rest of the team was already at his shoulder. 'Bob,' Firmin said, pointing with a bare index finger: 'make entry through that window with the sledge.' Bob C swung the business end of the hammer up high behind his head and sent it smashing through the window. He looked like Thor, god of thunder, having a bad day. There was an almighty crash as the head of the sledge hammer punched clean through the window. Splinters of glass and wood flew to all sides. If the six gunmen inside the embassy didn't know the SAS were on their case now, they never would.

Reaching in through the shattered glass, Bob C gave the rotating window catch a sharp twist. Then, grabbing the bottom of the sash, he shoved it up as far as it would go, posted a flash-bang into the room and climbed through. The stun grenade exploded in a blinding flash of light and sound. Clambering over the sill, he was acutely aware that he made a perfect target silhouetted against the daylight beyond. He had to hope the flash-bang worked as advertised.

Not exactly built like a runner, Bob C was straight in. Two seconds later, Firmin was in through the gap behind him, followed by the remaining eight men.

On the way in, he took a quick look back behind him: one of the reserves Trooper Robin H had moved up to stand by the low white wall with the rest of the reserve team. Firmin nodded to himself. Armed with one of only two silenced MP5-SDs the SAS used on the day, Trooper Robin H was in a good position outside the embassy to see and report everything to the abseilers in trouble on the second floor.

First part done. Call signs Bravo One, Bravo Two, Bravo Three, Bravo Five, Juliet One and Juliet Two were complete in the library. Looking down, Firmin saw blood on the palm of his left hand: he'd cut it making entry through the broken window. That would teach him to remember the gloves.

As he moved forward round the edges of the room, clearing it for hostiles and hostages, Firmin looked up. The library was in near darkness. There was a broad stretch of glass across the top of the far wall above a large bookcase. It looked like an inner window, positioned there to allow light in from the front hall. A table stood in front of it. Firmin thought, 'I'll jump up and take a look through it, see what's what in the hall.' He got an almighty shock. A figure dressed in black with a sub-machine gun was watching him. The shape looked menacing, unearthly. Firmin stared back. Then he realised: it was his own reflection. It wasn't an internal window: he was looking into a mirror. Certain that no one could have been ahead of him, he hadn't opened fire. Just as well. Turning, he jumped back down. He'd wasted enough time fannying about. Time to get on with the job.

No gunmen seen. No hostages. Shouting, 'Room Clear!' Firmin led the three two-man teams out into the hall. The Blue Team assaulters cleared the small rooms on the ground floor in double-quick time. Like clockwork, two of his men ran up the stairs and stopped at the landing, clearing visually to left and right. The stair head where it met the embassy's first-floor landing was the limit of exploitation for these call signs. The remaining six men in his team spread out with two men at the top, Firmin himself in the middle on the half-landing, and two more at the bottom in the hallway area.

They were now able to control all movement in and out of the heart of the building.

From his vantage point on the half-landing, Firmin commanded the whole of the hall and the embassy's front entrance; the library and basement doors; the stairs to the first floor and a large section of the first-floor landing. He would also be able to assist with command and control of the hostage evacuation, when – and if – it began.

There was shooting and screaming from the rooms above them, the rattle of sub-machine gun fire and the echoing blast of the stun grenades. The rest of the boys were busy. But for the moment, all the Bravo call signs on the stairs could do was watch and wait. Firmin got through to McVicar on the radio, but the signal was terrible, intermittent and crackling; there was no way of telling Sunray they'd cleared the basement and ground floor. Talk about frustrating!

■ ■ ■

Lined up behind Rusty Firmin's group was the basement team: Bravo Five. Snapper was at the front, while Takavesi – Juliet One – had command of Bravo Five at the rear. L/Cpl Davies, Juliet Two, and L/Cpl Rob T were in the middle. As they crouched behind the low white-painted wall at the rear of the embassy patio, waiting for the signal to attack, Snapper found himself repeating Paddy Mayne's dictum in his head: 'When you enter a room full of armed men, shoot the first person who makes a move, hostile or otherwise. He has started to think. Therefore he's dangerous.' On one level, the former SAS leader's words counted as good advice. But in this case, they were supposed to be rescuing the hostages, not shooting them.

A voice shouting: 'Go! Go! Go! Get in at the rear!' crackled in Snapper's earpiece. They were all up and running. It struck Snapper that he was at the front of the four-man team. 'Why me,' he thought wryly, 'when there are all these younger guys around? I've done my time – earned my place at the back with Tak.' Too late. There was a sharp, muted burst of machine-gun fire from somewhere inside the embassy. A woman screamed, a long, piercing shriek.

As he moved towards the library window, Snapper glimpsed an odd, swirling movement from overhead. He looked up. One of the abseil team was in trouble. The man was almost upside-down, kicking himself from side to side of a second-floor window, trying desperately to get free. Was that Red Team's leader? It looked like it, the distinctive size and shape of him, his leading position on the rope. That wasn't good. The second-floor team was crucial to the rescue's success.

There was a pulverising crash. Snapper looked back down. Bob C had smashed open the small right-hand window with the Equaliser. Firmin and his team were in and working, already clearing the library. Seconds later, Snapper and Bravo Five were in the embassy.

Snapper came out into the main hall. No gunmen. The cellar door was ahead and to the right of him. The gunmen had shoved a couple of step-ladders across the top of the stairs as a makeshift barricade. Snapper ran across and gave the barrier a quick once-over for booby-traps. He couldn't see any. And there wasn't time to do a thorough check. He'd just have to take the risk. Grabbing the first ladder, he wrenched it out of the barricade and threw it to one side. The other set of steps went the same way.

The way to the basement was now clear. Snapper tried the handle. The door was unlocked. Pushing it open, he pulled the pin on a flash-bang and chucked it down the stairs. The grenade bounced and exploded at the bottom. Gun-torches blazing, they went down after it – fast. Takavesi was still at the rear, covering the team's six o'clock. They hit the basement running. Snapper saw a dimly lit corridor ahead of them with doors leading off it to either side. They split into pairs and took one side each. They had no sledge hammers; no Remington shotguns; and no hooligan bars. There was only one thing for it: shoot the locks out with the MP5s and nine-millys. Snapper blasted a three-round burst from the MP5 into the first lock and booted the door with his right foot. As it flew back he chucked in a stun grenade, then hit the room. L/Cpl Davies went right, he went left. It was empty. 'Room clear!' shouted Snapper.

A voice to his left shouted almost at the same time: 'Room clear!' Takavesi and partner, confirming that the room they'd just swept was free of threat. The four men blasted through the basement fast and slick, clearing the rooms in series and doing it way faster than they'd ever managed in training. There were no terrorists in the cellars. Turning about face, the four assaulters ran back up to the ground floor.

They'd been in the cellars for less than five minutes, but as they came back out into the main hall, they saw that in the time they'd been down there, fire had started to take hold of the embassy. There was smoke everywhere. The sharp, acrid smell of it seeped through their gas masks.

They heard the rip of more gunfire from overhead, followed by a torrent of screams and shouts. With their own primary task now complete, Bravo Five, Juliet One and Juliet Two moved across and spread out with Firmin and the remaining Bravo call signs on the stairs and landing.

Ten men were now in position to control the hostage evacuation from the first floor, straight down the stairs and out through the back rooms where they had gained entry. The six-man reserve team, the eight-man reception team and the smoke team were all still outside at the back of the embassy, waiting to assist. The smoke team had a quiet day: Margaret Thatcher had decided that she wanted the world to see what the SAS could do.

All they needed now were the hostages.

■ ■ ■

There was a massive explosion from the embassy core. Glass rained down around them and the lights went out. When Salim dropped the field telephone and ran for the stairs, Lock knew he had to stop him. Lowering his right shoulder, he charged at the terrorist leader. The two men crashed back through the door into the Chargé d'Affaires' office. On the way in, Salim banged his right elbow hard against the jamb. A sharp, numbing pain shot through his arm. The Skorpion machine-pistol flew out of his hand, hit the floor and skittered away. As Salim moved to grab it, Lock hurled himself forward. The two men thudded to the floor, punching and kicking. Salim rolled, broke free, and scrabbled towards the machine-pistol. Lock caught hold of him, got an arm around his throat and hauled his head back. The terrorist leader kicked and bucked, but Lock held fast. 'You caused this,' he shouted. 'I gave you a fucking chance but you wouldn't take it, you bastard!'

'It wasn't me! It was the others!' Salim croaked.

Lock drew the police-issue five-shot .38 revolver from his waist holster. It was about time the weapon saw the light of day. So long as he'd been faced with six terrorists, the five-shot weapon had been about as much use as an ashtray on a motorbike. But if he was only going to have to deal with one . . .

Shoving the revolver's muzzle hard into Salim's right ear, he leaned forward: 'You're the leader! They'd have done what you fucking well told them!'

'Don't hurt me! Don't hurt me!' Salim pleaded. After six days of posturing, his abject terror now was pathetic.

. . .

Parry and McAleese stopped on either side of the office doorway. Macdonald and Deggs moved through them, wheeled sharp right and out on to the landing. They broke right here again, turning back towards the front of the building to clear the next room along on the right: the office of the Chargé d'Affaires' secretary. Parry and McAleese broke left to clear the room on the left: a small store room. They'd been told the wall adjoining the landing was a thin partition. As one they shoulder-charged it. The wall was solid brick. McAleese and Parry bounced off. It seemed wiser to use the door. Inside, it was dark. They had eyes everywhere, alert for the slightest hostile movement in the haze. Stacked with chairs and tables, it was some kind of lumber room where the embassy stored its unwanted furniture. It was empty. 'Room clear!' McAleese shouted.

He was still right up on Parry's shoulder. They reached the door to the ambassador's office. McAleese booted it open. Parry threw in a stun grenade. They both went in after it. There were shrieks and shouts from close by, and the sharp, staccato blasts of an MP5 firing short bursts. 'Tommo and Deggsy,' McAleese thought, 'doing the business.' His gaze probed the gloom. There was no sign of any hostages or gunmen. When they'd made certain the room was empty of everything except furniture, McAleese shouted, 'Room clear!' again. A quick shadow moved in the darkness behind them. They whipped round, trying to see what – or who – it was. A figure raced across the landing. Deggs turned and fired a snap burst from the hip with the MP5. The gunman paused for an instant, but then ran on. Reaching the door to the ambassador's room, the other large office across at the rear of the building, he pulled it open and vanished inside.

. . .

Lock looked down at the terrorist leader. Now it came to it, he couldn't bring himself to pull the trigger. He hadn't been trained to kill – it wasn't what he did. Besides, he'd be killing an unarmed human being who was begging for his life. That was the kind of thing terrorists did – not a uniformed policeman upholding the rule of law.

Lock moved the pistol up into the hollow beneath Salim's jaw. All he needed to do now was keep a grip of Salim, keep the gun to his head and control him until the SAS arrived. As if on cue, the office door crashed open. Two black-clad figures were in the room, the muzzles of their weapons describing neat, controlled arcs as they searched for targets.

Something moved in Lock's field of vision. He glanced down: two egg-shaped objects were rolling across the floor beside his right hip, their metal surfaces glinting a dull brassy yellow in the gathering gloom. 'Lemons,' Lock thought. 'That's strange.' The stun grenades exploded. The world evaporated in light and noise. The blast lifted Lock clear off Salim's back. The gunman crawled away.

Deafened and half-blind, Lock shook his head. His eyes were streaming and there was a roaring noise inside his head. He was gasping for breath: all the air seemed to have gone out of the room. Something terrible was attacking his eyes, nose and throat: gas. Through a blur, he saw Salim. For the second time, the terrorist was trying to get to the fallen gun. The Skorpion was a hand's-breadth from Salim's grasp. Jumping to his feet, Lock launched himself at the crawling man. They crunched into a flailing mass. As they grappled, one of the SAS men shouted: 'Trevor! Move over!' Lock broke free and rolled clear.

Salim was on top of the Skorpion. As his fingers closed around the weapon, Macdonald opened up. Gunfire ripped the room. A hail of bullets smashed into Salim. His back arched and then he lay still. Lock looked across at him. A neat seam of bullets crossed the gunman's body, starting at his left eye and running diagonally across his chest to the groin. There was no sign of blood. But Salim wasn't going to be storming any more embassies.

Macdonald and Deggs turned away from the dead man. Tommo shouted: 'Trevor! Are you all right?' Lock shook his head. Still numbed with shock and with his head ringing, he tried to show the men he was struggling for breath. Deggs said: 'Make for the window. Get some air!' Pulling clear the desk that had been shoved up against it as a barricade, Deggs and Macdonald helped Lock across to the window. He leaned out, sucking in great gulps of fresh air. Automatically, he'd picked up his uniform hat and put it on. He doffed the cap now with his left hand, as if he were making a bow to the world's press. In fact, he was wiping sweat from his forehead. The revolver was still in his right hand. Someone outside the embassy shouted: 'Trevor, get down!'

The men who had helped him pulled Lock back into the room. 'There are six terrorists,' he told them. 'Six of them.' They nodded. One of them walked to the door, leaned a bit and shouted: 'Room clear! PC confirms: six terrorists.'

Deggs and Macdonald hustled Lock to the head of the stairs. The first SAS call sign there grabbed hold of the policeman and threw him on to the next. Lock flew down the chain of men like a giant puppet. A few seconds later, he was safe on the embassy's rear lawn.

■ ■ ■

Blowing the window and clearing the Chargé d'Affaires' office, the first-floor landing and the small store room to the left had taken McAleese and Parry less than three minutes. They regrouped on the landing outside the office. There was more screaming, the sound of it almost continuous now. It seemed to be coming from the floor above them, in a room at the rear of the embassy. McAleese got down on one knee and leaned forward, peering through the smoke, dust and gas. It was extremely difficult to see anything. It was fucking outrageous that only about one in two men had torches fitted to their MP5s. Despite SAS supply supremo Fat-Wallet's repeated requests to the MoD for more, there still weren't enough of them to go round. With dust, smoke and gas thickening in the gloom around them, he needed one now. Badly.

The problem was getting worse. A noxious, swirling cloud of CS gas was now condensing in the confined space. McAleese was staring through a grey fog, barely able to see a gloved hand in front of his face. Bounching off the wall, he'd knocked his respirator slightly askew, breaking the seal with his skin. Unaware of the problem until now, he drew in a deep breath.

A rush of CS gas flooded his airways. The active ingredient of CS gas is O-chlorobenzylidene malonontrite, a lachrymator or tear-producing agent that causes severe irritation to the skin and the upper respiratory tract, as well as coughing, sneezing and disorientation. As McAleese now found, it worked just as well on SAS men as it did on anyone else. His eyes began to stream and his nose started running; the soft tissues of his throat and mouth swelled up and his tongue seemed to have doubled in size. It felt as if there were thick wooden sticks up his nose. His eyeballs were on fire.

A dizzying wave of sickness hit him and he began to choke. But all the time spent doing realistic training in a gas-filled environment was paying off; he'd endured this feeling lots of times before and it wasn't about to stop him completing his mission now. Stepping swiftly backwards out towards the stairwell and away from the gas, he dropped to one knee, ripped the respirator free with his left hand and retched. Despite being partly disabled, he was still watching and listening through his 360-degree arcs. He kept the MP5 up and ready to fire. Whatever the problem with his gas mask, he had no intention of getting shot. Or missing a chance to shoot one of the hostiles. He still had a job to do and he didn't want to fail.

The air by the stairwell was much clearer. McAleese gasped it down and quickly began to feel better. Although its immediate effects can be devastating, CS gas is short-acting. After cleaning the runny mess from his respirator, McAleese strapped it firmly back into place on his head. An anxious voice crackled to life in his earpiece: One of the command team: 'What's happening, what's happening?'

No one responded. With hostages still unaccounted for and gunmen still at large, there was no time. McAleese was watching along the corridor towards the stairwell. Parry went forward into the Ambassador's office alone. Something was wrong, McAleese could feel it, without knowing what it was. His head was going from side to side, eyes everywhere. Their work done, Deggs and Macdonald came back out of the Chargé d'Affaires' room to link up again.

There were so many armchair warriors making so much noise on the comms net now that the SAS teams inside the embassy could no longer use their radios. Radio reception was poor and patchy enough, without the head shed making all this extra racket. Raising his gas mask again, this time to make himself heard, McAleese shouted, 'What the fuck was that?'

'One of the X-rays,' Deggs said. 'I think I got him.' He nodded at the door across the landing. 'He ran into that room.'

There was a moment of complete silence. In that second, the four SAS men heard a deep groan from inside the ambassador's office. Most likely scenario: Deggs had hit him. But the fucker was still alive.

Parry was back outside on the landing. He raised his own mask and shouted across to the neighbouring SAS team, stopped at its limits of exploitation on the other side of the stairs. 'Anybody got a torch on their weapon? We need someone with a torch here!' One of the reserve team was at the head of the stairs, had a torch on his gun. He ran across to join them.

Parry, McAleese and Macdonald formed up behind him. With Deggs watching the rear arcs, the hybrid team moved across to the ambassador's door. Grabbing a stun grenade from his belt kit, Parry ripped out the safety-pin and threw the flash-bang in through the doorway. By the book, they went straight in behind the grenade: 'maximum speed, maximum aggression, maximum surprise and maximum effect.'

Parry and McAleese broke right inside the door, the other two broke left. The flash-bang – and the gas – should help to disorientate the fugitive. It might also make him shout, cough or react in some other way that betrayed his position. If they were really lucky, it might even make the gunman give up without a fight.

They weren't lucky. Parry spoke some Arabic. As they burst in through the door, he shouted: 'Who are you? Where are you from?' There was eerie silence bar the hiss of gas billowing from the canister and the snap and pop of flames taking hold in the building. The silence meant nothing: the flash-bangs often caused temporary deafness. The gunman was in there somewhere. But the room was stone dark.

Some of the CS gas had cleared, but a trickle of flame was beginning to run up one of the curtains. The four assaulters crabbed towards the rear windows. As the gun-torch's bright, guiding light sliced the thickening smoke, they spotted their quarry. The gunman was slumped on a battered chaise-longue at the back of the room. Bullets trickled in a slow stream from one of his pockets, thudding one by one to the floor. In the darkness and the smoke it was impossible to see if he had been hit. But there was no sign of blood seeping through his clothes.

It was bizarre. The terrorist looked relaxed – almost at ease, as if he'd just decided to lie down and take a nap.

Except for the semi-automatic pistol in his right hand.

The gunman looked up. He was facing four SAS men. Their MP5s were rock steady, trained on his centre mass and head. They were right on top of him, almost close enough to touch. The wise course of action would have been to shout: 'I surrender!' in every language he knew, especially English. Put the weapon down on the floor. Link his fingers on the top of his head.

Slowly.

Instead, the hand holding the pistol began to lift. The four SAS men opened fire as one. They had no idea how many rounds they put into the gunman. When they were done, there was no need to check if Abbas was dead.

■ ■ ■

By now the remaining gunmen were only too well aware that they were under attack. And that Salim was no longer leading them. They had fourteen male hostages in the telex room and four women at the rear of the building in Room 9A. A gunman stood guard outside the door of each room. Ron Morris was sitting just inside the entrance to the telex room, with Faruqi to his immediate right. Vahid Khabaz, Tabatabai and a third Iranian were beyond, with their backs to the right-hand wall. Afrouz and Dadgar sat in the middle of the room facing the door. The rest of the hostages huddled in a rough semi-circle near the window.

Hassan was trying to set fire to Room 8. Ali had been guarding the women in the cipher room. Panicking, he abandoned his post and ran across the landing into the telex room. Faisal and Makki followed him in.

Muhammad Faruqi heard a rustling sound and looked round. In the gloom, he saw a terrorist by the door: Faisal. Snarling and waving his arms, Faisal made all the Iranian hostages move up towards the window. As they scrabbled to obey, he cocked the Skorpion. Firing in short bursts, he opened up on the cowering men, the muzzle of the machine gun moving backwards and forwards in short, murderous arcs. A second man fired his Browning pistol into the terrified crowd.

Bullets sprayed around the room, slamming into telex machinery, furniture, walls – and people. The hostages scurried and squirmed to escape the hail of fire, burrowing under and behind the desks barricaded in front of the window. One man tried to wriggle in behind the back of the telex machine. Ali Akbar Samadzadeh didn't make it to cover. A round from the Skorpion caught him square in the chest. A second bullet smacked into one of his buttocks. He fell back dead.

As Faisal swung the weapon in a wild arc, more bullets smashed into Dr Afrouz. A bullet went through his nose, flinging him backwards and round. The wound started bleeding. As Afrouz slumped down next to a desk, he felt a sharp burn in his right leg. He'd been hit again; he wasn't sure how many times. Muhammad Moheb was lying next to him. 'I'm bleeding, I'm bleeding!' Afrouz moaned. 'I've been shot.'

'Try and be quiet,' said Moheb.

'I'm going to die,' thought Afrouz. 'I feel so hot. These are the last minutes of my life.' His other leg was on fire now; had they shot him through that, too? He thought the walls were going to crack and the ceiling was going to fall in. He still didn't know how many times he'd been shot. He only knew it hurt like hell and he didn't want to die.

The embassy's medical aide, Ahmed Dadgar, was huddled on the opposite side of the room. Six bullets ripped into him. The first hit him in the chest. The impact knocked him sprawling. More bullets hit him in the back, arms and legs, the final round lodging in his right hip. Dadgar slumped and lay back, groaning. He was very badly wounded. But amazingly, he was still breathing. Another bullet ripped through Tabatabai's shirt. He felt the hot wind of its passage against the skin of his chest, but when he looked down, there was no sign of any blood.

Doorman Abbas Fallahi was luckier still. A bullet hit a fifty-pence piece in his hip pocket, glanced off and ricocheted up into the ceiling. All he had to show for the strike was a massive bruise. And a hole in his pocket.

■ ■ ■

Palmer eyed the gunman on the floor at the back of Room 8. The room was long and wide. The X-ray didn't seem to have noticed him, despite the fact Palmer knew he must be outlined in black against the sky. Tough shit for him. Whether by accident or design, the window had already been smashed in. Palmer stuck a leg over the sill, climbed through and put the MP5 on the crouching man. His quarry was down on one knee scrabbling in the dust, intent on whatever he was doing, his hands close together in front of him.

There was one thing for certain: he wasn't praying.

Palmer saw the bright flare of an igniting match and smelled something new on the air. Not smoke or CS gas: an accelerant. Petrol or something in the same family; now he'd caught the scent, it was really strong. He took a couple of steps and felt something squelch underfoot. The rug! The fucker was trying to set fire to the magnificent Persian rug on the floor. And with it the whole office. Create a fire barrier, while he did what? Killed the hostages? Not on Tommy Palmer's watch.

The MP5 was steady on the kneeling man. Palmer squeezed the trigger. The working parts of the machine gun snapped forward. The firing-pin struck against the detonator buried in the base of the chambered round. There was a loud clack of metal meeting metal – and then silence. The round in the breech was a dud. He'd had a misfire, the dreaded 'dead man's click'.

Hassan looked up at the sound. He was staring down the muzzle of a sub-machine gun. A man who most definitely knew how to use it stared back at him. Panic flared in the gunman's eyes. Dropping the matches he'd been holding, he jumped to his feet, raised the pistol in his hand and fired. Two bullets spat over Palmer's head and buried in the top of the wall behind.

Palmer let the MP5 fall free against its sling. He drew the Browning from its holster in a fast, easy movement. Two could play at this game.

But he wasn't fast enough. Cat-quick, the X-ray had already turned. He ran back out through the door, made a snap-turn to the right and disappeared. Furious, Palmer gave chase. He'd had the gunman bang to rights: all he'd needed was a short burst from the MP5. But in the second or two it had taken him to change weapons, his target had fired at him and got away. Now Palmer felt a different kind of heat: hunting instinct. The hostile might have run away. But that didn't mean he was going to let him escape.

Eyes watering from the smoke and gas, Palmer raced in the steps of the fleeing man. Rounding the door-post on to the landing, he caught a glimpse of the fugitive. The man was just disappearing into a room on the left. From the floor plans he'd committed to memory, Palmer already knew it was the telex room. Where most, if not all of the male hostages were still being held prisoner. As he ran forward, he heard shooting and screaming from inside. Shit! The bastard was killing the hostages! He ran faster. Shouts and screams and groans echoed in the wake of the gunfire. Palmer hit the room, broke right and made a snap scan. There was total chaos in the room. For a long instant it was hard to make any sense at all out of what was happening.

■ ■ ■

A wide-eyed, breathless figure ran into the room: Hassan. Stepping over the hostages in his path, he moved to the far left-hand corner, took out a hand grenade and put his index finger through the pin. Staring at Faisal, Hassan shook his head. There were British commandos everywhere. It was over.

Seeing that, his three fellow gunmen lost their nerve. Waving his pistol in the air, Ali started running around like a freshly decapitated chicken. Then he dropped the weapon and squirmed down among the hostages on the floor. Faisal flung down his smoking Skorpion.

Delving into his pockets, he began flinging handfuls of bullets out as fast as he could.

Faruqi watched the gunmen out of the corner of his eye. It was plain they'd only stopped firing because they were afraid. He felt a wave of disgust and contempt. Soon – he hoped *very* soon – it would be their turn to cower and run. Turning his head, he saw Faisal. Who looked extremely scared. Having emptied his pockets of bullets, he now crossed the room, found a small space and lay down among the hostages.

Makki scooped up Faisal's Skorpion and some of the other weapons, took them to the window and, together with his own pistol, threw them out on to Princes Gate. Then he, too, moved back in among the crowd of men and lay face down. Like his fellow gunmen, he had decided this was their only chance of getting out of that embassy alive.

Hassan was the only gunman still standing. Slowly, he raised the hand grenade in his fist and went for the pin. 'Don't kill us all!' an Iranian shouted in Farsi. 'It's no use! Everybody is finished.' At this, the whole room erupted as one: shouts of *'Tasleem, tasleem!'* [we surrender] rang out in Farsi. There was a blur of movement at the door. A man clothed in black stood in the doorway. Raising the pistol in his hand, he pointed it straight at Hassan.

■ ■ ■

Palmer saw the telex room was full of men. Most of them were lying face down on the floor; some had taken refuge under desks and behind bits of furniture. At first glance, it was impossible to tell if any of the gunmen were hiding among them. But the one he'd chased in here was standing at the back of the room. Their eyes met.

The X-ray was standing left side on to him, holding something in his left hand. From the long, shiny detonator pin sticking up from the top of the man's fist, Palmer knew at once what it was: a Russian fragmentation grenade. Hassan's right index finger was curled around the locking pin; he began to raise his elbow.

Palmer aimed the Browning's muzzle at the terrorist's head and squeezed off a single shot. The gunman fell boneless to the floor. The grenade rolled from his grasp and came to a stop near his splayed feet. Palmer ran across and looked down at the fallen man. The bullet had ripped through the collar of Hassan's jacket, entered his skull just below the base of his left ear, ploughed diagonally across his brain and then exited through the right temple. The eyes were like the eyes of a dead fish: cloudy and staring wide. A big, ugly hole gaped in the side of his skull. There was no need to feel the man's pulse. The pin was still in the grenade. Palmer left it lying where it was, swung round and saw the Romeo Two call signs steaming in through the door.

■ ■ ■

Red Team leader was still going forward, doing the work that had to be done in spite of the ferocious pain. The priority for him and the rest of the second-floor team now was twofold: to identify and contain gunmen; and to get the hostages out before the building, which was now well alight, burned down around their ears. He told his men to start searching everyone in the telex room, strip them of any concealed weapons and then get them out to safety. Pausing only to ID and arrest any gunmen they detected in the process.

'I'm British!' shouted Ron Morris. Recognising him, two of the rescuers hauled the embassy manager up and led him out towards the landing. There were people milling everywhere, for a moment it was like being in a prison break. Other hostages turned their heads and shouted: 'I'm innocent!' One after another, the assaulters searched them, brought them to their feet and took them out to the head of the stairs. The chain of SAS men then manhandled the hostages down and out to the back garden.

Noticing he'd suffered a gunshot wound, Palmer took out a field dressing and used it to try and staunch the flow of blood from Ahmed Dadgar's chest.

Spotting his green combat jacket, Red Team leader put the MP5 on Makki. 'Lie face down on the floor! Put your arms out to either side and keep still!' he ordered. Makki lay down and spread his arms. He was now in a T shape. 'Who are you?' Where are you from?'

'Student! I am student!'

Pat G came up and went through Makki's pockets, then ran his hands up and down the back of the terrorist's body. No weapons. Pat G stood back, kicked Makki's legs wide and looked between them. A pistol magazine glinted under the gunman's thigh. Then he saw a holster at Makki's waist. Without warning, Makki twisted, brought his arms in towards his stomach and began to roll. Red Team leader, standing over him, opened fire with the MP5. Makki's back arched and then he fell forward.

They turned him over. There was a hand grenade under the gunman's belly. He'd been going for the pin. Too late.

In all of the noise and confusion, two gunmen, Faisal and Ali, had managed to slip out of the telex room unnoticed. They joined the throng of people hurtling down the stair chain to safety.

■ ■ ■

The drama of the SAS rescue went into action at peak viewing time on a Bank Holiday Monday. *Rio Lobo*, a Howard Hawks Western starring John Wayne, had just started on BBC1. On BBC2, the World Snooker Championships final between Hurricane Higgins and Cliff Thorburn was going right down to the wire. It was level-pegging at sixteen frames each, with one frame left to decide the match. The rival film over on ITV was *Detour to Terror*. Given what was happening at Princes Gate, it could hardly have been better named.

The BBC had strict rules about interrupting scheduled programmes. Only the death of a senior royal, or some great emergency of state counted as important enough. Even then, the Corporation's bosses knew from past and sometimes bitter experience that thousands of viewers would call to complain, especially if they cut off the snooker at a crucial moment. But the pictures coming in from the siege were so exceptional the BBC decided there was every reason they should show them instead of the snooker. Who cared about two blokes knocking a bunch of coloured balls around, when the world's most secretive and skilled Special Forces unit had exploded on to the screen?

The managers were right: the BBC's images of the SAS taking

the Iranian Embassy back were some of the most graphic and exciting ever seen on British television. Shot from a building in Exhibition Road, they showed the front of the Iranian Embassy from the right. Despite the distance, the camera caught the action in dramatic focus – and brought it into half the world's living rooms. Snooker fans or not, almost everyone who saw the pictures watched transfixed as the little black figures on the screen climbed over on to the embassy balcony; climbed back; triggered a massive explosion and then hopped back across to join in the rescue. It was the first time the public had ever seen the SAS in action. In British life, at least, the moment has become iconic.

For everyone glued to their sets, the real-life rescue unrolling on screen was far more dramatic than anything *Rio Lobo* or *Detour to Terror* could hope to offer. By the time they'd watched the rescue replayed on the late news a couple of times, many people were wondering if they'd actually been watching another film. That was because the footage was so compelling. ITN's coverage was so good, Goldsmith and the ITN team won a BAFTA for it.

■ ■ ■

Their work in the ambassador's room done, Bravo Four ran back out on to the landing. Bright orange tongues of flame were licking up on all sides. The acrid smell of smoke was hot on the air. Parry thought: 'We have to get the rescue done and get out, before the whole building burns down around our ears.'

McAleese stopped dead in his tracks. He'd forgotten the man at the window. The bloke who'd urged them to 'get the bastards' as they'd gone in. Signalling to Parry, he ran back through to the front first-floor room. Harris was sitting up. His hair was on end, his eyes staring wide and he looked like he'd been electrocuted. But he was still functioning. He still seemed to be aware of what was happening. McAleese and Parry picked him up bodily, shoved him out through the hole where the window had been and dumped him on the balcony. Parry shouted: 'Stay put here until you're rescued. OK?'

Harris nodded. 'OK.' But already, smoke and flames were guttering out from the room he had just quit. They were clawing ever closer towards him. As if that wasn't bad enough, bits of flaming debris were raining down on his unprotected head from the upper floors. The empty balcony to his immediate right looked inviting, for the very simple reason it was out of the fire. He stood in a half-crouch, with the idea of moving there. 'That's Harris! That's Harris!' a voice shouted up from Princes Gate. And then: 'Get down! Stay flat!' Harris dropped flat. He didn't want to get shot by a sniper after all that.

He looked back over his shoulder. The blaze in the room beyond was worse than ever. The sofa was burning fiercely, sending out a cloud of toxic fumes. One of the curtains hung blazing from a broken rod. Another piece of burning debris landed on his shoulder. He brushed it off. The heat was intense: it felt as if he was being roasted alive. Raising his head, he shouted: 'I'm going to burn to death. I'm burning.'

The same relentless voice shouted: 'Stay where you are, Harris. Stay flat.'

Parry and McAleese hopped back through the burning room and out to the first-floor landing to rejoin the rescue. Hostages were now appearing from all sides, in ones and twos and small groups. The rest of the SP team had already started the evacuation. As if to confirm it, the radio spat a new order: 'Hostages out on black.' It was a timely call: with no one fighting it, the fire already had a greedy-fingered grasp of the embassy's opulent furnishings. Soon, it would be into the building's fabric. The fire brigade was on standby a street away, but until they were certain it was safe and clear of gunmen, the firefighters couldn't come up to do their work.

Things were getting hairy. As they reached the head of the stairs on the first floor, McAleese and Parry saw that a stair chain had pre-empted the radio call. Their mates were hurling the hostages from man to man, almost throwing them down the stairs in the race to beat the fire. More troopers were bundling hostages out of the telex room.

From their vantage point at the top of the stairs, Parry and McAleese had a grandstand view of the evacuation. It was like watching several different action films playing at the same time. They helped move a couple of the arriving hostages across to the head of the stair chain and then stood back. The boys were doing it so fast and so well there was no need for extra hands.

Fast was good. Everyone had run out of time. The fire was flaring everywhere now, really taking hold. It was getting so bad Parry could feel the heat starting to come up through the soles of his boots. Fearing for their safety, the stair team was pretty much throwing the hostages from hand to hand. One female hostage dressed in white shirt and black trousers slipped on a patch of broken glass on the stairs, fell and bared most of her top half. It couldn't be helped. The immediate risk to life and limb overrode everything else.

For the second time in the space of a few minutes, McAleese remembered the BBC sound man, Harris. He was still out there on the balcony, waiting for the order to move. And like everyone else, he was now in real danger.

McAleese signalled to Parry. Together, the two men ran back to the room where they'd made entry. It wasn't just the heavy drapes – the windows, furniture and walls of the Chargé d'Affaires' office were now on fire, too. Peering through the smoke billowing around them, McAleese could just make out a figure curled up on the balcony outside. The BBC man looked in a bad way. His arms were wrapped around his head as he tried to shield himself from the blazing debris that was peppering him. McAleese realised they couldn't bring Harris back into the embassy through Afrouz's office. There was way too much smoke, way too much fire and heat.

They sprinted back out on to the inner landing, hooked a sharp right and headed for the secretarial room next door. To their relief, they saw that the fire hadn't caught in there yet, although parts of the office were smouldering. Racing to the window, McAleese heaved the lower section up, climbed out on to the balcony and shouted: 'Come over here, mate! Come over!' at the cowering sound man.

Harris looked up. Despite the rain of fire, he didn't want to go back inside a blazing building. If he entered that inferno, what guarantee did he have that he'd get out alive?

McAleese beckoned urgently. 'Come on, mate! It's OK! Come over.' Harris stood up. Adrenaline-propelled, he jumped up on to the balcony rail, took a flying leap that would have done credit to an Olympic hurdler, did a Tarzan-style swing on the intervening flagpole and sailed through the air towards McAleese. As he came within reach, the SAS man grabbed him and pulled him down. Harris smelled of heat, smoke and ash. They'd remembered him in the nick of time.

Hustling Harris in through the window, they half-carried, half-dragged him across the room and slung him at the first man in the stair chain. In the same way as Lock and all the other hostages, Harris went down like a big sack of potatoes, tumbling and banging from man to man until he reached the entrance hall. Other hands propelled him out towards the garden. It might not have been the most comfortable way to travel. But it was the fastest route to the rest of his life.

Still on the alert for any surviving gunmen, Bravo Four regrouped on the first-floor landing. The stairwell arrowed straight down from where they were now standing, then turned through ninety degrees to the left at the half-landing, twenty or thirty steps below. At that moment, McAleese spotted a tall man with a black beard in an olive-green combat jacket. He was in the crush on the stairs, trying to look over the balcony. The olive jacket, the man's slightly furtive look, his height and the distinctive Afro hair all rang alarm bells for McAleese. Then it hit him: he was looking at a terrorist. A sleeper. Pretending to be a hostage, the X-ray was hoping to escape in the mêlée. Ripping his gas mask up clear of his mouth, McAleese leaned forward. 'There's one of the fuckers there!' he yelled, pointing. 'He's one of them!'

Macdonald and Parry had also spotted Faisal. They shouted almost in the same breath.

Faisal heard them, all right. He looked up at McAleese. Terror and hatred combined in his face.

Firmin too recognised the man with the Afro hair: Shakir Abdullah Radhil, aka Faisal. Like a pantomime villain, the X-ray was holding the collar of his jacket up across the lower half of his face. His right hand, down by his side, remained hidden.

Snapper was about to bundle Faisal down to the next man in the stair chain. The X-ray was peering past the hostages next to him, trying to see over the banisters and down into the hall. Winner heard McAleese's shout and brought up his weapon. But even with the MP5's low muzzle velocity, he felt he couldn't shoot – the gunman was too close. There was a risk the rounds would pass clean through and hit a hostage. Or another call sign. In any case, in the basement he'd shot out so many locks he'd run out of ammunition. But Snapper was nothing if not quick-thinking. He brought the butt of his MP5 up and round in a flat, vicious arc. It hit the gunman hard on the back of the skull. Faisal's head snapped down and he stumbled forwards.

Firmin had moved up from the half-landing. In the same moment Snapper hit him, Firmin grabbed hold of Faisal's left arm. Despite the alarm calls, he couldn't just assume he was dealing with one of the terrorists, and not a hostage: he had to make sure for himself. Gripping the man's cuff, Firmin swung him sharply round. He caught a glint from the corner of his eye. A green metallic object gleamed in the suspect's right hand: a Russian assault grenade. That put the matter beyond doubt. There were no other SP team members in his line of sight. Holding him at arm's length, Firmin brought up the muzzle of his MP5, fired two short bursts into the gunman's centre mass and let go of his arm. The gunman flew backwards down the stairs and crashed in a heap at the bottom. Firmin went after him. As Faisal hit the floor, three more soldiers opened fire. Crouching, Firmin laid two fingers against the side of Faisal's neck. There was no pulse. The bursts from the MP5 had done their work.

Someone shouted, 'Grenade!' Firmin looked down and to the left. He hadn't seen the hand grenade leave Faisal's hand. It was lying in the hallway next to him. For a split-second, the world stopped. Then they all realised: the pin was still in place.

With gunfire, gas and grenades in their midst, some of the hostages on the stairs started screaming again. There was no time to try and reassure them. All the stair team could do was keep on hustling them out of that blazing, gas-and-smoke-filled space. While they did that, Bravo Four made a quick final search of the first floor to make sure there were no stragglers. Above them, using the specialist caving ladders, other teams had cleared the embassy's top floors.

With the last of the hostages clear of the stairs, Firmin and the Bravo call signs took up position on the ground floor area to control the exit from the burning building. One of the assault team picked up the fallen grenade and gave it to Firmin. He put it in his ops waistcoat; he would hand it in to the police as soon as he was clear of the building. All the hostages were accounted for. It was time for the SAS to vacate the embassy. Looking round, he saw a couple of reserve team members, Robin H and Dave Y armed with the only two Blue Team silenced MP5s. Although they hadn't been required on the initial assault they did assist with the hostage evacuation at the rear of the building.

The embassy behind Firmin now fell eerily quiet. With a final glance back, he saw Faisal lying motionless at the bottom of the stairs. It was the last thing he remembered seeing.

Firmin hadn't been the first man into the embassy – but he was definitely the last man out.

■ ■ ■

In the rear garden, more SAS call signs and a large contingent of police stood ready. Aided by some of the Squadron Head Quarters (SHQ) element, the hostage reception team would also continue to act as the rear cut-off group for any hostile runners.

As the hostages came tumbling out, the garden team grabbed them, told them to lie face down on the grass and cuffed their hands behind their backs with plastic ties. Readily identifiable in his uniform, PC Lock was the only exception. Coughing and spluttering, their eyes watering, some of the hostages were still suffering the effects of gas inhalation.

After six days inside, most of the hostages were just grateful to be alive, free and out in the fresh air. The grass felt beautifully cool on their cheeks, the smell of it was wonderfully sweet.

If you're genuinely innocent and six terrorists have been holding you at gunpoint for six agonising days, the face down and handcuff treatment doesn't sound very friendly. Standard procedure, it was designed to be assertive: no one knew for sure if all of the terrorists had been killed. There could still be more sleepers trying to escape in the throng. The SAS had just detected one terrorist – plus grenade – attempting to mingle with innocent hostages on the stairs. The pattern of behaviour suggested the terrorists had all been told – or agreed – to detonate grenades as an action of last resort. It was therefore essential to identify every single one of the people now lying face down on the embassy lawn.

The last surviving gunman, the baby-faced Ali, had made it all the way out to the garden. With his neat haircut and khaki-coloured chinos, he'd always looked the most innocent of the gunmen. Ali had been careful to dispose of all his weapons and ammunition, not just some of them. Cuffed and prone on the grass, he looked out of the corner of his eye. One of the tough-looking men in black who'd killed his comrades was coming towards him. With his fluent Farsi, he was hoping to pass as an Iranian hostage, convince the police of his innocence and melt away. His only hope was that none of the hostages would betray him.

With each passing second, his heart-rate increased and his breathing shortened. A large hand touched his shoulder – surprisingly gentle. 'What's your name? Do you speak English?' One of the men in black stood over him. There was a large clipboard in his hand. Ali glimpsed an array of photographs. His heart jumped into his throat: he'd just caught a glimpse of his own face.

'Student,' Ali whispered, his liquid brown eyes wide. 'I am student.' They'd all decided to say that as a last, final fig-leaf of cover.

'No!' a voice roared from close by. 'He's one of them! He's one of the terrorists!'

Ali's guts turned to jelly. He looked wildly around, trying to spot the man who had betrayed him. A big, angry face was staring back at him: the face of Sim Harris, the BBC sound man. Ali was lying near one of the female hostages, holding the edge of her blouse. The man with the clipboard said: 'Are you sure he's a terrorist?'

'Too right he's a bloody terrorist. He's one of them!'

Two SAS men seized Ali and hauled him bodily to his feet. 'Don't hurt him!' the woman cried out. 'Please don't hurt him!' Ali was young, he was handsome, and as their guard for most of the time he'd been uniformly kind and charming to the female hostages. On one of them, at least, he'd left a definite impression.

Ali's head was down and he dragged his feet as a pair of uniformed officers led him round the front of the embassy towards a waiting police van.

■ ■ ■

Sim Harris was still lying face down in the embassy gardens. A young policeman knelt by his side. 'Let me help you up, sir. You need to follow the others to the street.' Elated to be out of the burning embassy, Harris smiled as he got to his feet. 'Bloody hell, did what happened just happen?' He walked through the garden, a spring in his tired step: the fresh air felt wonderful after being cooped up in frowsy rooms for so long. And after the gas and fire and carnage of the past few minutes. How many had died? He could see Morris ahead of him, looking dazed and dishevelled. He could hear some of the women crying, if now in sheer relief.

A fleet of ambulances lined Princes Gate. Ushered aboard, the hostages were whisked to St Stephen's. Its A&E department had been isolated for their reception. A rather loud and fearsome nurse greeted Harris. 'Hello,' she boomed. 'Doo yoou speeek English?'

For a moment, Harris felt confused. 'Er, yes,' he replied. 'Fluently, thank you. I am English.'

'Oh goodness,' the nurse replied, blushing bright red, 'they told me you were all Iranians!'

Not all the hostages had escaped with minor injuries. Ahmed Dadgar was in intensive care. Shot six times through the back, lungs, left hand, hip and leg, he had felt the full force of the gunmen's firepower. He would remain in hospital for a further eight weeks, but like Dr Afrouz would go on to make a full recovery.

The more fortunate hostages escaped with cuts, bruises and burns. Once these were treated, the police moved them outside and on to a coach. 'Hey, where are we going?' asked Morris, looking around for Lock. Trevor always knew what was what. Where was he when they needed him?

Harris called out: 'Where are you taking us? We need to call our families, tell them we are OK. Why aren't we free to go?' A policeman came and sat next to the two men. 'We are taking you to Hendon Police College for a full debriefing. You can rest before we begin tomorrow morning.'

The hostages were astonished. They had just been held captive for six days and now, when they were supposedly free, they were once again being held against their will, this time as guests of the Metropolitan Police. Angry and dismayed, many protested. To make matters worse for Harris, in particular, on its way from central London to Hendon, the coach went right past BBC Television Centre. Cool as a cucumber for much of the siege, Harris was incensed. His colleagues would be waiting for him, ready with a couple of beers. And more importantly, there'd be a phone to call his wife and children. What on earth did the police think they were playing at?

Despite his protests, the coach kept right on going. The hostages had supper at Hendon, and then doctors dispensed Valium to help them sleep. At least the beds were comfortable, Harris thought – but he still wasn't allowed to make any contact with the outside world.

The next morning, he took a senior policeman to one side. 'Look, this is bloody ridiculous. I want to help you. I kept a diary during the siege which I am happy to share with you. But I won't tell you a thing until I can speak to my family.'

The officer looked at him impassively. 'What were you doing in the embassy that morning? You and your producer, Cramer?'

'I already told you a hundred times: we were trying to get visas for Iran.'

'And the siege just happened to start while a BBC TV news crew was in there. By complete coincidence?'

Harris understood: the police suspected that he and Cramer might have had advance knowledge of the plot. The idea was so absurd, he laughed outright. 'You're barking up the wrong tree,' he said. 'We just happened to be there. That's exactly what it was – a complete coincidence. We didn't have a camera or any recording equipment with us – it's not like we made a programme in there. Now, please: I absolutely have to let my family know I'm well.'

He got his way. A few moments later, he was on the line to Helen.

Following several hours of debriefing, Harris and the rest of the hostages were finally freed. It was only now he was out that Harris realised how gruelling and terrible the ordeal of the siege had been. But he also realised he had much to be thankful for: unlike Lavasani and Samadzadeh, he had escaped with his life.

■ ■ ■

As they walked back into the accommodation at Regent's Park Barracks, Sgt Peter Scholey met each man of the assault team in turn at the door with a cold can of beer. Part of the Regiment's operations research department, and the man who had made sure the frame charges, stun grenades and all the other essential kit was in good shape, Scholey knew the squadron was going to need a bit of a pick-me-up after the embassy do. He'd been out and bought twenty-six cases of lager. With his own money.

To John McAleese, it was one of the sweetest beers he'd ever drunk. After all the noise, heat, gas, smoke and dust of the embassy, the cool golden liquid was like nectar. Rusty Firmin drank his almost as fast as the fuze delay on a stun grenade.

But the SAS also faced a much more formal reception committee in the form of a Metropolitan Police forensics team. As each SAS man came in, officers handed him a clear polythene evidence bag. All the weapons that had been fired had to be sent for forensic examination, so the police could match any rounds found in the dead gunmen with the weapons and the people – each member of the SAS had a personal Regiment ID number – who had fired them. The mission had been to rescue the hostages using only such force as might be necessary. Murder had not been part of the mission statement. Murder is against the law.

Collecting the weapons was one thing, but however thorough they might be, it was going to be tough for the forensic scientists: before the fire brigade could get it under control, the blaze had consumed much of the embassy. On the upper floors, almost every room was a sea of charred and molten debris, wrecked furniture, ash and soot. A large section of the building's roof had burned away.

Once the police had departed, everything calmed down. Someone put the TV on to find out what had happened in the snooker. The room went quiet: the BBC had interrupted the snooker final to report on the siege. The camera showed a white first-floor balcony. There were three small figures in black moving about on it. One was holding something awkward and odd out in front of him. It took McAleese a second or two to realise it was him. The little man in black carefully placed what looked like a large picture frame up against a window, legged it back over the parapet and turned to face the wall. 'That was a bomb – that was a bomb!' yelped a voice on the audio track. The room gave a loud cheer. Even McAleese was impressed by the size of the explosion. Seeing yourself on screen, he'd just decided, was one of the strangest things in the world.

There was general disappointment when the announcer said that Thorburn had won the snooker. But in the context of a brilliantly successful day, it was a very small defeat.

■ ■ ■

McAleese was just pulling his sweatshirt over his head when there was a sudden commotion at the back of the room. Some burly plain-clothes bodyguard types came in through the door, followed by Lt-Col Rose and William Whitelaw. For some reason, the Home Secretary was weeping real tears, not the crocodile tears most politicians cry when they think it might serve them. Whitelaw said, 'Well done, lads. You saved us.' And he went round the room shaking everyone by the hand. Though Whitelaw might have been a perfectly nice bloke and well-meaning into the bargain – a lot of the SAS men in the room found the patronising 'lads' comment out of place: there was no connection between them and him. They were separate from the rest of the world, a warrior tribe. One that no huffle-puffle politician could ever join.

Whitelaw stopped crying, and for the first time everybody saw there was someone else with him: a small woman with a big hairdo who walked in a slightly stilted way. She was carrying a large, trademark handbag. Parry thought: 'You wouldn't want to get in the way if she took a swing at you with that.'

Lt-Col Rose said: 'Gentlemen – the Prime Minister.' Margaret Thatcher worked the room like the pro she was, pressing the flesh and thanking each member of the squadron personally and without talking down to them.

The only problem arose when the late news came on. Having made their circuit of the room, Thatcher and her entourage ended up standing directly in front of the television. When the news report came on, they naturally turned to the screen. It was the first time they'd seen the action, too.

'The main news, with Jan Leeming,' announced the portentous voice. And then, as the screen filled with footage of the explosion and a great billowing cloud of smoke, Leeming said: 'The dramatic end of the six-day siege. Nineteen hostages, including three Britons, are safe. The end came with an assault on the building by the army's Special Air Services Regiment, the SAS, not long after gunmen had killed two hostages and pushed the body of one out on to the embassy's steps. They'd threatened to kill another hostage every half hour. It ended with three gunmen dead, one in hospital and another in police custody.' She was almost right.

'Typical,' McAleese thought. 'I get my fifteen minutes of fame and there's a big fat head in the way, blocking my bloody view.' Without thinking, he shouted: 'Person at the front! Move your fucking head!'

The head in question belonged to Margaret Thatcher. Without turning a platinum hair, she moved.

With the bulletin over, Thatcher and her husband Denis went round and chatted to as many people as they could. As B Squadron and the six attached A and D Squadron snipers stood there knocking back the beers, she made a speech. It was short and to the point. 'Courage, and confidence – a brilliant operation,' she said. 'It made us all – *all* – proud to be British.' Thatcher knew how to work a crowd – even a crowd of exhausted and elated SAS men. When she stopped talking, they gave her a small cheer. To the members of the SP team, it felt like an ending.

■ ■ ■

At 2008 hrs, the Metropolitan Police reported that PC Trevor Lock was safe and well. A few minutes later, DAC Nievens announced: 'The siege has ended ... The Special Air Service Regiment was deployed in the final stage.' Most of Britain already knew that. Riveted to their television screens, they'd watched the men in black do their stuff.

At 2050 hrs, the Home Secretary held a press conference. Whitelaw was triumphant, overjoyed and flushed with Operation Nimrod's success. 'I would like,' he said, 'on behalf of the government and I believe the people of this country, to pay a very considerable tribute to the way the police handled this action.' The world's press jostled and shouted for more.

Well might the Home Secretary be chuffed: Operation Nimrod had taken just eleven minutes from initiation to completed hostage evacuation. Nineteen hostages had been rescued during the assault phase, five had been released before that. Five terrorists had been killed and one captured. The SAS had suffered only two casualties: the burns to the Red Team leader's legs; and another man armed with an MP5-K who'd accidentally shot an extra crease in his finger. In the days before Heckler & Koch modified the MP5-K with a front guard, that was easily done.

On the down side of the ledger, the terrorists had murdered two hostages: Abbas Lavasani and Ali Samadzadeh – one before and one during the rescue. They had also severely injured two more.

## GO! GO! GO!

When it was his turn, Metropolitan Police Commissioner Sir David McNee had a bit more to say:

> It is a matter of deep regret that the siege had to be ended by violence. Police waited and negotiated patiently over six days and tried every possible means except giving in to terrorism. This was not and never will be considered by us as an option. Over the last few days, five hostages were released by negotiation. We were determined that police would not be the first, if it came to aggression. Today, two people were reported killed. And there was a real threat that one hostage would be killed every half hour by the terrorists unless their demands were met.
>
> I appealed to them with a direct personal message. They refused to respond to it. A decision had to be taken urgently to avoid further bloodshed. I had no alternative, therefore, but, with the approval of the Home Secretary, for the SAS to take action. They acted promptly and efficiently. The hostages have been through a grim ordeal. They have my great sympathy. I do not wish to say any more at present than that I'm naturally delighted that Constable Trevor Lock came through safely. His conduct throughout was heroic and won the admiration of all.

■ ■ ■

Nejad – he had told the police his real name was not 'Ali' – had been convinced his life was over – terrified that when they discovered he was one of the gunmen, the SAS would drag him back into the burning embassy and shoot him. Instead, once he'd stopped shaking in fear, the police had searched him for the umpteenth time and then locked him into a basement cell at Paddington Green police station. He was left alone for several hours to sweat it out. At 0140 hrs, he was taken upstairs for interrogation. Five detectives sat waiting. One spoke fluent Arabic. Nejad told the police everything he knew.

When the embassy was first stormed, he said, the gunmen thought it was the police. 'I was on the second floor and Makki was outside the women's room. Hassan was standing on the stairs which led up to the third floor. Faisal was outside the men's room. I was walking backwards and forwards outside and then the glass broke above the stairs next to the women's room and Makki said the police were attacking. They threw a smoke grenade through the broken glass. Then Makki shouted, "Go into the room with the men and shut the door!"

'After we were in the room, within a matter of a minute, the building shook. I felt the explosion but I didn't see anything. I threw my gun out of the window and fell face down on to the floor. I had no other weapons. Faisal gave his automatic pistol to a hostage to throw out of the window, which I think the hostage did. The last thing I saw was Makki and Hassan behind the door with their guns still. But it started to get so dark and I couldn't breathe. I lay on the floor between the hostages. Then everyone came in shouting. The SAS shouted for the terrorists to stand up. Faisal and Hassan did and they were told to kneel facing the wall on the opposite side of the room. Their hands were put on the wall and then the people were taken out and we heard shots. I never saw them again.'

The discrepancy between the two versions of what happened in the telex room was and remains, very wide. But Ali did see his brothers once more. Early the next morning he was driven to the Westminster Mortuary. He let out a wail when he saw the five broken, bullet-ridden bodies on the metal slabs. Tears streaming down his face, he knelt beside each of his friends as he identified them. This was not supposed to have happened. Salim, Faisal, Abbas, Makki and Hassan dead. So far from home. He didn't even want think of how and where their bodies would be buried.

A 2155 hrs on Wednesday, 7 May, the police charged Fowzi Badavi Nejad with two counts of murder; conspiracy to murder Gholam-Ali Afrouz; Abdul Fazi Ezzati; Ahmed Dadgar and others; assaulting Police Constable Trevor Lock and, 'unlawfully and injuriously imprisoning him for six days against his will'.

'I did not kill them,' Nejad protested.

■ ■ ■

The SAS learned a number of valuable lessons from the debrief or 'wash-up' it held after Operation Nimrod. Not least among these was the need to improve the assault kit. Changes included: the introduction of ceramic helmets; Nomex fire-resistant coveralls to replace the bog-standard tank regiment coveralls; fire-resistant balaclavas; heat-resistant underwear; armoured cod-pieces (sorry, we made that one up); better gloves; ceramic shields for protection during assaults; and enough small, high-powered integrated weapons torches for all. And a key change: identification flashes to ID each individual call sign.

But there were plenty of things that had worked and did not need changing. Chief among these was the high standard of the individual SAS soldier; and the operational flexibility that individuals, sub-units, and the squadron as a whole demonstrated throughout the siege.

One of the soldiers who took part in Operation Nimrod, identified only as 'Soldier J' said: 'Princes Gate was a turning point. It demonstrated to the powers that be what the Regiment could do and just what an asset the country had; but it also brought a problem we wished to avoid: the media spotlight. In addition, for the first few years after the siege, Selection courses were packed with what seemed like every man in the British Army wanting to join the SAS. We just couldn't cope with the numbers ...

'Now, many years later, there are loads of blokes going around saying they were at Princes Gate. The security industry attracts them like flies. At the last count, I interviewed some seven hundred blokes who "took part at the Iranian Embassy".'

Every bugger and his dog wanted to be part of a resounding success. One that had made the SAS, little known before the siege, a household name. And ensured that from then on, they got all the kit they needed.

■ ■ ■

For many of the hostages, getting back to normal life proved difficult. A group including Chris Cramer, Ahmed Dadgar, Muhammad Faruqi, Sim Harris, Mustapha Karkouti, Trevor Lock, Ron Morris and Ali Tabatabai, met up a few months after the siege. They shared a need to talk about their experience. Each man revealed he was trying to cope with powerful emotional aftershocks: nightmares, depression, guilt, aggression, obsession and a difficulty in relating to friends and family. It was enormously helpful to come together and be able to talk about it openly and honestly.

Cramer suffered from huge feelings of guilt after being released on the second day. The son of a soldier, he felt he should have been strong enough, should have had the mettle to tough it out. To overcome this, he gave up drinking and shed forty pounds in weight. 'It was a feeling that, if I had been in better condition, mentally and physically, I might have been able to stand up to the strain a lot better.' Guilt, combined with feelings of inadequacy, made Cramer more determined to focus on his life ahead.

He went on to enjoy an illustrious career. As President of CNN International, he became one of the most powerful people in global news-gathering. Hugely respected for his recognition of the trauma and stress journalists often suffer in hot spots, Cramer has worked tirelessly to minimise the risk his team face. He is often quoted as saying that his compassion for those who suffer from Post Traumatic Stress Disorder comes directly from his experience as a hostage in the Iranian Embassy.

Ecstatic to be back with his wife and daughters, Sim Harris rode the wave of post-siege euphoria that swept Britain. 'I enjoy the popularity and publicity, the pop-star image of someone who had come through all of it and had a story to tell.' As interest in the siege inevitably waned, Harris became if anything more obsessed with it. In 1982, he wrote *Hostage* with Chris Cramer, a blow-by-blow account of the incident based on the diary he'd kept during the siege. Writing the book helped Harris lay the embassy ghost. He went on to enjoy a successful career in broadcasting.

Muhammad Faruqi, too, adjusted to normal life better than some. Perhaps this was because, from the outset, he viewed the siege not as a terrifying ordeal, but as a prime journalistic opportunity. It meant he kept a certain detachment. The man Lock had nicknamed 'Scoop' said: 'It was a very valuable time of my life. I saw it as a fascinating insight into a terrorist incident.' Devoutly religious, Faruqi also believed that his trust in God had helped him. But he was deeply saddened by so many deaths. 'The gunmen chose to ride a tiger and it took them to their graves.'

Ahmed Dadgar was the most severely wounded of the surviving hostages. Doctors told his family: 'His mind is strong, but his body is almost dead. Prepare for the worst.' Yet Dadgar made a miraculous physical recovery. The emotional and psychological side-effects of the siege were to stay with him for a lot longer. Even from his hospital bed, Dadgar was convinced that Faisal was on guard outside the ward, his Skorpion at the ready to shoot him if he tried to leave the room.

As the nightmares refused to leave him, Dadgar experienced anger, bitterness and fear of a kind that he had never known. As the Old Bailey trial date loomed, Dadgar was worried he would not be able to contain his rage when he saw Nejad in the dock. But surprisingly, when it came to the day, he felt a wave of compassion. 'I felt sorry for him being alive. He was so powerful when he was with the other gunmen, brandishing his weapons. But in the dock he was nothing.' For Dadgar, it was a turning point. He even expressed support for Nejad's release in 2008.

PC Trevor Lock became a national hero after the siege. On welcoming him back to Scotland Yard, Sir David McNee burst into tears. Lock's face – 'Siege Hero!' – adorned the front pages of the British newspapers for weeks. He was awarded the George Medal 'for civilian gallantry in the face of enemy action'.

The only surviving hostage allowed to visit the SAS men who had rescued him, Lock said: 'I never knew which one of them saved my life, but I was able to thank them all. It was strange, knowing that one of the men in front of me had saved my bacon and not knowing exactly which one it was.'

Lock, too, suffered from aftershocks, or 'kickbacks' as he called them. Travelling on the London Underground a short time after the siege had ended, he caught the smell of Dadgar's aftershave that Salim had worn in the embassy. He had to hurry away and get up into the fresh air.

Recognised in the street, hunted down for autographs and sound bites, Lock became a reluctant celebrity. He won 'Man of the Year' and was made a Freeman of the City of London. Never one to seek the limelight, he found this part of post-siege life increasingly difficult to accept. He relied on his wife Doreen and their children for love and support.

Officially warned not to talk freely about the siege or any of the other hostages until after Nejad's trial, Lock never returned to the DPG. After a spell on office duties, he spent some time advising foreign heads of state on security. Later he became an observer on board a police helicopter.

■ ■ ■

Controversy surrounding events in the telex room has lingered. Some commentators – then and now – have alleged that the SAS used undue force, or even executed in cold blood gunmen who'd surrendered. The substance for these allegations seems to have come from accounts given by some of the hostages and Nejad. Muhammad Faruqi's is a good example.

In his statement to the police, Muhammad Faruqi alleged: 'One of the terrorists was sitting on the floor. When he was pointed out by the Iranians to the commandos, they asked him to stand up and then shot him.' He was apparently referring to Faisal. But Faisal's body was recovered from the foot of the stairs with multiple bullet wounds to the trunk, not the head. And other hostages, and not just SAS men, had seen him on the stairs.

In the subsequent inquest at Westminster Coroner's Court, independent forensic experts gave their professional opinions as to how and where the gunshot injuries had been inflicted. We can do no better than include that evidence as detailed in the appendix to the official Home Office report on the Iranian Embassy siege.

■ ■ ■

On 2 November, under armed police escort, Fowzi Nejad appeared at the Old Bailey to face trial for the murders of Abbas Lavasani and Ali Akbar Samadzadeh; conspiracy to murder; falsely imprisoning PC Trevor Lock and being in possession of firearms with the intent to endanger life.

To the first and most serious charges of murder, Nejad pleaded not guilty. To all the other charges, he pleaded guilty.

An interesting picture of the siege developed over the next few days. In his evidence, Nejad revealed there had been a split between the gunmen. Throughout the siege, Salim had refused to tell the others what the police were saying. Then, despite the agreement they'd made before the start of the mission that they would not kill anyone, Salim had changed his mind. By Day Five, according to Nejad, he was intent on murder. 'Me and some of the other gunmen protested – but Salim told us he would shoot us if we went against him. He had the power in the group. We had to obey him.'

In court, Nejad was repentant. 'Now I am ashamed of what we did and of my own actions. I had been willing to die when we took the embassy. I had been cheated in Iraq and wanted freedom for my people.' At the beginning of the fifth day of his trial, there was shock in the courtroom as Nejad changed his plea from not guilty of murder, to a plea of guilty of manslaughter. The Crown accepted this. The jury retired to consider the evidence. They found him guilty on all counts. Mr Justice Park sentenced Nejad to life imprisonment.

The judge acknowledged that Nejad was not the actual killer of the two dead hostages in that he had not pulled the trigger, but he had taken part in 'an outrageous criminal enterprise'. He ended his sentencing by telling Nejad: 'You and your fellow exiles subjected every one of those hostages, day after day, to unspeakable terror and caused the greatest possible mental anguish and distress.' Even though he had learned some English, this was too much for Nejad to understand. A translator relayed the judge's comments – and the sentence. After that, officers led Nejad away in handcuffs, to begin his time in a maximum security prison.

Nejad made the most of life inside. Known as Fozzy, he was liked by his fellow inmates, kept fit and worked hard at educating himself. When he had learned speak and write fluently in English, he issued apologies to the hostages, again acknowledging that he had done wrong. After he had served twenty years, his lawyers submitted new evidence that had not come to light during his trial. In interviews for television, some of the hostages stated that Nejad had been instrumental in preventing more deaths during the siege. Nejad said he had been duped by Iraqi intelligence into taking part in the siege – and that one of the main reasons he had agreed to join the operation was fear of Iraqi reprisals against his family.

In 2001 Lord Woolf, the Lord Chief Justice, recommended that Nejad's sentence be reduced to twenty-two years. By then, he'd spent twenty-one years in prison. David Blunkett, the Home Secretary, ignored Woolf's advice. Incensed by what he called this 'disturbing inactivity' Lord Woolf intervened again. The decision not to reduce Nejad's tariff was overturned. But then, owing to administrative complications, a further two years went by before he made it to an open prison.

When Charles Clarke became Home Secretary he was more sympathetic. Iran had called for Nejad's release and return to face trial for the murder of the two Iranian hostages. Under the recently adopted European Convention of Human Rights, it would have been illegal for the British government to send him back to face torture or execution. He had to remain in the UK. In October 2008, twenty-eight years after the siege, Nejad was finally set free. Granted political asylum and given safe housing, he now lives in South London.

Nejad's release has divided opinion. PC Trevor Lock told the BBC: 'For such a serious crime, life should have meant life. For him to be able to come out and then be considered for political asylum – what a situation! He has committed this major crime, gone to prison, comes out and then is allowed to stay in this country where he committed that crime? He was here as a visitor and he has abused that hospitality.'

Ahmed Dadgar took a different view. 'I personally forgive him ... I think he has been punished enough.'

But the shadow of the Iranian Embassy siege hangs in Nejad's mind. As it does with all those who were there and who survive.

In September 1980, Iraqi forces invaded Iran. In the eight-year war that followed, more than half a million people died.

A warrant is still out for the arrest of Sami Mohammed Ali, aka 'The Fox'. He has never been found.

# Coroner's Report

INCIDENT AT THE IRANIAN EMBASSY
(30 APRIL – 5 MAY 1980)

RESUMED INQUEST ON THE FIVE TERRORISTS

WESTMINSTER CORONERS COURT:
3/4 FEBRUARY 1981

The Coroner, Dr Knapman, considered written statements from SAS soldiers designated as J, H, HH, G, S, LL, E and X. Oral evidence was given by two soldiers referred to as CC and I. PC Lock gave evidence as to the circumstances in which Salim met his death and Mr Morris was also called. From among the Iranian hostages Mr Dadgar, Mr Fallahi and Mr Tabatabai gave evidence. The Coroner made the point that, if other hostages had not been called it was because their statements had no light to shed on the question of how the terrorists met their deaths, or, in the case of Mr Faruqi, they were no longer in the country. He was at pains to point out that the witnesses had not been 'handpicked', and that where the jury was hearing written statements, they were hearing the whole statement and not selected bits. He also drew attention to the preamble to each statement in which the person making it acknowledged his liability to prosecution if he gave false evidence.

2. The evidence about the deaths was as follows:

<u>Salim</u> (the leader)

PC Lock described how he was stuggling with Salim in the Minister/Counsellor's room on the first floor when the SAS came in. He was in pain and his eyes were hurting from the effect of the stun grenade and he was trying to stop Salim getting to his gun. He knew that Salim had carried a grenade and had Sellotaped a spare magazine to the one in his gun so that he would have two ready for use. PC Lock said that all the terrorists felt that they would gain prestige if they died as martyrs. The soldier HH's statement described how he pushed Lock away and hit Salim with a long burst from his smg. Both he and his colleague J, who also fired saw Salim's gun. Lock confirmed to them that there were 6 terrorists, and he was helped to the window to get air. Dr West, the forensic pathologist, (who confirmed that he had no connection with the police or MOD) gave the cause of death as firearm wounds to head and chest caused by two bursts of automatic fire. There were 15 entry and exit wounds.

<u>Abbas</u>

Written statements were read from soliders J, H, G and S the gist of which was that Abbas was blown by a stun grenade across the doorway of the Ambassador's Office on the first floor and was seen to be holding a Browning type pistol in his hand. Soldier J hit him in the chest with a controlled burst and Abbas moved back into the room. The soldier knew that he had been hit but was still alive because he could hear him groaning. The room was in darkness and they called for G, who had a torch fixed to his weapon. Four soldiers went into the room and located Abbas half lying on the sofa with a gun in his hand which they all took to be a 9mm Browning. They all saw some ammunition drop out of his clothing. Abbas made a movement with the gun which H, the leader of the group, interpreted as hostile to himself and the other soldiers, and he hit him with a controlled burst of fire from 2–3 yards. The others also fired. The pathologist: gave the cause of death as firearm wounds to the chest and abdomen. There were 21 entry wounds and 18 exit wounds. Supt Churchill-Coleman said that Abbas' Browning had not been found. He pointed out that the room had been badly damaged by fire and it was possible that the gun was in the ruins. Three Brownings belonging to the terrorists had been found although Nejad, the survivor, had said that there were 4 in all and that Abbas certainly had one. A charred air pistol was found in the room. It was not possible to say whether this had anything to do with the terrorists, or, alternatively, whether Abbas had actually been waving it at the soldiers and it had been mistaken, in the torchlight, for something more lethal. [In fact, we now know, it belonged to Ron Morris.]

## Shai*

Shai's body was found in the telex room on the second floor where the hostages were, together with that of Makki and the dead hostage Samadzadeh who was shot by the terrorists as the SAS went in. Sgt Cogbill, who was in an adjacent block of flats, saw the flash of gunfire directed from the top floor down on to the SAS who were going in at the back. This was believed to be Shai. Soldier LL described how he and his colleagues went in via the second floor rear. He chased Shai into the telex room. His machine gun jammed and he drew his Browning. Shai was on the left hand side of the room and had a grenade in his hand. He moved to detonate it and soldier LL fired one round. Shai was shot in the head and killed. Dr West gave the cause of death as a firearm wound to the head. There was only one such wound. The bullet had entered below the left ear and come out at the right temple. The former hostage Mr Fallahi said that an SAS man held Shai's head under his arm and shot him at point blank range. When questioned about this, Dr West said that this was quite impossible on the evidence and the ballistics expert, Mr Arnold, concurred. In the first place it would not be possible to inflict such a wound at point blank range without the soldier blowing his own arm off. More importantly, a shot at close range would have left unmistakeable burn and other marks on the head of the deceased. There were no such marks, either on him or on the anorak collar

* Hassan

through which the bullet had passed. It was clear that the shot which killed Shai had not been fired from close range. The Coroner reminded the jury that Mr Fallahi's evidence had been rather confused and that he had had language difficulties (despite the fact that he had had the benefit of an interpreter). All the Iranian witnesses emphasised the noise, smoke and confusion in the room and none of them had seen the shot. Supt Churchill-Coleman said that a grenade was found within inches of Shai's body.

Faisal

There seemed initially to be a conflict of evidence about the manner and place of Faisal's death since Mr Tabatabai, a former hostage, seemed at first to imply that he had seen Faisal shot in the back of the head at point blank range by an SAS soldier in the telex room. Evidence was then given that Faisal had been brought out of the telex room after the hostages, had pulled a grenade and had been shot at the bottom of the stairs. When questioned again Mr Tabatabai said that he had not said that he had seen Faisal actually shot. He had seen him being held by his hair by an SAS man who was holding a gun but he had been moved out with his fellow hostages at that point and could not say how or where Faisal actually died. Soldier I gave oral evidence about the scuffle at the top of the stairs where Faisal was identified as a terrorist, and the warning shouted from his colleagues that he had a grenade. Soldier I saw an olive green Russian type grenade in Faisal's right hand as he came down the stairs and hit him on the head with the butt of his gun. He could not open fire because of the other soldiers around. Soldiers HH, E, X and H fired on Faisal at the bottom of the stairs. His grenade was picked up and given to DI Lewis. Dr West gave the cause of death as multiple firearm wounds. There were 39 entry wounds and 33 exit wounds. Mr Arnold, the ballistics expert, said that the 11 bullets recovered from the body had come from 4 different SAS guns. The Coroner decided not to read the statements of soldiers K and U which said essentially the same thing.

<u>Makki</u>

Makki was the last to be killed in the telex room at the point where nearly all the hostages were out and the building was well alight. He was identified as a terrorist by soldier VV who ordered him to lie down and covered him while soldier CC, who gave oral evidence, searched him for weapons. Makki was lying in a T position with his arms out and was told not to move. He understood English because when asked who he was he replied that he was a student. When CC parted Makki's legs, he saw what looked like the magazine for an automatic pistol (subsequently found under his body) and a holster. At this point Makki pulled his arms in towards his stomach and turned over. Soldier CC thought that he was going for a grenade and moved back. His colleague VV gave Makki a burst of fire in the small of the back. Dr West said that the cause of death was firearm wounds to the neck and pelvis and that Makki must have been moving when shot. A grenade was found near his body.

3. In the course of his summing up, the Coroner pointed out that sending in the army implied that the situation required action which was over and above what the police were trained to do. The SAS knew when they went in that one hostage had been killed and it was thought possible that another death had occurred. The jury had seen a letter from the terrorists in which they threatened to blow up the Embassy. They had also seen a letter from the Commissioner urging them to surrender. It was known that the terrorists had automatic machine pistols, Brownings and grenades. It was possible that the whole building was booby-trapped and that one false move could blow the whole place up. The jury were required only to find how, when and by what means each terrorist came by his death. They were precluded from framing a verdict in any way which might seek to determine matters of civil or criminal liability. The reason for the delay in concluding the inquest was that the DPP had asked him not to resume it until the conclusion of criminal proceedings against the surviving terrorist.

4. The jury were told that they must consider whether the SAS acted reasonably in all circumstances. They were asked to imagine the atmosphere of confusion noise and terror which the hostages had described at the moment the soldiers went in. The building was shortly on fire, the rooms were full of smoke and CS gas, and all the hostage witnesses had suffered from its effects. Some had been wounded or thought themselves wounded. During the assault the terrorists opened fire on them, killing one and wounding two.

5. The terrorists died of multiple wounds in all cases except one. In regard to the number of shots fired, the jury were reminded that the SAS weapons fired 10 rounds per second. They were to imagine the soldiers spotting the terrorists through the smoke, unable to be sure whether they were carrying concealed weapons or grenades, and ask themselves whether it was reasonable to shoot first and ask questions afterwards. The SAS took no chances.

6. The Coroner then described the possible verdicts in the following terms:

(a) Justifiable homicide

Section 3 of the Criminal Law Act 1967 provides that a person may use such force as is reasonable in the circumstances in the prevention of a crime. It was for the jury to say what degree of force was reasonable and they should ask themselves two questions: 1) whether the force used in this case was necessary, and 2) whether it was in proportion to the evil to be avoided. DAC Dellow had said that the situation had become so desperate that the police had handed control to a specialised branch of the Army. One hostage was known to have been murdered. The terrorists had threatened to kill the hostages and, if attacked, blow up the building with everyone in it. The jury might feel that this answered those questions.

(b) Unlawful killing

The jury could return this verdict if they considered that the conduct of the SAS had been totally unreasonable. He mentioned this verdict

225

only for the sake of completeness and pointed out that, if evidence had emerged which suggested that an offence of murder or manslaughter had been committed, he would have had to adjourn the inquest and send the papers to the DDP, having heard the evidence and considering the special job which the SAS had been asked to do (i.e. to rescue the hostages) he thought that the jury would not wish to give too much consideration to this verdict.

### (c) Misadventure

This verdict would be appropriate in a situation where a lawful act unexpectedly takes an unfortunate turn leading to death. In this case the jury could return this verdict if they thought that the soldiers had not intended to shoot at the terrorists but that they had, as it were, been caught in the cross-fire. However it seemed clear from the evidence that the soldiers were aiming at the terrorists.

### (d) Open verdict

This would be appropriate if the jury thought that there was insufficient evidence to record any of the other verdicts.

7. The jury recorded unanimous verdicts of justifiable homicide in each case. The Coroner's inquisition therefore records the cause of death (i.e. various types of firearm wounds) for each terrorist and the fact that he was shot on 5 May 1980 when members of the SAS stormed the Embassy at 16 Princes Gate where the deceased and other terrorists were holding the Embassy staff hostage.

### Points of Interest

8. The former hostage Mr Morris (who insisted on shaking hands with one of the SAS men and thanking him) gave evidence that, having fired on the hostages when the SAS began their assault, the terrorists in the telex room then panicked and began to throw down their guns. Some were thrown out of the window. Subsequent evidence showed that they had not necessarily divested themselves of all their weapons (the gun held by Abbas) and they certainly still had grenades

on them (Faisal, Shai and Makki). A grenade was dropped from the telex room on to the first floor balcony below, where the SAS were coming in. Fortunately it still had its pin. The allegation that the hostages helped the soldiers by identifying the terrorists was denied. It was Mr Fallahi the hostage, and not a terrorist, who waved something white out of the window as the assault went in. The Coroner said that the original statements made by the hostages to the police after the event had been brief. He noted that they had been 'embellished' in recent weeks in the press. In court the Iranian hostages denied saying that they had seen the terrorists shot after surrendering and the only one who had actually witnessed a killing was Mr Fallahi, who thought that he had seen Shai killed in a way which did not accord with the evidence of the pathologist.

9. The pattern of the evidence seemed to suggest that, while Salim, Abbas and Shai could be said to have died in the course of the fighting, the other two, Faisal and Makki need not have died. They were both 'taken alive' in the telex room. If Faisal had not produced his grenade on the stairs, and if Makki had obeyed the order to lie still and had not moved in a way which suggested that he too was going for a grenade, it is possible that neither would have been shot.

10. Supt Churchill-Coleman gave evidence about the arrest of the surviving terrorist Nejad. He said that Nejad was identified as a terrorist by soldiers and police as he came out of the building and that he was immediately taken apart from the other hostages to be searched. At no time was there any suggestion or possibility of his being taken back inside the Embassy for any purpose whatever.

# Acknowledgements

A special mention to Nigel McCrery who first came up with the idea for this book. Nigel worked with a number of the SAS men who were at the siege and their compelling stories have added a unique voice to the narrative.

Among those, the voice of John McAleese – the 'Man on the Balcony' – rings out true and clear. His detailed testimony and sharp recall have helped bring the assault to life. Thanks are also due to Pete Winner; Tom Macdonald; Stuart McVicar; Dusty Gray; Tak Takavesi; Mel Parry and Peter Scholey and all the other members of the assault team.

Our special thanks also go to hostages Sim Harris, Chris Cramer and Mustapha Karkouti. Sim's first-hand account of his time inside the Embassy has been invaluable, as has his and Chris Cramer's permission to use *Hostage*, their memoir of the siege.

We would also like to thank Max Wakefield, Andrew Granath, Ian Morrison, Gaynor Aaltonen and Rupert Walters for their advice and contributions.

Thanks also to literary agents Robert Kirby and Mark Lucas and our publishing team at Orion – Alan Samson, Lucinda McNeile and Martha Ashby. Thanks for the use of the bunker! And many thanks to Forouzan Jafari, our first-rate Farsi–English translator.

Rusty Firmin, Will Pearson and Gillian Stern